Forging the American Character

Fourth Edition

Forging the American Character

Volume II
Readings in United States
History Since 1865

John R. M. Wilson
Vanguard University
Editor

Prentice
Hall

Upper Saddle River, NJ 07458

Library of Congress Cataloging-in-Publication Data

Forging the American character: readings in United States history/[compiled by] JOHN R. M. WILSON—4th ed.
   p. cm.
  Includes index.
  Contents: v. 1. To 1877—v. 2. Since 1865.
  ISBN 0-13-097765-9 (v. 1)—ISBN 0-13-097766-7 (v. 2)
   1. United States—Civilization.   I. Wilson, John R. M.

E169.1 .F745 2003
973—dc21   2002066285

VP, Editorial Director: *Charlyce Jones Owen*
Acquisitions Editor: *Charles Cavaliere*
Assistant Editor: *Emsal Hasan*
Editorial Assistant: *Adrienne Paul*
Editorial/Production Supervision: *Joanne Riker*
Prepress and Manufacturing Buyer: *Sherry Lewis*
Marketing Manager: *Chris Ruel*
Marketing Assistant: *Scott Rich*
Cover Art Director: *Jayne Conte*
Cover Designer: *Bruce Kenselaar*

This book was set in 10/12 Palatino by Interactive Composition Corporation and was printed and bound by Courier Companies, Inc. The cover was printed by Coral Graphics.

 © 2003, 2000, 1997, 1991 by Pearson Education, Inc.
Upper Saddle River, New Jersey 07458

Printed in the United States of America
10 9 8 7 6 5 4 3 2 1

ISBN 0-13-097766-7

Pearson Education LTD., *London*
Pearson Education Australia PTY, Limited, *Sydney*
Pearson Education Singapore, Pte. Ltd
Pearson Education North Asia Ltd, *Hong Kong*
Pearson Education Canada, Ltd., *Toronto*
Pearson Educación de Mexico, S.A. de C.V.
Pearson Education—Japan, *Tokyo*
Pearson Education Malaysia, Pte. Ltd
Pearson Education, *Upper Saddle River, New Jersey*

For
Allison, Natalie, Emily
Gwen, and Matthew

Contents

Preface

A long United States history textbook may run to 1000 pages. Although that length may seem intimidating to students, it still does not allow extended treatment of a wide variety of fascinating topics. A book of readings, however, does. The theme of this reader is the American character. I trust that the concept will illuminate American history without being overly restrictive.

A reader like this one enables students to explore subjects ranging from the influence of Indians and the Spanish on the American experience to the debate over multiculturalism at the turn of the new millennium, from the horrors of life and death in the Civil War to the myths that grew up around the Vietnam War. The nature of the selections varies. Some offer cutting-edge interpretations of the past; others introduce readers to new findings; a few synthesize the writings in a historical subfield; and several are classic statements of enduring value. The readings do not pretend to cover every possible topic; rather, they explore various areas that shed light on the American character yet suffer comparative neglect in many textbooks.

Trying to define the American character can be very frustrating. No one has been able to develop a widely accepted definition of the concept. Authors often use different meanings in the same piece of writing—for instance, referring interchangeably to the character of the individual American and to the character of the mass of Americans. National character, especially in a country as big and heterogeneous as the United States, can be useful only as a large-scale generalization to cover the most prominent characteristics of the national culture. Some scholars have criticized efforts to capture the national character, suggesting that in many cases they may merely be intellectually sophisticated forms of racial stereotyping. Yet the practice persists, perhaps because it is so convenient to group people and thus make them more manageable. Perhaps the most useful definition is that national character means generalizations about a nation or nationality developed to clarify the ways in which it is distinctive.

A national character suggests tendencies on the part of a people, not fixed positions held by everyone. It means that, all things being equal, the people of a given nation are more likely to believe or behave in a certain way than those of another nation. There is an inherent comparison implied in suggesting a national character, although studies of the American character generally tend not to explicitly explore other nationalities.

The genre began very early in the history of the United States with the publication in 1782 of J. Hector St. John de Crevecouer's *Letters from an American Farmer*; the immigrant asked the famous question, "What then is this American, this new man?" Crevecouer's pioneering inquiry into the American character ran up against geographical and cultural heterogeneity, which has become a vastly greater obstacle in the succeeding two centuries. The most famous inquiry came in the 1830s when Alexis de Tocqueville wrote *Democracy in America* and provided penetrating French insight into the nature of the conforming, religious, liberty-loving joiners he observed. Over the years, historians and other social observers have sought to explain American distinctiveness through such characteristics as abundance, exposure to the frontier, pragmatism, belief in progress, and mobility. They have debated the relative influence of mother England and the wilderness and, in so doing, have illuminated American self-understanding without providing any final answers. The quest continues, as the popularity of *Habits of the Heart* attests. That 1985 study by Robert Bellah and associates focuses on the strains between American individualism and the need for community and offers the most thorough recent analysis of the American character.

This collection suggests that Americans have defined themselves not only by what they are but also by what they are not, and the latter negative definition is an important component of Americanism. By and large, Native Americans have not been allowed to share their heritage with Europeans, despite their significant contributions to the lives of colonists in the New World. For other nationalities, conformity to the English cultural model was long required for acceptance in the United States, although a more pluralistic, open society seems to be emerging as the nation has moved into a new millennium. Yet over the past half century, the increasingly diverse American population has frequently defined itself less by what it is than by what it is not—as antifascist and, especially, anticommunist.

This book should help to clarify some of the various forces, ideologies, people, and experiences that have helped forge today's distinctive American character. If, as Socrates said, the unexamined life is not worth living, then this excursion into the life of a people should help make it more worthwhile.

In closing, I wish to thank the reviewers for their thoughtful suggestions: Louis Schmier, Valdosta State University; Charles T. Johnson, Valdosta State University; Dwight D. Watson, Southwest Texas State University; and Brooke D. Simpson, Arizona State University.

John R. M. Wilson
Costa Mesa, California

Forging the American Character

1

The New View of Reconstruction

ERIC FONER

Eric Foner (1943–), both educated and educator at Columbia University, is one of the fine scholars engaged in exploring the gaps between perception and reality in the Civil War and Reconstruction era. He takes particular interest in blacks and radicalism. Two of his books indicate his area of expertise: *Politics and Ideology in the Age of the Civil War* (1981) and *Nothing but Freedom: Emancipation and Its Legacy* (1983). In 1988 he published a full-length and well-received treatment of the subject of this article: *Reconstruction: America's Unfinished Revolution, 1863–1877.*

In this 1983 selection from *American Heritage*, Foner offers a clear picture of the view of Reconstruction that prevailed from the 1870s through the 1950s and explains why it is no longer convincing. Reconstruction provides a good case study of historiography, the history of history. As long as white racism was the social and historical norm, radical northern attempts to force black equality on the South during Reconstruction appeared misguided, if not downright malevolent. The civil rights movement in the 1950s and 1960s forced historians to reevaluate both their attitudes toward current racial issues and their interpretations of the past. This new look led to a shift in the roles of heroes and villains in Reconstruction. Now the Radical Republicans became the good guys and President Andrew Johnson and southern obstructionists the obstacles to racial progress.

Foner suggests that a new, more radical, view has emerged: Reconstruction was simply not extreme enough. The failure of the Radical Republicans to provide "forty acres and a mule" or any economic stake in the new postwar society left the freedmen at the mercy of their former masters—with the resultant economic gap lasting to the present. Nevertheless, the door of hope was opened and blacks have been struggling through it ever since what W. E. B. DuBois termed the "splendid failure" of Reconstruction.

The American character is not static. Frederick Jackson Turner argued that the frontier was the most important factor in forging it. Foner's article depicts human, political attempts to reshape it. The debate over Reconstruction is in part a debate over whether the Radical Republicans, promoting greater racial equality, or the Southern Redeemers, seeking continued racial supremacy, were truer to what the American character has been—or could be.

In the past twenty years, no period of American history has been the subject of a more thoroughgoing reevaluation than Reconstruction—the violent, dramatic, and still controversial era following the Civil War. Race relations, politics, social life, and economic change during Reconstruction have all been reinterpreted in the light of changed attitudes toward the place of blacks within American society. If historians have not yet forged a fully satisfying portrait of Reconstruction as a whole, the traditional interpretation that dominated historical writing for much of this century has irrevocably been laid to rest.

Anyone who attended high school before 1960 learned that Reconstruction was an era of unrelieved sordidness in American political and social life. The martyred Lincoln, according to this view, had planned a quick and painless readmission of the Southern states as equal members of the national family. President Andrew Johnson, his successor, attempted to carry out Lincoln's policies but was foiled by the Radical Republicans (also known as Vindictives or Jacobins). Motivated by an irrational hatred of Rebels or by ties with Northern capitalists out to plunder the South, the Radicals swept aside Johnson's lenient program and fastened black supremacy upon the defeated Confederacy. An orgy of corruption followed, presided over by unscrupulous carpetbaggers (Northerners who ventured south to reap the spoils of office), traitorous scalawags (Southern whites who cooperated with the new governments for personal gain), and the ignorant and childlike freedmen, who were incapable of properly exercising the political power that had been thrust upon them. After much needless suffering, the white community of the South banded together to overthrow these "black" governments and restore home rule (their euphemism for white supremacy). All told, Reconstruction was just about the darkest page in the American saga.

Originating in anti-Reconstruction propaganda of Southern Democrats during the 1870s, this traditional interpretation achieved scholarly legitimacy around the turn of the century through the work of William Dunning and his students at Columbia University. It reached the larger public through films like *Birth of a Nation* and *Gone With the Wind* and that bestselling work of myth-making masquerading as history, *The Tragic Era*, by Claude G. Bowers. In language as exaggerated as it was colorful, Bowers told how Andrew Johnson "fought the bravest battle for constitutional liberty and for the preservation of our institutions ever waged by an Executive" but was overwhelmed by the "poisonous propaganda" of the Radicals. Southern whites, as a result, "literally were put to the torture" by "emissaries of hate" who manipulated the "simple-minded" freedmen, "inflaming the negroes' egotism" and even inspiring "lustful assaults" by blacks upon white womanhood.

In a discipline that sometimes seems to pride itself on the rapid rise and fall of historical interpretations, this traditional portrait of Reconstruction enjoyed remarkable staying power. The long reign of the old interpretation is not difficult to explain. It presented a set of easily identifiable heroes and villains. It enjoyed the imprimatur of the nation's leading scholars. And it accorded with the political and social realities of the first half of this century. This image of Reconstruction helped freeze the mind of the white South in unalterable opposition to any movement for breaching the ascendancy of the Democratic party, eliminating segregation, or readmitting disfranchised blacks to the vote.

Nevertheless, the demise of the traditional interpretation was inevitable, for it ignored the testimony of the central participant in the drama of Reconstruction—the black freedman. Furthermore, it was grounded in the conviction that blacks were unfit to share in political power. As Dunning's Columbia colleague John W. Burgess put it, "A black skin means membership in a race of men which has never of itself succeeded in subjecting passion to reason, has never, therefore, created any civilization of any kind." Once objective scholarship and modern experience rendered that assumption untenable, the entire edifice was bound to fall.

The work of "revising" the history of Reconstruction began with the writings of a handful of survivors of the era, such as John R. Lynch, who had served as a black congressman from Mississippi after the Civil War. In the 1930s white scholars like Francis Simkins and Robert Woody carried the task forward. Then, in 1935, the black historian and activist W. E. B. DuBois produced *Black Reconstruction in America*, a monumental reevaluation that closed with an irrefutable indictment of a historical profession that had sacrificed scholarly objectivity on the altar of racial bias. "One fact and one alone," he wrote, "explains the attitude of most recent writers toward Reconstruction; they cannot conceive of Negroes as men." DuBois's work, however, was ignored by most historians.

It was not until the 1960s that the full force of the revisionist wave broke over the field. Then, in rapid succession, virtually every assumption of the traditional viewpoint was systematically dismantled. A drastically different portrait emerged to take its place. President Lincoln did not have a coherent "plan" for Reconstruction, but at the time of his assassination he had been cautiously contemplating black suffrage. Andrew Johnson was a stubborn, racist politician who lacked the ability to compromise. By isolating himself from the broad currents of public opinion that had nourished Lincoln's career, Johnson created an impasse with Congress that Lincoln would certainly have avoided, thus throwing away his political power and destroying his own plans for reconstructing the South.

The Radicals in Congress were acquitted of both vindictive motive and the charge of serving as the stalking-horses of Northern capitalism. They emerged instead as idealists in the best nineteenth-century reform tradition. Radical leaders like Charles Sumner and Thaddeus Stevens had worked for the rights of blacks long before any conceivable political advantage flowed from such a commitment. Stevens refused to sign the Pennsylvania Constitution of 1838 because it disfranchised the state's black citizens; Sumner led a fight in the 1850s to integrate Boston's public schools. Their Reconstruction policies were based on principle, not petty political advantage, for the central issue dividing Johnson and these Radical Republicans was the civil rights of freedmen. Studies of congressional policy-making, such as Eric L. McKitrick's *Andrew Johnson and Reconstruction,* also revealed that Reconstruction legislation, ranging from the Civil Rights Act of 1866 to the Fourteenth and Fifteenth Amendments, enjoyed broad support from moderate and conservative Republicans. It was not simply the work of a narrow radical faction.

Even more startling was the revised portrait of Reconstruction in the South itself. Imbued with the spirit of the civil rights movement and rejecting entirely the racial assumptions that had underpinned the traditional interpretation, these historians evaluated Reconstruction from the black point of view. Works like Joel Williamson's *After Slavery* portrayed the period as a time of extraordinary political, social, and economic progress for blacks. The establishment of public school systems, the granting of equal citizenship to blacks, the effort to restore the devastated Southern economy, the attempts to construct an interracial political democracy from the ashes of slavery, all these were commendable achievements, not the elements of Bowers's "tragic era."

Unlike earlier writers, the revisionists stressed the active role of the freedmen in shaping Reconstruction. Black initiative established as many schools as did Northern religious societies and the Freedmen's Bureau. The right to vote was not simply thrust upon them by meddling outsiders, since blacks began agitating for the suffrage as soon as they were freed. In 1865 black conventions throughout the South issued eloquent, though unheeded, appeals for equal civil and political rights.

With the advent of Radical Reconstruction in 1867, the freedmen did enjoy a real measure of political power. But black supremacy never existed.

In most states blacks held only a small fraction of political offices, and even in South Carolina, where they comprised a majority of the state legislature's lower house, effective power remained in white hands. As for corruption, moral standards in both government and private enterprise were at low ebb throughout the nation in the postwar years—the era of Boss Tweed, the Credit Mobilier scandal, and the Whiskey Ring. Southern corruption could hardly be blamed on former slaves.

Other actors in the Reconstruction drama also came in for reevaluation. Most carpetbaggers were former Union soldiers seeking economic opportunity in the postwar South, not unscrupulous adventurers. Their motives, a typically American amalgam of humanitarianism and the pursuit of profit, were no more insidious than those of Western pioneers. Scalawags, previously seen as traitors to the white race, now emerged as "Old Line" Whig Unionists who had opposed secession in the first place or as poor whites who had long resented planters' domination of Southern life and who saw in Reconstruction a chance to recast Southern society along more democratic lines. Strongholds of Southern white Republicanism like east Tennessee and western North Carolina had been the scene of resistance to Confederate rule throughout the Civil War; now, as one scalawag newspaper put it, the choice was "between salvation at the hand of the Negro or destruction at the hand of the rebels."

At the same time, the Ku Klux Klan and kindred groups, whose campaign of violence against black and white Republicans had been minimized or excused in older writings, were portrayed as they really were. Earlier scholars had conveyed the impression that the Klan intimidated blacks mainly by dressing as ghosts and playing on the freedmen's superstitions. In fact, black fears were all too real: the Klan was a terrorist organization that beat and killed its political opponents to deprive blacks of their newly won rights. The complicity of the Democratic party and the silence of prominent whites in the face of such outrages stood as an indictment of the moral code the South had inherited from the days of slavery.

By the end of the 1960s, then, the old interpretation had been completely reversed. Southern freedmen were the heroes, the "Redeemers" who overthrew Reconstruction were the villains, and if the era was "tragic," it was because change did not go far enough. Reconstruction had been a time of real progress and its failure a lost opportunity for the South and the nation. But the legacy of Reconstruction—the Fourteenth and Fifteenth Amendments—endured to inspire future efforts for civil rights. As Kenneth Stampp wrote in *The Era of Reconstruction*, a superb summary of revisionist findings published in 1965, "If it was worth four years of civil war to save the Union, it was worth a few years of radical reconstruction to give the American Negro the ultimate promise of equal civil and political rights."

As Stampp's statement suggests, the reevaluation of the first Reconstruction was inspired in large measure by the impact of the second—the modern civil rights movement. And with the waning of that movement in recent years, writing on Reconstruction has undergone still another transformation. Instead of seeing the Civil War and its aftermath as a second American Revolution (as Charles Beard had), a regression into barbarism (as Bowers argued), or a golden opportunity squandered (as the revisionists saw it), recent writers argue that Radical Reconstruction was not really very radical. Since land was not distributed to the former slaves, they remained economically dependent upon their former owners. The planter class survived both the war and Reconstruction with its property (apart from slaves) and prestige more or less intact.

Not only changing times but also the changing concerns of historians have contributed to this latest reassessment of Reconstruction. The hallmark of the past decade's historical writing has been an emphasis upon "social history"—the evocation of the past lives of ordinary Americans—and the downplaying of strictly political events. When applied to Reconstruction, this concern with the "social" suggested that black suffrage and officeholding, once seen as the most radical departures of the Reconstruction era, were relatively insignificant.

Recent historians have focused their investigations not upon the politics of Reconstruction but upon the social and economic aspects of the transition from slavery to freedom. Herbert Gutman's influential study of the black family during and after slavery found little change in family structure or relations between men and women resulting from emancipation. Under slavery most blacks had lived in nuclear family units, although they faced the constant threat of separation from loved ones by sale. Reconstruction provided the opportunity for blacks to solidify their preexisting family ties. Conflicts over whether black women should work in the cotton fields (planters said yes, many black families said no) and over white attempts to "apprentice" black children revealed that the autonomy of family life was a major preoccupation of the freedmen. Indeed, whether manifested in their withdrawal from churches controlled by whites, in the blossoming of black fraternal, benevolent, and self-improvement organizations, or in the demise of the slave quarters and their replacement by small tenant farms occupied by individual families, the quest for independence from white authority and control over their own day-to-day lives shaped the black response to emancipation.

In the post–Civil War South the surest guarantee of economic autonomy, blacks believed, was land. To the freedmen the justice of a claim to land based on their years of unrequited labor appeared self-evident. As an Alabama black convention put it, "The property which they [the planters] hold was nearly all earned by the sweat of our brows." As Leon Litwack showed in *Been in the Storm So Long*, a Pulitzer Prize–winning account of the black response to emancipation, many freedmen in 1865 and 1866 refused to sign labor contracts, expecting the federal government to give them land. In some localities, as one Alabama overseer reported, they "set up claims to the plantation and all on it."

In the end, of course, the vast majority of Southern blacks remained propertyless and poor. But exactly why the South, and especially its black population, suffered from dire poverty and economic retardation in the decades following the Civil War is a matter of much dispute. In *One Kind of Freedom*, economists Roger Ransom and Richard Sutch indicted country merchants for monopolizing credit and charging usurious interest rates, forcing black tenants into debt and locking the South into a dependence on cotton production that impoverished the entire region. But Jonathan Wiener, in his study of postwar Alabama, argued that planters used their political power to compel blacks to remain on the plantations. Planters succeeded in stabilizing the plantation system, but only by blocking the growth of alternative enterprises, like factories, that might draw off black laborers, thus locking the region into a pattern of economic backwardness.

If the thrust of recent writing has emphasized the social and economic aspects of Reconstruction, politics has not been entirely neglected. But political studies have also reflected the postrevisionist mood summarized by C. Vann Woodward when he observed "how essentially nonrevolutionary and conservative Reconstruction really was." Recent writers, unlike their revisionist predecessors, have found little to praise in federal policy toward the emancipated blacks.

A new sensitivity to the strength of prejudice and laissez-faire ideas in the nineteenth-century North has led many historians to doubt whether the Republican party ever made a genuine commitment to racial justice in the South. The granting of black suffrage was an alternative to a long-term federal responsibility for protecting the rights of the former slaves. Once enfranchised, blacks could be left to fend for themselves. With the exception of a few Radicals like Thaddeus Stevens, nearly all Northern policy-makers and educators are criticized today for assuming that, so long as the unfettered operations of the marketplace afforded blacks the opportunity to advance through diligent labor, federal efforts to assist them in acquiring land were unnecessary.

Probably the most innovative recent writing on Reconstruction politics has centered on a broad reassessment of black Republicanism, largely undertaken by a new generation of black historians. Scholars like Thomas Holt and Nell Painter insist that Reconstruction was not simply a matter of black and white. Conflicts within the black community, no less than divisions among whites, shaped Reconstruction politics. Where revisionist scholars, both black and white, had celebrated the accomplishments of black political leaders, Holt, Painter, and others charge that they failed to address the economic plight of the black masses. Painter criticized "representative colored men," as national black leaders were called, for failing to provide ordinary freedmen with effective political leadership. Holt found that black officeholders in

South Carolina mostly emerged from the old free mulatto class of Charleston, which shared many assumptions with prominent whites. "Basically bourgeois in their origins and orientation," he wrote, they "failed to act in the interest of black peasants."

In emphasizing the persistence from slavery of divisions between free blacks and slaves, these writers reflect the increasing concern with continuity and conservatism in Reconstruction. Their work reflects a startling extension of revisionist premises. If, as has been argued for the past twenty years, blacks were active agents rather than mere victims of manipulation, then they could not be absolved of blame for the ultimate failure of Reconstruction.

Despite the excellence of recent writing and the continual expansion of our knowledge of the period, historians of Reconstruction today face a unique dilemma. An old interpretation has been overthrown, but a coherent new synthesis has yet to take its place. The revisionists of the 1960s effectively established a series of negative points: the Reconstruction governments were not as bad as had been portrayed, black supremacy was a myth, the Radicals were not cynical manipulators of the freedmen. Yet no convincing overall portrait of the quality of political and social life emerged from their writings. More recent historians have rightly pointed to elements of continuity that spanned the nineteenth-century Southern experience, especially the survival, in modified form, of the plantation system. Nevertheless, by denying the real changes that did occur, they have failed to provide a convincing portrait of an era characterized above all by drama, turmoil, and social change.

Building upon the findings of the past twenty years of scholarship, a new portrait of Reconstruction ought to begin by viewing it not as a specific time period, bounded by the years 1865 and 1877, but as an episode in a prolonged historical process—American society's adjustment to the consequences of the Civil War and emancipation. The Civil War, of course, raised the decisive questions of America's national existence: the relations between local and national authority, the definition of citizenship, the balance between force and consent in generating obedience to authority. The war and Reconstruction, as Allan Nevins observed over fifty years ago, marked the "emergence of modern America." This was the era of the completion of the national railroad network, the creation of the modern steel industry, the conquest of the West and final subduing of the Indians, and the expansion of the mining frontier. Lincoln's America—the world of the small farm and artisan shop—gave way to a rapidly industrializing economy. The issues that galvanized postwar Northern politics—from the question of the greenback currency to the mode of paying holders of the national debt—arose from the economic changes unleashed by the Civil War.

Above all, the war irrevocably abolished slavery. Since 1619, when "twenty negars" disembarked from a Dutch ship in Virginia, racial injustice had haunted American life, mocking its professed ideals even as tobacco and cotton, the products of slave labor, helped finance the nation's economic development. Now the implications of the black presence could no longer be ignored. The Civil War resolved the problem of slavery but, as the Philadelphia diarist Sydney George Fisher observed in June 1865, it opened an even more intractable problem: "What shall we do with the Negro?" Indeed, he went on, this was a problem *"incapable* of any solution that will satisfy both North and South."

As Fisher realized, the focal point of Reconstruction was the social revolution known as emancipation. Plantation slavery was simultaneously a system of labor, a form of racial domination, and the foundation upon which arose a distinctive ruling class within the South. Its demise threw open the most fundamental questions of economy, society, and politics. A new system of labor, social, racial, and political relations had to be created to replace slavery.

The United States was not the only nation to experience emancipation in the nineteenth century. Neither plantation slavery nor abolition were unique to the United States. But Reconstruction was. In a comparative perspective Radical Reconstruction stands as a remarkable experiment, the only effort of a society experiencing abolition to bring the former slaves within the umbrella of equal citizenship. Because the Radicals did not achieve everything they wanted, historians have lately tended to play down the stunning departure represented by black suffrage and officeholding. Former slaves, most fewer than two years removed from bondage, debated the fundamental questions of the polity: What is a republican form of government? Should the state provide equal education for all? How could political equality be reconciled with a society in which property was so unequally distributed? There was something inspiring in the way such men met the challenge of Reconstruction. "I knew nothing more than to obey my master," James K. Greene, an Alabama black politician later recalled. "But the tocsin of freedom sounded and knocked at the door and we walked out like free men and we met the exigencies as they grew up, and shouldered the responsibilities."

"You never saw a people more excited on the subject of politics than are the negroes of the south," one planter observed in 1867. And there were more than a few Southern whites as well who in these years shook off the prejudices of the past to embrace the vision of a new South dedicated to the principles of equal citizenship and social justice. One ordinary South Carolinian expressed the new sense of possibility in 1868 to the Republican governor of the state: "I am sorry that I cannot write an elegant stiled letter to your excellency. But I rejoice to think that God almighty has given to the poor of S.C. a Gov. to hear to feel to protect the humble poor without distinction to race or color. . . . I am a native borned S.C. a poor man never owned a Negro in my life nor my father before me. . . . Remember the true and loyal are the poor of the whites and blacks, outside of these you can find none loyal."

Few modern scholars believe the Reconstruction governments established in the South in 1867 and 1868 fulfilled the aspirations of their humble constituents. While their achievements in such realms as education, civil rights, and the economic rebuilding of the South are now widely appreciated, historians today believe they failed to affect either the economic plight of the emancipated slave or the ongoing transformation of independent white farmers into cotton tenants. Yet their opponents did perceive the Reconstruction governments in precisely this way—as representatives of a revolution that had put the bottom rail, both racial and economic, on top. This perception helps explain the ferocity of the attacks leveled against them and the pervasiveness of violence in the postemancipation South.

The spectacle of black men voting and holding office was anathema to large numbers of Southern whites. Even more disturbing, at least in the view of those who still controlled the plantation regions of the South, was the emergence of local officials, black and white, who sympathized with the plight of the black laborer. Alabama's vagrancy law was a "dead letter" in 1870, "because those who are charged with its enforcement are indebted to the vagrant vote for their offices and emoluments." Political debates over the level and incidence of taxation, the control of crops, and the resolution of contract disputes revealed that a primary issue of Reconstruction was the role of government in a plantation society. During presidential Reconstruction, and after "Redemption," with planters and their allies in control of politics, the law emerged as a means of stabilizing and promoting the plantation system. If Radical Reconstruction failed to redistribute the land of the South, the ouster of the planter class from control of politics at least ensured that the sanctions of the criminal law would not be employed to discipline the black labor force.

An understanding of this fundamental conflict over the relation between government and society helps explain the pervasive complaints concerning corruption and "extravagance" during Radical Reconstruction. Corruption there was aplenty; tax rates did rise sharply. More significant than the rate of taxation, however, was the change in its incidence. For the first time, planters and white farmers had to pay a significant portion of their income to the government, while propertyless blacks often escaped scot-free. Several states, moreover, enacted heavy taxes on uncultivated land to discourage land speculation and force land onto the market, benefiting, it was hoped, the freedmen.

As time passed, complaints about the "extravagance" and corruption of Southern governments found a sympathetic audience among influential Northerners. The Democratic charge that universal suffrage in the South was responsible for high taxes and governmental extravagance coincided with a rising conviction among the urban middle classes of the North that city government had to be taken out of the hands of the immigrant poor and returned to the "best men"—the educated, professional, financially independent citizens unable to exert much political influence at a time of mass parties and machine politics. Increasingly the "respectable" middle classes began to retreat from the very notion of universal suffrage. The poor were no longer perceived as honest producers, the backbone of the social order; now they became the "dangerous classes," the "mob." As the historian Francis Parkman put it, too much power rested with "masses of imported ignorance and hereditary ineptitude." To Parkman the Irish of the Northern cities and the blacks of the South were equally incapable of utilizing the ballot: "Witness the municipal corruptions of New York, and the monstrosities of negro rule in South Carolina." Such attitudes helped to justify Northern inaction as, one by one, the Reconstruction regimes of the South were overthrown by political violence.

In the end, then, neither the abolition of slavery nor Reconstruction succeeded in resolving the debate over the meaning of freedom in American life. Twenty years before the American Civil War, writing about the prospect of abolition in France's colonies, Alexis de Tocqueville had written, "If the Negroes have the right to become free, the [planters] have the incontestable right not to be ruined by the Negroes' freedom." And in the United States, as in nearly every plantation society that experienced the end of slavery, a rigid social and political dichotomy between former master and former slave, an ideology of racism, and a dependent labor force with limited economic opportunities all survived abolition. Unless one means by freedom the simple fact of not being a slave, emancipation thrust blacks into a kind of no-man's land, a partial freedom that made a mockery of the American ideal of equal citizenship.

Yet by the same token the ultimate outcome underscores the uniqueness of Reconstruction itself. Alone among the societies that abolished slavery in the nineteenth century, the United States, for a moment, offered the freedmen a measure of political control over their own destinies. However brief its sway, Reconstruction allowed scope for a remarkable political and social mobilization of the black community. It opened doors of opportunity that could never be completely closed. Reconstruction transformed the lives of Southern blacks in ways unmeasurable by statistics and unreachable by law. It raised their expectations and aspirations, redefined their status in relation to the larger society, and allowed space for the creation of institutions that enabled them to survive the repression that followed. And it established constitutional principles of civil and political equality that, while flagrantly violated after Redemption, planted the seeds of future struggle.

Certainly, in terms of the sense of possibility with which it opened, Reconstruction failed. But as DuBois observed, it was a "splendid failure." For its animating vision—a society in which social advancement would be open to all on the basis of individual merit, not inherited caste distinctions—is as old as America itself and remains relevant to a nation still grappling with the unresolved legacy of emancipation.

QUESTIONS TO CONSIDER

1. Prior to the modern civil rights movement, whom did historians describe as the "good guys" and "bad guys" of Reconstruction? Why?
2. What caused that long-lived interpretation to crumble?
3. What was the focal point of Reconstruction, according to Foner and Sydney George Fisher?
4. In the long run, how did Reconstruction most fail the freedmen? Why did that failure occur and why was it critical?
5. Does Foner conclude that Reconstruction was a success or a failure? What do you conclude?

2

Ten-Gallon Hero

DAVID BRION DAVIS

Reprinted from *American Quarterly*,
© 1954, Trustees of the University
of Pennsylvania.

David Brion Davis (1927–   ), a professor of history at Yale, has won renown as a specialist in the history of slavery. His profound and original studies—*The Problem of Slavery in Western Culture* (1966), *The Problem of Slavery in the Age of Revolution* (1975), and *Slavery and Human Progress* (1984)—earned him a reputation as one of the nation's foremost scholars. His interest in the broader field of nineteenth-century cultural and intellectual history led him in 1954 to write this article on the cowboy.

Davis explains how the mythical cowboy was a synthesis of the myths of the western scout and the antebellum southern gentleman. The cowboy, Davis maintains, outlasted such earlier nostalgic frontier images because he embodied the last of American frontiers. Owen Wister's classic portrait *The Virginian* (1902) appeared just nine years after Frederick Jackson Turner's famous paper presented at 1893 AHA convention in Chicago on the significance of the frontier on American history, itself occasioned by the "end" of the frontier disclosed by the 1890 census. Through a combination of commercial exploitation and psychological need, the cowboy became a symbol of American individualism, not only to Americans, but also to the world.

Since "Ten-Gallon Hero" appeared, the cowboy has fallen from his preeminent position on television and in the movies. He is most evident today in commercials for beer, cigarettes, and pickup trucks, where he continues to embody the ultimate independent, free man. He has been replaced as a hero for preadolescents by Luke Skywalker and other "space cowboys" who are pursuing the final frontier, free even from the constraints of earth. Another hero of today's youth is the independent, uncontrollable law enforcer in the mold of Dirty Harry. The new generation has paid a price for changing its heroes. Whereas the cowboy was quite clearly escapist in nature, the contemporary setting and plausibility of the violent cops-and-robbers shows have made heavy viewers far more fearful about the world in which they live. Thus, the American character is being continually forged, not only by great ideas, but also by such commonplace things as one's choice of entertainment and heroes.

In 1900 it seemed that the significance of the cowboy era would decline along with other brief but romantic episodes in American history. The Long Drive lingered only in the memories and imaginations of old cowhands. The "hoemen" occupied former range land while Mennonites and professional dry farmers had sown their Turkey Red winter wheat on the Kansas prairies. To be sure, a cattle industry still flourished, but the cowboy was more like an employee of a corporation than the free-lance cowboy of old. The myth of the cowboy lived on in the Beadle and Adams paper-back novels, with the followers of Ned Buntline and the prolific Colonel Prentiss Ingraham. But this seemed merely a substitution of the more up-to-date cowboy in a tradition which began with Leatherstocking and Daniel Boone. If the mountain man had replaced Boone and the forest scouts, if the cowboy had succeeded the mountain man, and if the legends of Mike Fink and Crockett were slipping into the past, it would seem probable that the cowboy would follow, to become a quaint character of antiquity, overshadowed by newer heroes.

Yet more than a half century after the passing of the actual wild and woolly cowboy, we find a unique phenomenon in American mythology. Gaudy-covered Western or cowboy magazines decorate stands, windows, and shelves in "drug" stores, bookstores, grocery stores, and supermarkets from Miami to Seattle. Hundreds of cowboy movies and television shows are watched and lived through by millions of Americans. Nearly every little boy demands a cowboy suit and a Western six-shooter cap pistol. Cowboys gaze out at you with steely eye and cocked revolver from cereal packages and television screens. Jukeboxes in Bennington, Vermont, as well as Globe, Arizona, moan and warble the latest cowboy songs. Middle-age folk who had once thought of William S. Hart, Harry Carey, and Tom Mix as a passing phase, have lived to see several Hopalong Cassidy revivals, the Lone Ranger, Tim McCoy, Gene Autry, and Roy Rogers. Adolescents and even grown men in Maine and Florida can be seen affecting cowboy, or at least modified cowboy garb, while in the new airplane plants in Kansas, workers don their cowboy boots and wide-brimmed hats, go to work whistling a cowboy song, and are defiantly proud that they live in the land of lassos and sixguns.

When recognized at all, this remarkable cowboy complex is usually defined as the distortion of once-colorful legends by a commercial society. The obvious divergence between the real West and the idealized version, the standardization of plot and characters, and the ridiculous incongruities of cowboys with automobiles and airplanes, all go to substantiate this conclusion.

However, there is more than the cowboy costume and stage setting in even the wildest of these adventures. Despite the incongruities, the cowboy myth exists in fact, and as such is probably a more influential social force than the actual cowboy ever was. It provides the framework for an expression of common ideals of morality and behavior. And while a commercial success, the hero cowboy must satisfy some basic want in American culture, or there could never be such a tremendous market. It is true that the market has been exploited by magazine, song, and scenario writers, but it is important to ask why similar myths have not been equally profitable, such as the lumbermen of the early northwest, the whale fishermen of New Bedford, the early railroad builders, or the fur traders. There have been romances written and movies produced idealizing these phases of American history, but little boys do not dress up like Paul Bunyan and you do not see harpooners on cereal packages. Yet America has had many episodes fully as colorful and of longer duration than the actual cowboy era.

The cowboy hero and his setting are a unique synthesis of two American traditions, and echoes of this past can be discerned in even the wildest of the modern horse operas. On the one hand, the line of descent is a direct evolution from the Western scout of Cooper and the Dime Novel; on the other, there has been a recasting of the golden myth of the antebellum South. The two were fused sometime in the 1880s. Perhaps there was actually some basis for such a union. While the West was economically tied to the North as soon as the early canals and railroads broke the river-centered traffic, social ties endured longer. Many Southerners emigrated West and went into the cattle business, and of course, the Long Drive originated in Texas. The literary synthesis of two traditions only followed the two social movements. It was on the Great Plains that the descendants of Daniel Boone met the drawling Texas cowboy.

Henry Nash Smith has described two paradoxical aspects of the legendary Western scout, typified in Boone himself. This woodsman, this buckskin-clad wilderness hunter is a pioneer, breaking trails for his countrymen to follow, reducing the savage wilderness for civilization. Nevertheless, he is also represented as escaping civilization, turning his back on the petty materialism of the world, on the hypocritical and self-conscious manners of community life, and seeking the unsullied, true values of nature.

These seemingly conflicting points of view have counterparts in the woodsman's descendant, the cowboy. The ideal cowboy fights for justice, risks his life to make the dismal little cowtown safe for law-abiding, respectable citizens, but in so doing he destroys the very environment which made him a heroic figure. This paradox is common with all ideals, and the cowboy legend is certainly the embodiment of a social ideal. Thus the minister or social reformer who rises to heroism in his fight against a sin-infested community would logically become a mere figurehead once the community is reformed. There can be no true ideal or hero in a utopia. And the civilization for which the cowboy or trailblazer struggles is utopian in character.

But there is a further consideration in the case of the cowboy. In our mythology, the cowboy era is timeless. The ranch may own a modern station wagon, but the distinguishing attributes of cowboy and environment remain. There is, it is true, a nostalgic sense that this is the last great drama, a sad knowledge that the cowboy is passing and that civilization is approaching. But it never comes. This strange, wistful sense of the coming end of an epoch is not something outside our experience. It is a faithful reflection of the sense of approaching adulthood. The appeal of the cowboy, in this sense, is similar to the appeal of Boone, Leatherstocking, and the later Mountain Man. We know that adulthood, civilization, is inevitable, but we are living toward the end of childhood, and at that point "childness" seems eternal; it is a whole lifetime. But suddenly we find it is not eternal, the forests disappear, the mountains are settled, and we have new responsibilities. When we shut our eyes and try to remember, the last image of a carefree life appears. For the nation, this last image is the cowboy.

The reborn myth of the antebellum South also involves nostalgia; not so much nostalgia for something that actually existed as for dreams and ideals. When the Southern myth reappeared on the rolling prairies, it was purified and regenerated by the casting off of apologies for slavery. It would focus all energies on its former role of opposing the peculiar social and economic philosophy of the Northeast. This took the form of something more fundamental than mere agrarianism or primitivism. Asserting the importance of values beyond the utilitarian and material, this transplanted Southern philosophy challenged the doctrine of enlightened self-interest and the belief that leisure time is sin.

Like the barons and knights of Southern feudalism, the large ranch owners and itinerant cowboys knew how to have a good time. If there was a time for work, there was a time for play, and the early rodeos, horse races, and wild nights at a cowtown were not occasions for reserve. In this respect, the cowboy West was more in the tradition of fun-loving New Orleans than of the Northeast. Furthermore, the ranch was a remarkable duplication of the plantation, minus slaves. It was a hospitable social unit, where travelers were welcome even when the owner was absent. As opposed to the hardworking, thrifty, and sober ideal of the East, the actual cowboy was overly cheerful at times, generous to the point of waste, and inclined to value friendly comradeship above prestige.

The mythical New England Yankee developed a code of action which always triumphed over the more sophisticated city slicker, because the Yankee's down-to-earth shrewdness, common sense, and reserved humor embodied values which Americans considered as pragmatically effective. The ideal cowboy also had a code of action, but it involved neither material nor social success. The cowboy avoided actions which "just weren't done" because he placed a value on doing things "right," on managing difficult problems and situations with ease, skill, and modesty. The cowboy's code was a Western and democratic version of the Southern gentleman's "honor."

In the early years of the twentieth century, a Philadelphia lawyer, who affected a careless, loose-tied bow instead of the traditional black ribbon and who liked to appear in his shirt sleeves, wrote: "The nomadic bachelor west is over, the housed, married west is established." In a book published in 1902 he had, more than any other man, established an idealized version of the former, unifying the Southern and Western hero myths in a formula which was not to be forgotten. Owen Wister had, in fact, liberated the cowboy hero from the Dime Novels and provided a synthetic tradition suitable for a new century. The Virginian became a key document in popular American culture, a romance which defined the cowboy character and thus the ideal American character in terms of courage, sex, religion, and humor. The novel served as a model for hundreds of Western books and movies for half a century. In the recent popular movie "High Noon" a Hollywood star, who won his fame dramatizing Wister's novel, reenacted the same basic plot of hero rejecting heroine's pleas and threats, to uphold his honor against the villain Trampas. While this theme is probably at least a thousand years old, it was Owen Wister who gave it a specifically American content and thus explicated and popularized the modern cowboy ideal, with its traditions, informality, and all-important code.

Of course, Wister's West is not the realistic, boisterous, sometimes monotonous West of Charlie Siringo and Andy Adams. The cowboy, after all, drove cattle. He worked. There was much loneliness and monotony on the range, which has faded like mist under a desert sun in the reminiscences of old cow hands and the fiction of idealizers. The Virginian runs some errands now and then, but there are no cattle-driving scenes, no monotony, no hard work. Fictional cowboys are never bored. Real cowboys were often so bored that they memorized the labels on tin cans and then played games to see how well they could recite them. The cowboys in books and movies are far too busy making love and chasing bandits to work at such a dreary task as driving cattle. But then the Southern plantation owner did no work. The befringed hero of the forests did not work. And if any ideal is to be accepted by adolescent America, monotonous work must be subordinated to more exciting pastimes. The fact that the cowboy hero has more important things to do is only in keeping with his tradition and audience. He is only a natural reaction against a civilization which demands increasingly monotonous work, against the approaching adulthood when playtime ends.

And if the cowboy romance banishes work and monotony, their very opposites are found in the immensity of the Western environment. To be sure, the deserts and prairies can be bleak, but they are never dull when used as setting for the cowboy myth. There is always an element of the unexpected, of surprise, of variety. The tremendous distances either seclude or elevate the particular and significant. There are mirages, hidden springs, dust storms, hidden identities, and secret ranches. In one of his early Western novels William MacLeod Raine used both devices of a secret ranch and hidden identity, while Hoffman Birney combined a hidden ranch, a secret trail, and two hidden identities. In such an environment of uncertainty and change men of true genius stand out from the rest. The evil or good in an individual is quickly revealed in cowboy land. A man familiar with the actual cowboy wrote that "brains, moral and physical courage, strength of character, native gentlemanliness, proficiency in riding or shooting—every quality of leadership tended to raise its owner from the common level."

The hazing which cowboys gave the tenderfoot was only preliminary. It was a symbol of the true test which anyone must undergo in the West. After the final winnowing of men, there emerge the heroes, the villains, and the clowns. The latter live in a purgatory and usually attach themselves to the hero group. Often, after the stress of an extreme emergency, they burst out of their caste and are accepted in the elite.

While the Western environment, according to the myth, sorts men into their true places, it does not determine men. It brings out the best in heroes and the worst in villains, but it does not add quality to the man who has none. The cowboy is a superman and is adorable for his own sake. It is here that he is the descendant of supernatural folk heroes. Harry Hawkeye, the creator of an early cowboy hero, Calvin Yancey, described him as:

> straight as an arrow, fair and ruddy as a Viking, with long flowing golden hair, which rippled over his massive shoulders, falling nearly to his waist; a high, broad forehead beneath which sparkled a pair of violet blue eyes, tender and soulful in repose, but firm and determined under excitement. His entire face was a study for a sculptor with its delicate aquiline nose, straight in outline as though chiselled from Parian marble, and its generous manly mouth, with full crimson and arched lips, surmounted by a long, silken blonde mustache, through which a beautiful set of even white teeth gleamed like rows of lustrous pearls.

While the Virginian is not quite the blond, Nordic hero, he is just as beautiful to behold. His black, curly locks, his lean athletic figure, his quiet, unassuming manner, all go to make him the most physically attractive man Owen Wister could describe. Later cowboy heroes have shaved their mustaches, but the great majority have beautiful curly hair, usually blond or red, square jaws, cleft chins, broad shoulders, deep chests, and wasplike waists. Like the Virginian, they are perfect men, absolutely incapable of doing the wrong thing unless deceived.

Many writers familiar with the real cowboy have criticized Wister for his concentration on the Virginian's love interest and, of course, they deplore the present degeneration of the cowboy plot, where love is supreme. There were few women in the West in the Chisholm Trail days and those few in Dodge City, Abilene, and Wichita were of dubious morality. The cowboy's sex life was intermittent, to say the least. He had to carry his thirst long distances, like a camel, and in the oases the orgies were hardly on a spiritual plane. Since earlier heroes, like the woodsman, led celibate lives, it is important to ask why the cowboy depends on love interest.

At first glance, there would seem to be an inconsistency here. The cowboy is happiest with a group of buddies, playing poker, chasing horse thieves, riding in masculine company. He is contemptuous of farmers, has no interest in children, and considers men who have lived among women as effete. Usually he left his own family at a tender age and rebelled against the restrictions of mothers and older sisters. Neither the Virginian nor the actual cowboys were family men, nor did they have much interest in the homes they left behind. Thus, it would seem that courting a young schoolteacher from Vermont would be self-destruction. At no place is the idealized cowboy further from reality than in his love for the tender woman from the East. Like the law and order he fights for, she will destroy his way of life.

But this paradox is solved when one considers the hero cowboy, not the plot, as the center of all attention. Molly Wood in *The Virginian*, like all her successors, is a literary device, a *dea ex machina* with a special purpose. Along with the Western environment, she serves to throw a stronger light on the hero, to make him stand out in relief, to complete the picture of an ideal. In the first place, she brings out qualities in him which we could not see otherwise. Without her, he would be too much the brute for a real folk hero, at least in a modern age. If Molly Wood were not in *The Virginian*, the hero might seem too raucous, too wild. Of course, his affair with a blonde in town is handled genteelly; his boyish pranks such as mixing up the babies at a party are treated as good, clean fun. But still, there is nothing to bring out his qualities of masculine tenderness, there is nothing to show his conscience until Molly Wood arrives. A cowboy's tenderness is usually revealed through his kindness to horses, and in this sense, the Eastern belle's role is that of a glorified horse. A woman in the Western drama is somebody to rescue, somebody to protect. In her presence, the cowboy shows that, in his own way, he is a cultural ideal. The nomadic, bachelor cowboys described by Andy Adams and Charles Siringo are a little too masculine, a little too isolated from civilization to become the ideal for a settled community.

While the Western heroine brings out a new aspect of the cowboy's character, she also serves the external purpose of registering our attitudes toward him. The cowboy ideal is an adorable figure and the heroine is the vehicle of adoration. Female characters enable the author to make observations about cowboys which would be impossible with an all-male cast. This role would lose its value if the heroine surrendered to the cowboy immediately. So the more she struggles with herself, the more she conquers her Eastern reservations and surmounts difficulties before capitulating, the more it enhances the hero.

Again, *The Virginian* is the perfect example. We do not meet Molly Wood in the first part of the book. Instead, the author, the I, who is an Easterner, goes to Wyoming and meets the Virginian. It is love at first sight, not in the sexual sense, of course (this was 1902), but there is no mistaking it for anything other than love. This young man's love for the Virginian is not important in itself; it heightens our worship of the hero. The sex of the worshiper is irrelevant. At first the young man is disconsolate, because he cannot win the Virginian's friendship. He must go through the ordeal of not knowing the Virginian's opinion of him. But as he learns the ways of the West, the Virginian's sublime goodness is unveiled. Though increasing knowledge of the hero's character only serves to widen the impossible gulf between the finite Easterner and the infinite, pure virtue of the cowboy, the latter, out of his own free grace and goodness recognizes the lowly visitor, who adores him all the more for it. But this little episode is only a preface, a symbol of the drama to come. As soon as the Virginian bestows his grace on the male adorer, Molly Wood arrives. The same passion is reenacted, though on a much larger frame. In this role, the sex of Molly is important, and the traditional romance plot is only superficial form. Molly's coyness, her reserve, her involved heritage of Vermont tradition, all go to build an insurmountable barrier. Yet she loves the Virginian. And Owen Wister and his audience love the Virginian through Molly Wood's love. With the male adorer, they had gone about as far as they could go. But Molly offers a new height from which to love the Virginian. There are many exciting possibilities. Molly can save his life and nurse him back to health. She can threaten to break off their wedding if he goes out to fight his rival, and then forgive him when he disobeys her plea. The Virginian marries Molly in the end and most of his descendants either marry or are about to marry their lovely ladies. But this does not mean a physical marriage, children, and a home. That would be building up a hero only to destroy him. The love climax at the end of the cowboy drama raises the hero to a supreme height, [and] the audience achieves an emotional union with its ideal. In the next book or movie the cowboy will be the carefree bachelor again.

The classic hero, Hopalong Cassidy, has saved hundreds of heroines, protected them, and has been adored by them. But in 1910 Hopalong, "remembering a former experience of his own, smiled in knowing cynicism when told that he again would fall under the feminine spell." In 1950 he expressed the same resistance to actual marriage:

"But you can't always move on, Hoppy!" Lenny protested. "Someday you must settle down! Don't you ever think of marriage?" "Un-huh, and whenever I think of it I saddle Topper and ride. I'm not a marrying man,

Lenny. Sometimes I get to thinkin' about that poem a feller wrote, about how a woman is only a woman but—" "The open road is my Fate!" she finished. "That's it. But can you imagine any woman raised outside a tepee livin' in the same house with a restless man?"

The cowboy hero is the hero of the preadolescent, either chronologically or mentally. It is the stage of revolt against femininity and feminine standards. It is also the age of hero worship. If the cowboy romance were sexual, if it implied settling down with a real *girl*, there would be little interest. One recent cowboy hero summarized this attitude in terms which should appeal strongly to any ten-year-old: "I'd as soon fight a she-lion barehanded as have any truck with a gal." The usual cowboy movie idol has about as much social presence in front of the leading lady as a very bashful boy. He is most certainly not the lover-type. That makes him lovable to both male and female Americans. There can be no doubt that Owen Wister identified himself, not with the Virginian, but with Molly Wood.

While some glorifiers of the actual cowboy have maintained that his closeness to nature made him a deeply religious being, thus echoing the devoutness of the earlier woodsman hero who found God in nature, this tradition has never carried over to the heroic cowboy. Undoubtedly some of the real cowboys were religious, though the consensus of most of the writers on the subject seems to indicate that indifference was more common. Intellectualized religion obviously had no appeal and though the cowboy was often deeply sentimental, he did not seem prone to the emotional and frenzied religion of backwoods farmers and squatters. Perhaps his freedom from family conflicts, from smoldering hatreds and entangled jealousies and loves, had something to do with this. Despite the hard work, the violent physical conflicts, and the occasional debaucheries, the cowboy's life must have had a certain innocent, Homeric quality. Even when witnessing a lynching or murder, the cowboy must have felt further removed from total depravity or original sin than the farmer in a squalid frontier town, with his nagging wife and thirteen children.

At any rate, the cowboy hero of our mythology is too much of a god himself to feel humility. His very creation is a denial of any kind of sin. The cowboy is an enunciation of the goodness of man and the glory which he can achieve by himself. The Western environment strips off the artifice, the social veneer, and instead of a cringing sinner, we behold a dazzling superman. He is a figure of friendly justice, full of self-reliance, a very tower of strength. What need has he of a god?

Of course, the cowboy is not positively antireligious. He is a respecter of traditions as long as they do not threaten his freedom. The Virginian is polite enough to the orthodox minister who visits his employer's ranch. He listens respectfully to the long sermon, but the ranting and raving about his evil nature are more than he can stand. He knows that his cowboy friends are good men. He loves the beauty of the natural world and feels that the Creator of such a world must be a good and just God. Beyond that, the most ignorant cowboy knows as much as this sinister-voiced preacher. So like a young Greek god leaving Mount Olympus for a practical joke in the interest of justice, the Virginian leaves his role of calm and straightforward dignity, and engages in some humorous guile and deceit. The minister is sleeping in the next room and the Virginian calls him and complains that the devil is clutching him. After numerous sessions of wrestling with his conscience, the sleepy minister acting as referee, morning comes before the divine finds he has been tricked. He leaves the ranch in a rage, much to the delight of all the cowboys. The moral, observes Wister, is that men who are obsessed with evil and morbid ideas of human nature had better stay away from the cowboy West. As Alfred Henry Lewis put it, describing a Western town the year *The Virginian* was published, "Wolfville's a hard practical outfit, what you might call a heap obdurate, an' it's goin' to take more than them fitful an' o'casional sermons I aloodes to,—to reach the roots of its soul." The cowboy is too good and has too much horse sense to be deluded by such brooding theology. Tex Burns could have been describing the Virginian when he wrote that his characters "had the cow hand's rough sense of humor and a zest for practical jokes no cow hand ever outgrows."

Coming as it did at the end of the nineteenth century, the cowboy ideal registered both a protest against orthodox creeds and a faith that man needs no formal religion, once he finds a pure and natural environment. It is the extreme end of a long evolution of individualism. Even the individualistic forest scout was dependent on his surroundings, and he exhibited a sort of pantheistic piety when he beheld the wilderness. The mighty captain of industry, while not accountable to anyone in this world, gave lip-service to the generous God who had made him a steward of wealth. But the cowboy hero stood out on the lonely prairie, dependent on neither man nor God. He was willing to take whatever risks lay along his road and would gladly make fun of any man who took life too seriously. Speaking of his mother's death, a real cowboy is supposed to have said:

> With almost her last breath, she begged me to make my peace with God, while the making was good. I have been too busy to heed her last advice. Being a just God, I feel that He will overlook my neglect. If not, I will have to take my medicine, with Satan holding the spoon.

While the cowboy hero has a respect for property, he does not seek personal wealth and is generous to the point of carelessness. He gives money to his friends, to people in distress, and blows the rest when he hits town on Saturday night. He owns no land and, in fact, has only contempt for farmers, with their ploughed fields and weather-beaten buildings. He hates the slick professional gambler, the grasping Eastern speculator, and railroad man.

How are these traits to be reconciled with his regard for property rights? The answer lies in a single possession—his horse. The cowboy's horse is what separates him from vagabondage and migratory labor. It is his link with the cavalier and plumed knight. More and more, in our increasingly property-conscious society, the cowboy's horse has gained in importance. A horse thief becomes a symbol of concentrated evil, a projection of all crime against property and, concomitantly, against social status. Zane Grey was adhering to this tradition when he wrote, "in those days, a horse meant all the world to a man. A lucky strike of grassy upland and good water . . . made him rich in all that he cared to own." On the other hand, "a horse thief was meaner than a poisoned coyote."

When a cowboy is willing to sell his horse, as one actually does in *The Virginian*, he has sold his dignity and self-identity. It is the tragic mistake which will inevitably bring its nemesis. His love for and close relationship with his horse not only make a cowboy seem more human, they also show his respect for propriety and order. He may drift from ranch to ranch, but his horse ties him down to respectability. Yet the cowboy hero is not an ambitious man. He lacks the concern for hard work and practical results which typifies the Horatio Alger ideal. Despite his fine horse and expensive saddle and boots, he values his code of honor and his friends more than possessions. Because the cowboy era is timeless, the hero has little drive or push toward a new and better life. He fights for law and order and this implies civilization, but the cowboy has no visions of empires, industrial or agrarian.

One of the American traits which foreign visitors most frequently described was the inability to have a good time. Americans constantly appear in European journals as ill-at-ease socially, as feeling they must work every spare moment. Certainly it was part of the American Protestant capitalistic ethic, the Poor Richard, Horatio Alger ideal, that spare time, frivolous play, and relaxation were sins which would bring only poverty, disease, and other misfortunes. If a youth would study the wise sayings of great men, if he worked hard and made valuable friends but no really confidential ones, if he never let his hair down or became too intimate with any person, wife included, if he stolidly kept his emotions to himself and watched for his chance in the world, then he would be sure to succeed. But the cowboy hero is mainly concerned with doing things skillfully and conforming to his moral code for its own sake. When he plays poker, treats the town to a drink, or raises a thousand dollars to buy off the evil mortgage, he is not aiming at personal success. Most cowboy heroes have at least one friend who knows them intimately, and they are seldom reserved, except in the presence of a villain or nosey stranger.

Both the hero and real cowboy appear to be easy-going and informal. In dress, speech, and social manner, the cowboy sets a new ideal. Every cowboy knows how to relax. If the villains are sometimes tense and nervous, the hero sits placidly at a card game, never ruffled, never disturbed, even when his arch rival is behind him at the bar, hot with rage and whisky. The ideal cowboy is the kind of man who turns around slowly when a pistol goes off and drawls, "Ah'd put thet up, if Ah were yew." William Macleod Raine's Sheriff Collins chats humorously with some train robbers and maintains a calm, unconcerned air which amuses the passengers, though he is actually pumping the bandits for useful information. Previously, he had displayed typical cowboy individualism by flagging the train down and climbing aboard, despite the protests of the conductor. Instead of the eager, aspiring youth, the cowboy hero is like a young tomcat, calm and relaxed but always ready to spring into action. An early description of one of the most persistent of the cowboy heroes summarizes the ideal characteristics which appeal to a wide audience:

> Hopalong Cassidy had the most striking personality of all the men in his outfit; humorous, courageous to the point of foolishness, eager for fight or frolic, nonchalant when one would expect him to be quite otherwise, curious, loyal to a fault, and best man with a Colt in the Southwest, he was a paradox, and a puzzle even to his most intimate friends. With him life was a humorous recurrence of sensations, a huge pleasant joke instinctively tolerated, but not worth the price cowards pay to keep it. He had come onto the range when a boy and since that time he had laughingly carried his life in his open hand, and . . . still carried it there, and just as recklessly.

Of course, most cowboy books and movies bristle with violence. Wild fist fights, brawls with chairs and bottles, gun play and mass battles with crashing windows, fires, and the final racing skirmish on horseback, are all as much a part of the cowboy drama as the boots and spurs. These bloody escapades are necessary and are simply explained. They provide the stage for the hero to show his heroism, and since the cowboy is the hero to the preadolescent, he must prove himself by their standards. Physical prowess is the most important thing for the ten- or twelve-year-old mind. They are constantly plagued by fear, doubt, and insecurity, in short, by evil, and they lack the power to crush it. The cowboy provides the instrument for their aggressive impulses, while the villain symbolizes all evil. The ethics of the cowboy band are the ethics of the boy's gang, where each member has a role determined by his physical skills and his past performance. As with any group of boys, an individual cowboy who had been "taken down a peg" was forever ridiculed and teased about his loss in status.

The volume of cowboy magazines, radio programs, and motion pictures would indicate a national hero for at least a certain age group, a national hero who could hardly help but reflect specific attitudes. The cowboy myth has been chosen by this audience because it combines a complex of traits, a way of life, which they consider the proper ideal for America. The actual drama and setting are subordinate to the grand figure of the cowboy hero, and the love affairs, the exciting plots, and the climactic physical struggles present opportunities for the definition of the cowboy code and character. Through the superficial action, the heroism of the cowboy is revealed, and each repetition of the drama, like the repetition of a sacrament, reaffirms the cowboy public's faith in their ideal.

Perhaps the outstanding cowboy trait, above even honor, courage, and generosity, is the relaxed, calm attitude toward life. Though he lives intensely, he has a calm self-assurance, a knowledge that he can handle anything. He is good-humored and jovial. He never takes women too seriously. He can take a joke or laugh at himself. Yet the cowboy is usually anti-intellectual and antischool, another attitude which appeals to a younger audience.

Above all, the cowboy is a "good joe." He personifies a code of personal dignity, personal liberty, and personal honesty. Most writers on the actual cowboy represented him as having these traits. While many of these men obviously glorify him as much as any fiction writers, there must have been some basis for their judgment. As far as his light-hearted, calm attitude is concerned, it is amazing how similar cowboys appear, both in romances and nonfiction. Millions of American youth subscribed to the new ideal and yearned for the clear, Western atmosphere of "unswerving loyalty, the true, deep affection, and good-natured banter that left no sting." For a few thrilling hours they could roughly toss conventions aside and share the fellowship of ranch life and adore the kind of hero who was never bored and never afraid.

Whether these traits of self-confidence, a relaxed attitude toward life and good humor, have actually increased in the United States during the past fifty years is like asking whether men love their wives more now than in 1900. Certainly the effective influence of the cowboy myth can never be determined. It is significant, however, that the cowboy ideal has emerged above all others. And while the standardization of plot and character seems to follow other commercial conventions, the very popularity of this standard cowboy is important and is an overlooked aspect of the American character. It is true that this hero is infantile, that he is silly, overdone, and unreal. But when we think of many past ideals and heroes, myths and ethics; when we compare our placid cowboy with say, the eager, cold, serious hero of Nazi Germany (the high-cheek-boned, blond lad who appeared on the Reichsmarks); or if we compare the cowboy with the gangster heroes of the thirties, or with the serious, self-righteous and brutal series of Supermen, Batmen, and Human Torches; when, in an age of violence and questioned public and private morality, if we think of the many possible heroes we might have had—then we can be thankful for our silly cowboy. We could have chosen worse.

QUESTIONS TO CONSIDER

1. How is the cowboy complex usually defined?
2. What does Davis see as the function of the cowboy myth?
3. Why has the cowboy image in particular been so enduring?
4. What was the significance of Owen Wister's *The Virginian*?
5. How accurate is the myth's reflection of the realities of work and monotony in the West?
6. Describe the cowboy's attitude toward religion and the reasons for it.
7. What is the cowboy's attitude toward property?

3

Suburban Men and Masculine Domesticity, 1870–1915

MARGARET MARSH

Margaret Marsh, "Suburban Men and Masculine Domesticity," *American Quarterly*, June 1988, pp. 165–181. The American Studies Association. Reprinted by permission of the Johns Hopkins University Press.

While cowboys provided romance for easterners (and drudgery for themselves) in the 1870s and 1880s, the cutting edge of social change was in the cities. Urbanization transformed the national scene. In 1860 approximately 20 percent of the U.S. population was urban; by 1920 the percentage living in cities with a population over 2500 had shot up to over 51 percent. But not just cities grew. With the advent of improved transportation, especially the trolley, suburbs became not only potential new urban neighborhoods but also escapes from the cities and their temptations.

In this 1988 article, a precursor to her book *Suburban Lives*, Rutgers University administrator and former Temple University professor Margaret Marsh (1945–) argues that in the years after the Civil War, American families underwent a significant transformation. At midcentury, middle-class married couples led separate lives, segregated into distinctive spheres defined by ideology. What historian Barbara Welter termed the "cult of true womanhood" confined women in a behavioral straitjacket, requiring them to be submissive, pure, pious, and domestic. Men found the meaning in their lives in making a living, in a milieu outside the home. Yet by the turn of the twentieth century, several factors had combined to make companionate marriage the new model for those middle-class families. Increased occupational stability for middle-class men combined with the possibility of suburban living to transform the very nature of marriage, eroding the barriers that had kept spouses apart. If the family is the basic building block in American society, such an evolution tells us much about the nature of the American character in the twentieth century.

The home is man's affair as much as woman's.
                                   —Martha and Robert Bruère, 1909

There is no reason at all why men should not sweep and dust, make beds, clean windows, fix the fire, clean the grate, arrange the furniture. . . .
                                   —*American Homes and Gardens*, 1905

When historians think about American men at the turn of the twentieth century, among the images they usually conjure up are these: a bored clerk or middle-manager in some impersonal office of a faceless corporation, pushing papers or counting the company's money, longing nostalgically for a time when a man could find adventure and get rich at the same time—by becoming a robber baron, or conquering new frontiers; or Theodore Roosevelt, the delicate child who grew up to relish big-game hunting and war, and whose open disdain for softness and "effeminacy" made him the symbol of rugged masculinity in his own time.

We owe the association of the corporate drone with the flamboyant Rough Rider to an influential essay by John Higham, who argued that one of the most significant American cultural constructs at the turn of the century was a growing cult of masculinity, attended by the insecurities of middle-class men about their own virility and "manliness." Beginning in the 1890s, Higham argued, the country witnessed a national "urge to be young, masculine, and adventurous," when Americans rebelled against "the frustrations, the routine, and the sheer dullness of an urban-industrial culture." He cited the growing popularity of boxing and football, a disaffection from genteel fiction, and not least, the rise in the level of national bellicosity, as important indicators of a new public mood.

Higham's article, published in 1970, triggered an interest in the historical meaning of masculinity. His insights, and those of others who have followed his interpretive lead, have been of undeniable value. Nevertheless, his work defined an entire generation of middle-class men—young and middle-aged, married and single, urban, suburban, and rural—in terms of anxieties about manliness. Those anxieties, and the men who faced them, undoubtedly existed, but in the course of my research on suburban families, I have discovered a different manner of middle-class man. The evidence to date is scattered, but there is enough to suggest that historians supplement the image of the dissatisfied clerk with an additional picture of a contented suburban father, who enjoyed the security of a regular salary, a predictable rise through the company hierarchy, and greater leisure. This last prerequisite was facilitated by shorter commuting times—often thirty minute or less—to and from the suburbs of most cities. (With the exception of some New York lines, men could expect to spend less time going to and from work than had their fathers who had to rely on horse-drawn streetcars and omnibuses.)

Alongside the idea of the cult of masculinity, which offered an explanation for some elements of middle-class male culture, we should consider the model of masculine domesticity. Masculine domesticity is difficult to define; in some ways, it is easier to say what it was not than what it was. It was not equivalent to feminism. It was not an equal sharing of all household duties. Nor did it extend to the belief that men and women ought to have identical opportunities in the larger society. It was, however, a model of behavior in which fathers would agree to take on increased responsibility for some of the day-to-day tasks of bringing up children and spending their time away from work in playing with their sons and daughters, teaching them, taking them on trips. A domestic man would also make his wife, rather than his male cronies, his regular companion on evenings out. And while he might not dust the mantel or make the bed except in special circumstances, he would take a significantly greater interest in the details of running the household and caring for the children than his father was expected to do.

The evidence for the growth of masculine domesticity comes from a variety of places. Prescriptive literature is one important source. Tantalizing clues from domestic architecture, records of community groups in the suburbs themselves, letters, and diaries provide others. Among the former are the later writings of the influential literary domestic Harriet Beecher Stowe; the essays of Boston feminist and popular author of juvenile fiction Abby Morton Diaz; widely read child-rearing manuals; and the advice of successful men to their aspiring juniors in the Progressive Era, in this case from such disparate figures as the reformist senator Albert Beveridge and the sensationalist publisher and "physical culture" hero Bernarr Macfadden. If the image of domestic man came only from this prescriptive literature, it would still be important as a sign of changing cultural models. Yet suggestions of changing male roles also appeared in the reconfiguration of interior space in suburban houses, in the rise of suburban institutions which included both husbands and wives, and in the daily lives of suburban families.

Masculine domesticity required three conditions for its emergence: an ideal of marriage that emphasized companionship instead of either patriarchal rule or the ideology of domesticity, both of which encouraged gender separation; an economic system that provided sufficient job security for middle-class men so that husbands could devote more attention to their families; and a physical location in which the new attitudes toward family could find their appropriate spatial expressions. It was not until the power relations within middle-class marriage underwent subtle shifts, until the rise of the corporation provided relatively secure jobs with predictable patterns of mobility, and until suburbs began to be viewed as the appropriate space within which to create the companionate family, that the development of masculine domesticity was possible. By the early twentieth century, all three of the conditions had been met.

During the second third of the nineteenth century the patriarchal family, softened by love and mutual obligation, had served as the principal model for middle-class families. This ideal of family life had depended on what twentieth-century historians have come to call the ideology of domesticity, a social theory articulated most persuasively by Catharine Beecher in the 1840s. Building in part on the ideas of Sarah Josepha Hale and Horace Bushnell, Beecher attempted to unify the contradictions of a society that was both democratic and in many ways inegalitarian by minimizing class, racial, and ethnic differences while maximizing those of gender. The success of the ideology of domesticity required, in the words of Beecher's biographer, "the isolation of women in the home away from full participation in the society." To compensate them for their voluntary abdication of the right to a position in the world of men, women held sway within the home, thereby (at least theoretically) stabilizing society as a whole.

The belief in separate spheres was not universal, but during the middle years of the century it dominated ideas about gender. And as Mary Ryan has argued, "Any cultural construct that achieved such popularity bore some semblance to social reality." Ryan's study of Utica and Suzanne Lebsock's of Petersburg demonstrate the "social reality" of gender separation at mid-century for white, middle-class women. The doctrine of separate spheres began to break down after the Civil War. During the past two decades, historians have extensively chronicled the incursions of women into the masculine sphere. But changing roles for women also meant changes in male roles. As women entered the masculine world, men began to enter the sphere assigned to women.

We can begin to understand this phenomenon—which ended in the masculine domesticity of the Progressive Era—by looking first at changes in the kinds of advice given to young men about the organization of their lives. In the middle of the nineteenth century, male advice-writers (excluding the medical advice-givers who wrote marriage manuals) rarely concerned themselves with the role of husband or father. Instead, they emphasized economic and social mobility, urging young men to develop the qualities of sobriety, honesty, and a capacity for hard work because these qualities were essential to economic success, not because they would help a man become a better husband or father. Neither did these male writers offer suggestions on choosing a suitable wife, or on appropriate behavior toward one's children. Although the moral young man understood from these advice manuals what to avoid—prostitutes, gambling dens, and the questionable pleasures of urban life—they offered him no positive assistance in settling his personal life.

A British writer, William Rathbone Grey, who expressed anxieties about the future of marriage, suggested that prostitution made many men "lo[a]th to resign the easy independence, the exceptional luxuries, the habitual indulgences of a bachelor's career, for the fetters of a wife, the burden and responsibility of children, and the decent monotony of the domestic hearth." Grey's portrait of urban decadence was not unusual for the period, but his explicit expression of a fear that it would deter young men from marrying was. American writers of advice for young men generally contented themselves with painting lurid pictures of urban corruption, without correspondingly urging their readers to embrace "the decent monotony" of domesticity. Most male advice writers did not exhibit misgivings about their readers' future domestic lives in the 1840s and 1850s; books by women did, but they addressed a different audience. Catharine Sedgwick's *Home*, for example, portrayed the moral home as the only sure preventative against the dissipation that worried the male writers, but her book's readers were largely women.

One of the few men who dealt with the domestic duties of husbands at mid-century, temperance author T. S. Arthur, did so for *Godey's Lady's Book*. Arthur's series on "Model Husbands" explored the impact of a husband's temperament on domestic life. His "bad model" husband possessed a foul temper, was selfish and inconsiderate of his wife, left her alone every evening while he went out with his male cronies, and paid no attention to his children. A "better specimen," although he began his married life impatient with his bride's inability to manage the home to his satisfaction, learned to subdue his selfishness and thereby bring about an improvement in his wife's domestic abilities. If a "better specimen" was one who could learn to subdue his anger, a "good model" had none to subdue. The ideal husband took great delight in his family, spending his evenings at home reading with his wife and children. Arthur insisted that men had domestic obligations that included helping around the house in emergencies, as well as showing attentiveness to their wives and children, and taking their pleasures in the home with the family rather than in the city with their friends. T. S. Arthur's determined effort to combine male superiority with conjugal generosity was atypical; significantly, he published these articles in a magazine read primarily by women, not by men.

In fact, it was women writers who began first to refuse to pay even lip service to the patriarchal idea. Harriet Beecher Stowe, one of the nineteenth century's most popular writers, ridiculed patriarchal pretensions and praised domestic men in her last two novels. For example, one of her respected male characters in *My Wife and I* insisted that the opinions of his wife and sister were far more valuable to him than the views "of all the doctors of divinity." In the same novel Stowe asserted confidently that "sooner or later the true wife becomes a mother to her husband; she guides him, cares for him, teaches him, and catechizes him in the nicest way possible."

Stowe's novels found an echo in the advice literature of Abby Morton Diaz, a widely read author of juvenile fiction as well as a prominent Boston feminist, who tried in the mid-1870s to persuade men that egalitarian marriages were in their best interests. Long before the term "togetherness" was coined to describe an ideal marriage, Diaz insisted that "a sympathetic couple are to such a degree one that a pleasure which comes to either singly can only be half enjoyed, and even this half-joy is lessened by the consciousness of what the other is losing." Such a matrimonial state was possible only when the wife was "at least the equal of her husband" in intelligence, taste, and education. Women would have to be granted the rights of education and citizenship before there could be truly happy marriages.

By the 1890s, women advice-givers were arguing that men should help out around the house and stop expecting their wives to wait on them. As one of Margaret Sangster's friends complained, she was tired of picking up after her husband, who every day "manages to give my drawing room, sitting room, and library an appearance of having been swept by a cyclone. One traces him all over the house by the things he has heedlessly dropped. . . ." Sangster urged her friend to tell her husband to pick up after himself, since a good husband would surely make an effort to reform, at least "to some extent." Such advice, and the relationship that it implied, was far removed from a world in which a father's convenience was of principal importance.

These changes in attitude toward marriage, combined with the significant and growing public activity of middle-class women, contributed to women's greater self-consciousness that they had significant roles to play in the shaping of society. Even if she did not aspire to vote or to work at a career, a wife could justify having greater expectations of her husband. Whereas mid-century domestic writers had begged husbands not to "sear and palsy" their wives' hearts by a "tyrannical and overbearing manner," their counterparts at the turn of the twentieth century sharply informed men that husbands too "should rise above the petty . . . irritations of the day and speak with agreeable consideration for others. . . ." Furthermore, they insisted, the work of a housewife was "just as important" as the husband's breadwinning job, and therefore his wife was entitled to his income: "She earns it just as truly, and has just as much a right to it as he. . . ."

By the early twentieth century, male writers had begun to concur with many of these sentiments, particularly those having to do with the importance of family togetherness. As an anonymous father, writing in *The Independent* in 1906, argued, not only the family but the larger society, benefitted when "father and son . . . take their social enjoyments *en famille*." James Canfield expressed similar views in *Cosmopolitan*. Enumerating "the three controlling desires of every normal man," he gave first priority to male domestic needs: "His home must be more than a mere shelter. . . . He must be able to make his house a home by adding a hearth—and there is no hearth for a man but the heart of a woman."

The domestic lives of middle-class families reflected the changes in the attitudes toward marriage. On the surface, the majority of men's and women's lives did not appear to change much; for example, women did not hold down paid jobs outside the home to any appreciable extent. But as the twentieth century drew nearer, women increasingly spent more time beyond the confines of the home, whether in mothers' groups or women's clubs, in reform activities, or simply shopping in the downtown department stores. Husbands changed their behavior patterns as well. The golden age of male fraternal organizations had passed by the turn of the century, according to historian Mark Carnes. Male clubdom would rise again later in the century, but for the moment suburban men sought their leisure closer to home, in tennis and country clubs that welcomed the whole family, and in social groups that included their wives. In one New Jersey suburb, for example, during the first decade of the twentieth century, the Men's Civic Club had difficulty in attracting members, and the Women's Sewing Society was forced to disband completely in 1903; but the Penn Literary Society, the Debating group, and the Natural Science Club, all of which included both men and women and numbered many married couples in their ranks, flourished. So, too, did the new family-oriented tennis club, founded in the same period.

Women advice-givers at mid-century had urged women to spend time socializing with other women for their *own* well-being. By the 1908s the justification for the maintenance of women's outside interests was different, and emphasized the importance of the husband-wife bond. Absorption in one's domestic duties, argued the advice-givers, would damage a man's relationship with her husband. Women who confined themselves to the household and to the unremitting care of children were in danger of becoming inadequate wives. In the early twentieth century even moderate reformers urged women to get out of the house, to stop "fluttering about inside four walls under the delusion that these mark their proper sphere of activity," to cease thinking of the house as a "fortified citadel."

Advice to men had also changed. While male advice-givers rarely insisted that men take on the administrative or physical duties of running a household, they did urge them to trade the burdens of patriarchal authority and work-induced separation from family life for emotional closeness to their wives and the pleasures of spending time with their children as companions. Of course, not all men were in agreement with such advice. However, even criticism could inadvertently highlight the new domesticity of suburban men. Richard Harding Davis, writing for *Harper's* in 1894, found his married suburban friends boring because they had no interests beyond each other, their house, and their suburban pleasures. Davis found their contentment incomprehensible.

Companionate marriages need not have been entirely egalitarian to require new roles for both men and women. Martha Bruère, an influential Progressive Era home economist, and her economist husband Robert, investigated the households of early twentieth-century middle-class America, using actual case studies of urban, suburban, and farm families. Reformers who discouraged parsimony and encouraged consumption in the pursuit of cultivation and comfort, the Bruères believed that "the home is man's affair as much as woman's. . . . When God made homemakers, male and female created He them!"

There is a considerable cultural chasm between the middle-class society of the mid-nineteenth century, in which women took responsibility for the home and for the emotional tasks of parenthood while men took on the role of firm patriarch or detached observer, and that of the early twentieth, in which men could be referred to as "homemakers." The generational contrast between the father and husband of Harriet Beecher Stowe's heroine Eva in *My Wife and I* may serve to point up the beginnings of this change in the nature of masculine domestic involvement. The father, Mr. Van Arsdell, a well-to-do businessman who supported his family in a Fifth Avenue townhouse, "considered the household and all its works and ways as an insoluble mystery which he was well-pleased to leave to his wife." His role in the family was quite simply "yearly to enlarge his means of satisfying the desires and aspirations of his family," the domestic appurtenances of which "he knew little and cared less."

But if Mr. Van Arsdell was a shadow in his house, fleeing to his library and leaving everything else to his wife, his son-in-law, Harry Henderson, was a very different kind of man. Harry and Eva eschewed Fifth Avenue and urban fashion for a detached single family house; its yard had "trees, and English sparrows, and bird houses," not to mention flowers and grape vines, those necessary adjuncts to the late Victorian suburban house. Revelling in his domesticity, Harry spent his evenings with his wife planning new decorations and home improvements (to be carried out by the servants). He said of his house: During the day "I think of it . . . when I'm at work in my office, and am always wanting to come home and see it again." Harry was completely comfortable with domesticity, proclaiming, "There is no earthly reason which requires a man, in order to be manly, to be unhandy and clumsy in regard to the minutiae of domestic life."

Although Stowe's work suggests an incipient change in the ways in which men should make their presence known in the family, it is doubtful that the typical middle-class suburban husband in the 1870s could have emulated the fictional Harry Henderson. Maintaining a condition of affluence or stable respectability for a family without a hereditary income involved considerable risk. The salaried middle-class man with a secure corporate or bureaucratic position was still a rarity. William Robinson was a case in point. Robinson was a Massachusetts journalist of no more than local repute, about whose life historians would know little were it not for the papers left by his wife, Harriet Hanson Robinson, who after his death became a suffragist of state-wide importance. Of significance here is his struggle to provide moderate prosperity for his growing family in the third quarter of the nineteenth century. At one point, seemingly headed for upward mobility as a member of the Massachusetts State Legislature, he rose at 6:30 to take the train from his house in Lowell to Boston, returning home after eight in the evening. Then, since he was editing a weekly paper, he and his wife spent two to three hours each evening working on it. Later, he moved his family to Malden, a Boston suburb, which shortened his commuting time but not his workday. Wherever he worked he put in long hours, and there was at least one period when he remained without full-time employment for several years, supporting his family by free-lance work and part-time odd jobs.

William Robinson accepted the breadwinner role and its responsibilities, although the economic realities of the age meant that his work required his whole attention. Other men opted out altogether. David Lee Child, husband of abolitionist and domestic writer Lydia Maria Child, was perhaps an extreme example of an ineffectual provider, since he failed at every occupation he tried. Nevertheless, the reaction of his wife, a prominent public figure, indicates the great importance of masculine economic success in the mid-nineteenth century, even to a woman capable of providing for herself. Lydia Maria Child complained bitterly to David Child's sister after David died: "For the last forty-five years I have paid from my own funds, all the expenses . . . ; food, clothing, washing, fuel, taxes, etc. . . . [David] had no promptitude, no system in his affairs; hence everything went into confusion. After many years of struggling with ever recurring pecuniary difficulties, I reluctantly became convinced that there was *no help* for these difficulties." Lydia Maria Child, with a husband so absolutely unfit for the demands of the marketplace economy, took over and retained, with some considerable resentment, the role of breadwinner.

Child's resentment exemplifies the contradictions of this age for middle-class men and women. She was a talented (and reasonably well-paid) writer and first-rate editor, but having to support her husband because of his fecklessness angered her. Child was not alone. When Hattie Robinson, William Robinson's daughter, married Sydney Shattuck in 1878, she quit her job so that he could be the sole breadwinner. After a period of living with the bride's mother, the young couple bought a suburban house, and Shattuck, in business for himself, prospered. But his business failed, and although he spent years trying to recapture his early success, it always eluded him; at the time of his death the couple lived in a shabbily genteel boardinghouse, his wife having become a bitter, querulous, and nearly friendless woman. After his death, she was forced to throw herself on the charity of her niece.

These few examples, while they do not indicate that middle-class men were abandoning the breadwinner role in any numbers, nevertheless suggest the precarious nature of middle-class status in the middle years of the century. Statistical portraits have made a similar point. As Michael Katz has said of the male citizenry of Buffalo (a reasonably prosperous city which nevertheless witnessed a downward mobility rate of 27 percent in the 1850s and 43 percent in the 1860s), "Neither staying wealthy nor falling, many men struggled from year to year, their economic state marginal and fluctuating." Both men and women might be unable to live up to their assigned (or hoped-for) roles. When they failed to do so, men were likely to become dispirited and women resentful.

Yet Stowe's Harry Henderson did have some real-life counterparts. One was Charles Cumings, an insurance company executive whose family moved from Boston's South End to suburban Jamaica Plain in 1877. Charles Cumings was a precursor of the early twentieth-century domestic man. We know of him primarily because he made entries in his wife's daybook, entries that showed him to be intensely interested in the doings of his children and revealed his delight in their new suburban house. His joyful notes about the children's first steps, anxious ones about their illnesses, and proud little comments on the progress of the house and lawn are complemented by Augusta Cuming's remarks, including one written during one of his infrequent absences from home, when she noted that everyone, but especially three-year-old Gertrude, missed him very much. By the early twentieth century there would be more men like Charles Cumings. In the 1870s he was a rarity—an organization man during the heyday of entrepreneurialism; a private man during the great age of public male socializing; and a father involved in the details of his children's lives at a time when most men still believed that children were a mother's responsibility.

The connection between Cumings' occupation and his domesticity is significant. As the century came to a close, and the American upper middle class shifted away from its mid-nineteenth-century base of entrepreneurs, independent professionals, and clergy, other men could be like Charles Cumings. By then, particularly in the suburbs, the typical early twentieth-century, middle-class father was salaried and had some security in his position, more or less regular hours, and relatively predictable patterns of occupational mobility.

As middle-class men gained respite from the economic pressures that had plagued the previous generation, they had the time to give their families greater attention. This change, along with the prodding of feminists, triggered the recognition of the importance of male domestic responsibility. Abby Diaz had remarked in the 1870s that people were always asking her why, if women needed education for motherhood, men did not need similar training for fatherhood. Men, she responded, did indeed need such training, but she was too busy to provide it. She added derisively: "If men feel this need, there is nothing to prevent them from assembling . . . to inquire how they shall best qualify themselves to fulfill the duties of fatherhood. [I am] . . . under the impression that men's clubs do not meet especially with a view to such discussion." And Harriet Beecher Stowe, although less of a feminist than Diaz, remarked during the same period, "We have heard much said of the importance of training women to be wives." She would have liked "something to be said on the importance of training men to be husbands."

By the 1890s acerbic tones had diminished, to be replaced by sympathetic anecdotes about families in which the men shared domestic duties. Margaret Sangster approved of a family of her acquaintance in which "everyone shared the housework, even the boys . . . ," while in another household the son, "a manly young fellow," did the ironing. Martha and Robert Bruère took the idea of masculine domesticity at least as seriously as did Sangster, insisting that "a knowledge of housekeeping is not a matter of sex, but science," so "all ought to know [it], men and women alike." High schools, they argued, ought to require boys to take home economics courses, because men should also become "homemakers." But even the (male) editor of the suburban-oriented magazine *American Homes and Gardens* announced in 1905, "There is no reason at all why men should not sweep and dust, make beds, clean windows, fix the fire, clean the grate, arrange the furniture" and cook. The editor refers to domestic servants, not husbands. Still, he intended to make a point about male involvement in the home, and not merely about servants; he continued the same theme in his editorial for the following month: "The responsibility for the home is not [the woman's] alone," he insisted, "but is equally the husband's."

It is not clear that the average middle-class man, young or old, was induced to do the ironing because of examples like those cited by Margaret Sangster, or to take home economics courses on the advice of the Bruères. Men were, however, becoming more involved in the internal workings of the household, as Joan Seidl discovered. She has examined the personal papers of Minnesotans at the turn of the twentieth century, many living in suburban St. Paul, and found that husbands of the early twentieth century took a far greater interest in the home than did those of the 1880s. Her focus is on house decoration; in the earlier period men cared little about it, but by the first decade of the century they were active participants. The recently married Helen Sommers, for example, wrote her sister in 1909 about decorating the house which she and her husband had chosen: "Harry & I are working every thing out together. . . ." Household decoration, according to Seidl, was a symbol of the growing involvement of men in the home. "Most remarkable," she argues, "given the standard interpretations of the period, is the degree to which husbands took an active role in domestic arrangements. . . . Fixed hours of work allowed leisure for Walter Post to dry the dishes and for James Andrews to paste up the wallpaper."

Women, however, wanted men to do more than share in the process of making decisions about household furnishings. They also wanted them to be nurturing fathers. Some of them pinned their hopes on the next generation. Kate Wiggen, who before she wrote *Rebecca of Sunnybrook Farm* had been a kindergarten teacher, attempted to develop "the father spirit" in little boys. At school, her charges played a bird game, in which "we had always had a mother bird in the nest with the birdlings. . . ." Wiggin then introduced a "father bird" and similarly reorganized other games. Finally, she incorporated the boys into "doll's day," previously a girls' game only.

Wiggen asked one of the boys to play "father" and rock a doll to sleep. To her delight, all the other little boys then wanted to play.

Wiggin published her kindergarten techniques and they enjoyed wide circulation. Perhaps it was the imagined sight of thousands of little boys rocking dolls to sleep that encouraged men to start getting involved in rearing their children, in order to save their sons from such influences. In fact, some of the motivation for greater fatherly involvement with their children was surely to balance the preponderant female presence in the lives of young children. But the word is *balance*, not *overshadow*. Masculine domesticity, as it had evolved by the early twentieth century, was incorporated into the concept of manliness, as men became convinced that in order to have their sons grow up to be "manly" they should involve themselves more substantially in their children's upbringing.

Senator Albert Beveridge was one of a growing number of men who applauded masculine domesticity in the early twentieth century. These men encouraged fathers to form direct and immediate bonds with their children, by playing games with them, taking them on camping trips, and simply spending time with them. Of course, before the entrenchment of the ideology of domesticity in the second third of the nineteenth century, fathers had maintained a large role in family government, but in the early period the emphasis was on obedience, discipline, and the importance of the father's role as head of the household. In the early twentieth century the stress was on friendship: fathers were encouraged to be "chums" with their children, especially, but by no means exclusively, with their sons. Male writers on parenthood differed from their female counterparts in that they placed greater importance on independence, approving of boys having, from about the age of seven on, a sort of freewheeling companionship with other boys—a "gang" or "bunch," to use the terms of the period. They argued that fathers could encourage such freedom because the new closeness of father and son would prevent the boy from falling into evil ways. His father would play baseball with him, take him and his friends camping and swimming, and in general play the role of a caring older companion rather than a stern patriarch.

Within this new definition of fatherhood, aggressiveness was channeled into safe outlets. Indeed, the concepts of masculine domesticity and "manliness" seem more complementary than antipathetic: One might hypothesize that men, as their behavior within the family became less aloof (or patriarchal), and more nurturing and companionable, would develop a fantasy life that was more aggressive. The rage for football and boxing, and the reading of adventure novels, might have provided that vigorous fantasy life, masking but not contradicting masculine domesticity. That subject remains to be investigated. What is clear, however, is that some of the advocates of masculine domesticity did think about its implications for manliness, but stood their ground nonetheless. Senator Beveridge, in his advice book for young men, told the story of a "resourceful Oriental" who had suggested that "the influence of women on the Occidental man is effeminizing our civilization." Beveridge countered with his own view: "Even if what this Oriental assailant of our customs terms the overcharge of femininity in Occidental society does mellow us," he said, "it does not follow that it weakens us."

Bernarr Macfadden epitomized the connections between the cult of masculinity and masculine domesticity. Macfadden was a major figure in the mass culture of the early to mid-twentieth century, amassing a publishing empire based on his ownership of *The New York Daily News* and the magazines *True Story* and *True Romance*. In the second decade of the twentieth century he published *Physical Culture* and books on health and what we now call "fitness." A self-proclaimed savior, Macfadden addressed his gospel of "physical culture" to women as much as to men. And just as women ought to develop physical strength, so too men ought to develop their nurturant capacities, since both had emotional and nurturing functions within the family.

Macfadden insisted that husbands should even be present at childbirth, and he warned, "Whenever you find a man who is without an innate love for children, you may rest assured that there is something wrong with his character." An early authorized biographer of Macfadden claimed that his subject regularly devoted his evenings to his family, always leaving work "between five and seven. . . . He is a home-loving soul. . . . Sane, happy American family life is one of his ideals . . . and his own [seven] children are a constant source of pleasure to him." Whether Macfadden's biographer accurately described his subject's habits is less significant than that it mattered deeply to Macfadden that readers believe in the overarching importance of his family life. In the mid-nineteenth century, a self-made man like Macfadden would have stressed the tenacity and arduousness of his economic struggle, rather than his willingness to set it all aside at a specific time each day in order to be with his family.

The final condition for the development of masculine domesticity was spatial. The suburbs were assumed to be the natural habitat of domestic man. Macfadden claimed that the purchase of a "modest little home" would give the young married man a sense of stability, as well as the necessary physical distance from urban temptations. Having come to New York City from the midwest to make his fortune, Macfadden himself moved to the suburbs at the first opportunity, and held resolutely anti-urban sentiments. Albert Beveridge had expressed similar views. Devoting an entire chapter of his advice book for young men to "The New Home," he informed his readers that "'Apartments' cannot by any magic be converted into a home. . . . Better a separate dwelling with [a] dry goods box for a table and camp-stools for chairs than tapestried walls, mosaic floors, and all luxuriousness. . . ."

Furthermore, once the young man had got himself a wife, a nice suburban house, and some children (because "a purposely childless marriage is no marriage at all"), he "will spend all of [his] extra time at home," listening to his wife play the piano, reading, and not least, playing with the children.

Two things are important about the domestic advice of Macfadden and Beveridge. First, successful men advised their juniors to cultivate domestic habits. Second, they advised them to do so in the suburbs. Macfadden and Beveridge were among a growing number of Americans in the early twentieth century who viewed urban life as a direct threat to family happiness. As late as the 1880s, the city had still seemed redeemable to urban residents and social critics alike. When people moved to the urban fringe they were often waiting for the city to catch up to them, not trying to escape it. But by the turn of the century the suburban flow had an escapist quality to it; one symbol of that escapism, as Kenneth Jackson points out, was the decline of annexation as a means of holding suburbs and city together. And a number of sociologists who specialized in the study of the city during the first decade of the twentieth century contended that urban life and stable family life seemed incompatible. In 1909 the American Sociological Society devoted its annual meeting to questions about the family. While the scholars in attendance were not entirely agreed about the nature of the changes that were affecting the family, a number of the participants warned explicitly that city life and family togetherness had become contradictory.

The advice-givers and academics hoped that middle-class fathers, with more secure careers and houses in the suburbs, would spend their time with their wives and children rather than male friends. The great popularity of family-oriented recreational activities around the turn of the century and afterward suggests that suburban families wanted to play together. According to the most comprehensive study of American leisure, in this period croquet and roller skating were more popular than baseball (and many families, including the girls, apparently tried to play baseball on the lawn). Bicycling did not become a craze until it became a sport for women and girls as well as boys and men. Suburbs institutionalized the relationships that marked the companionate family by creating various kinds of clubs, such as "wheel clubs," athletic fields used by both sexes, and tennis and golf clubs. (If early twentieth-century photographs and real estate advertisements are reliable, men played golf with their wives, not business associates.)

Cordelia Biddle, from a wealthy and prominent Philadelphia family, was obviously not a typical child of the years immediately before World War I, but it was not solely because of her money: she spent much of her childhood in the boxing ring, because boxing was a favorite sport of her father, who taught her. "The center of activity at our house," she recalled, "was the boxing ring, . . . where I was initiated into the mysteries of the solar-plexus punch, the left jab, and the right cross. Instead of dolls, I played with barbells; instead of hopscotch and ring-o-levio, I was learning to patch up cuts under the eye." But if she remembered that boxing was an unusual sport for girls, she also remembered "that women of that period were so athletic." Biddle's parents belonged to a bicycling club called the "Century Club" because it "specialized in hundred-mile trips," during which her mother "easily kept up" with her father.

Togetherness meant more than sports and outdoor recreation. In suburban Haddonfield, New Jersey, where commuters to Camden and Philadelphia swelled the population from about 2700 in 1900 to more than 4000 by 1910, husbands and wives joined cultural and social clubs together to study nature, to talk about their family trips, even to debate each other on public issues. Such clubs were popular in the community—the debating group had over a hundred active members, and the literary society (which was mostly a social club) sometimes drew as many as forty people to its monthly gatherings. Men and women did not do everything jointly; they did not enjoy (or endure) absolute togetherness. What is at issue is the degree of change that occurred over the course of the last quarter of the nineteenth century or so. And if we compare these husbands and wives of the early twentieth century to the generation that preceded them, the change is apparent. In Haddonfield, even the Mothers and Teachers Club, which normally met in the afternoon, scheduled two of its eight meetings in the evenings for the convenience of the fathers.

In the light of all this, we must be skeptical of assertions like those of Peter Stearns, who has remarked that while it was true that suburbanization weakened patriarchy, it also, in "increas[ing] the physical separation of the man from his home . . . left the woman in greater effective control." The decline of patriarchy did not lead to a decline of masculine interest in the home in the early twentieth century. Elaine Tyler May offers a contrasting view. In her comparative study of marriage and divorce in Victorian and Progressive Era America, she illustrates the ways in which Los Angeles, a suburbanized city composed principally of residential subdivisions, dealt with the early twentieth-century fears about the collapse of the family. In Los Angeles, middle-class Americans created an intense family life in a suburban environment that they hoped would both protect the family from the dangers of urban life and allow its members to enjoy its material blessings.

Architectural evidence supports May's arguments. The most striking thing about the middle-class domestic architecture produced in the second and third quarters of the nineteenth century, as Gwendolyn Wright has pointed out, was its design for separation. The most striking thing about suburban houses in the early twentieth century was their design for family togetherness. In middle- to upper-middle-class homes, the living room replaced the separate parlor, study (commonly considered a male refuge), and sitting room that had characterized Victorian upper-middle-class houses. Both modest and fairly expensive new houses had more open floor plans. Architects in the early twentieth century, ranging from the iconoclastic

Frank Lloyd Wright to the very conservative Joy Wheeler Dow, explicitly designed houses for family togetherness. And architectural writers made the same statement in home magazines. Families no longer maintained segregated social space, but the rage for marking off children's areas with special wallcoverings and accessories announced, perhaps obliquely, that women and children would no longer automatically share the same space. Such a change, one might speculate, might have made it more possible for men and women to share private space.

The evidence described above may not convince historians to abandon entirely the notion of an early twentieth-century cult of masculinity, and there is no reason that they should; nevertheless, during the last years of the nineteenth century and the early years of the twentieth century masculine domesticity cropped up in advice literature by men and women, in architectural design, in recreational patterns, in Progressive Era analyses of middle-class households, and in the personal papers of eastern and midwestern suburbanites. Taken as a whole this data does suggest that we need to seek more historical information about the domestic role of American men.

This study does not pretend to be comprehensive; questions about the pervasiveness of masculine domesticity, and especially about the exact ways in which it connected to, or existed in tension with, the cult of masculinity, still await answers. For example, the popularity during the early twentieth century of boxing, football, and adventure novels is seen by historians as indicators of a heightened male aggressiveness, an aggressiveness that also manifested itself in national belligerence. But they may have served more a symbolic function for middle-class American men during this period, overlaying the intensified male participation in what had been defined as women's sphere.

The redefinition of manliness to include some traditional female functions, one suspects, represented a collective masculine response to feminists like Charlotte Perkins Gilman, who insisted that the traditional family was anachronistic in an urban society, and who demanded that women seek for themselves the sense of individual achievement and separate identity that had been reserved for men. Urban feminists endorsed Gilman's ideas. Her writings and lectures received considerable attention in the periodical press of the day, although it is unlikely that all middle-class men knew her by name. Whether they could identify her, however, is not the point; no one who read the newspapers could have been ignorant of the views she espoused. On the whole, men responded to those views by moving their families to the suburbs. There, fathers would draw themselves into the domestic circle, where individual needs could take second place to the needs of the family.

Masculine domesticity, in that sense, served as a male reply to the feminists' insistence that women had as much right to seek individual achievement as did men. It offered an alternative to feminism: men would acknowledge the importance of the domestic sphere, not only rhetorically, but also by assuming specific responsibilities within it. Women, however, shared only partially in the world of men. Reform activities, mothers' clubs, even voting became acceptable, but taking on roles in the larger society identical to those of men did not. Men who espoused masculine domesticity, it seems logical to speculate, deflected feminist objectives. Suburbanism was neither incidental or accidental to this process. Suburban advocates in the early twentieth century preached that removal from the city would both encourage family unity and discourage excessive attention to one's individual wants. The suburb served as the spatial context for what its advocates hoped would be a new form of marriage. Husbands and wives would be companions, not rivals, and the specter of individualist demands would retreat in the face of family togetherness.

QUESTIONS TO CONSIDER

1. Against what image of turn-of-the-century men is Marsh arguing? What is her alternative?
2. What arguments does Marsh present to show that marriages were becoming companionate rather than patriarchal, with women relegated to domestic separation?
3. How did changing economic conditions for middle-class men encourage masculine domesticity? What was masculine domesticity?
4. What is the spatial argument for masculine domesticity?
5. What was the cult of masculinity? How does Marsh suggest that one might reconcile her theory with it?
6. How does Marsh relate masculine domesticity to feminists like Charlotte Perkins Gilman?

4

Rural Radicals

CATHERINE McNICOL STOCK

The Founding Fathers modeled the new United States on the Roman Republic, admiring its government's separation of powers and the fact that Rome was a nation under the rule of law. In the United States, when times were tough, the unfortunate did not foment revolution—they worked within the political system. And so it was with the farmers of the late nineteenth century. One reason people moved to the cities and the suburbs, as Margaret Marsh has noted, was that they were fleeing the countryside and its exasperating economic problems. But many remained on the land.

Thomas Jefferson argued that the small, independent yeoman farmer was the backbone of the new republic, the key to the American character. The farmer exemplified self-reliance, independence, responsibility, and virtue. But the agricultural world changed dramatically after the Civil War. Farmers moved from independence and self-sufficiency to participation in the complex interrelationships of a cash economy. They found their livelihood threatened not only by the vagaries of nature but also by economic forces over which they had no control. Chief among the villains were the railroads, vital for shipping their crops to market, and the banks, crucial for the credit necessary to operate increasingly large and mechanized farms. In a philosophical turnabout from their belief in the early nineteenth century that the less government the better, farmers turned in desperation to the government as the only power that could solve their problems. The political revolt climaxed in the 1896 election when the Populist Party, the voice of the farmers, joined the Democrats and endorsed William Jennings

Bryan for president. Thus the farmer, a cornerstone of American individualism, had dramatically altered his character, moving from fierce independence to recognition of the necessity of government regulation in a modern economy.

This chapter is taken from Catherine McNicol Stock's full-length book *Rural Radicals* (1996). Stock is an associate professor of history and director of the American Studies Program at Connecticut College. She has also written *Main Street in Crisis: The Great Depression and the Old Middle Class on the Northern Plains.*

When, in the midst of war, the United States Congress passed the Homestead Act in 1862 and opened up much of the Midwest, Great Plains, and Southwest for settlement, it set the stage for both the largest frontier migration in United States history and one of the most dramatic expansions of agricultural production in the world. Between 1870 and 1900 the number of farms in every region of the United States increased. Overall, the number of farms more than doubled, jumping from 2.7 million to 5.7 million. So did the numbers of acres of land in farms and the total value of farm property. More land was privately purchased and improved between 1870 and 1900 [than] had been privately purchased and improved in all the years between the European colonization of North America and the Civil War. So huge was the growth in the Great Plains and Northwest that in 1889 six new western states entered the Union—more than at any other time since the Revolution. Even in the devastated South, economic progress was swift. Production of cotton expanded throughout the former Confederacy, increasing from four million bales to ten million bales in less than thirty years.

But ironically, when this tremendous, multiregional expansion of agriculture began, the age of the farmer was already rapidly slipping away. In fact, conditions of life in the nation in 1865 were staggeringly different from what they had been in the time of Jefferson and Jackson, so recently passed. Some changes stemmed in small or large part from the division of the Union and the dawn of the bloody Civil War. Between 1861 and 1865 thousands of rural men and boys left the homes and communities where their families had lived for generations and never returned. This tragedy had an immediate impact on agricultural productivity and also had long-term effects on the distribution of the rural population. In the South, farms were ruined and families made homeless; poor white farmers who survived the devastation looked to Texas and Kansas to begin their lives anew. So did freed slaves whose dreams of "forty acres and a mule" would soon be replaced by a social oppression that was the moral equivalent of slavery. In the North, rural boys and men who went to war also experienced more of the world and its grim realities than they had ever planned. Some used these experiences as opportunities to migrate to places they had seen or heard about. Others migrated not because they wanted to keep marching but because they couldn't stop. Life would never get back to normal for them or for anybody else who lived in the United States.

But the Civil War accentuated and accelerated changes in American society other than the geographic distribution of its rural population. It also hastened economic, political, and cultural changes whose roots, as we have seen, lay in antebellum society but whose branches would now directly challenge the viability of small producerism. The postbellum era would bring new organizational structures to business, politics, and government. It would lead even more people to the nation's cities than to its farms, and it would encourage them to think about themselves and their futures in ways altogether foreign to rural ways of life. None of these changes, however, would escape the view of those Americans who still held fast to the dream of small production and local control. The changes would instead propel farmers—male and female—to seek out new ways to make their dreams come true. Moreover, the changes would encourage them to choose a strategy linking the futures of black and white and farmer and laborer together. At the intersection between urbanization, industrialization, and bureaucratization and a burgeoning and shifting agricultural population came the most widespread, articulate, and inclusive rural radical movement in the history of the United States.

Chief among all of the challenges faced by farmers in the postbellum era was the consolidation of industrial capitalism. Most rural people in the United States had never been entirely self-sufficient, that is, without some rudimentary links to the market or cash economy. On the other hand, many had long been opposed to "bigness," the corruption that came with too much land, too much wealth (especially from nonproductive labor), and too much political influence. And they had resisted all kinds of dependencies with their lives. Nevertheless, as early as the mid-eighteenth century, parts of the rural East and its people also served as a staging ground for the transformation of premodern capitalism to industrial capitalism, which was encouraged by Jeffersonian and Jacksonian liberal economics. In the same years that mid-Maine farmers fought for land from the Great Proprietors, they also began sending their daughters to work in the new textile mills in Lynn and Lowell, Massachusetts. Eastern Massachusetts farmers who may have sympathized with the western Shaysites took in piecework for shoemakers, hatmakers, and weavers. Even the cantankerous Whisky Rebels in Pennsylvania read, and perhaps answered, recruiting advertisements from a large manufacturer in Delaware. In this way, many farmers in the East were already both "in" and "of" the marketplace by 1800.

The East was the vanguard of industrialization in rural America, of course. Because economic development never happens all at once, many pockets of the Far West, Midwest, and South remained immune to industrialization until mid-century. Some pockets in Appalachia may have even maintained a precapitalist economy of domestic consumption and barter. Nevertheless, between 1865 and 1900 the transition of the American economy to an advanced, centralized, and state-supported industrial-capitalist system was completed in every region—from the arid Great Plains of the West to the humid bayous of the former Confederacy. This meant that just as Americans on the frontier, freed slaves, and poor southern whites thought that they were beginning lives of economic independence, they became surrounded by what Patricia Nelson Limerick calls the new dependencies of the industrial era.

Some of these dependencies came in unexpected packaging. For example, when the Republican Congress opened up many acres of the public domain to pioneer settlement in 1862, it also passed the Pacific Railroad Act, which provided hundreds of millions of acres of better land and substantial government loans to railroad corporations. Pioneers who could afford to bought land from the railroads instead of the government. But railroads also held monopolies on the transportation of their crops. Farmers in the West and South also became dependent on banks and furnishing merchants to finance seed, implements, and domestic goods. Some freedmen leased the same lands they had tilled as slaves and "shared" their crops with the same men who had owned them. All creditors pressured farmers to plant as much of their land in market crops as possible and as little in the traditional "safety first" crops grown exclusively for domestic consumption. To do so, however, required farmers to purchase even more domestic products from the merchant.

New labor-saving technologies complicated the postbellum farmer's autonomy as well. One hundred and sixty acres—the typical size of a homestead grant—quickly proved to be too small a plot to farm successfully in most of the West. As soon as possible, pioneer farmers bought more land either on credit or through the Timber Culture Act or the Desert Land Act. More land was more easily worked with horse-drawn machinery like the self-binding reaper and header, and in some places, the steam-powered thresher. These machines increased production but they did not contribute to an atmosphere of pastoral agrarianism. One Kansas observer thought that with the new technology his "vast farming region has more the appearance of an enormous manufacturing center than a quiet, unobtrusive, unparalleled grain-raising community." Expensive machinery also required expensive financing, as did irrigation equipment in the Far West and new fertilizers introduced in the Old South. Increasingly, credit problems cost farmers both the ideal and the reality of autonomy. Tenancy—as feared as ever by small producers—increased in every region between 1870 and 1900. So did the number of former agriculturists employed in wage labor or extractive industry. Collapsing farm prices—common enough in the emerging global marketplace where speculators bought and sold crops as commodities—pushed many farm families to the brink of starvation.

American political culture also changed in the wake of the Civil War. By 1840 the partisan politics that Anti-Federalists had helped to fashion had thoroughly captured the political imagination of white men in America. In fact, in a time of increasing mobility and urbanization, political parties served as new kinds of collective communities. As a result, nineteenth-century men were not interested in politics only at election time as they are today—if they still are at all. They considered partisan politics to be part of their personal identities and part of the ongoing civic culture of their communities. Huge percentages of eligible Americans voted in the smallest local and the largest national contests. Moreover, the location of most political activity moved from indoors, the traditional location of the elite, to out-of-doors, the traditional location of the people, thus incorporating that space within the political structure. Lavish parades, festivals, songs, and pageants accompanied the electoral process. Millions of Americans including Native Americans, Asian Americans, African Americans, and women were still disenfranchised, of course, and their disenfranchisement still upheld the independence of white men. Nevertheless, as Michael McGerr notes, "American politics from roughly the 'thirties to the 'nineties demanded the legitimacy conferred by all classes of the people." Governance by a few wealthy aristocrats who thought that they knew best for all the rest was the politics of the past, as far as nineteenth-century men were concerned.

The war did not change the fervor with which men participated in politics but it did change the reasons why they felt allegiance to their parties. In the 1830s and 1840s men essentially voted with their pocketbooks: those who associated themselves with the needs of small producers, including farmers and urban artisans, voted with Jackson or, after 1840 in the North, with the Whigs. Those associated with large business voted decidedly Republican. The war that broke so many bodies also crushed these economically and ideologically based political divisions. Between 1860 and 1880 seven of the eight major voting blocks in the North and South "waved the bloody shirt" with their ballots. Although voters in the Far West were somewhat less partisan in their voting patterns, for a quarter of a century after the Civil War the Solid South and Republican North could not be broken by interregional economic or political issues. As late as 1892, an Alabama congressman who dared to change his party allegiance remarked, "My own father would not hear me speak and said he would rather make my coffin with his own hands and bury me than to have me desert the Democratic Party." In time, many would come together and vow to "join hands against a common foe . . . without regret for the past or fear for the future." Such a feat would be anything but easy, however.

The form and function of the government also began to change in these years, as it mirrored the emerging centralization and subsequent fragmentation and bureaucratization of the modern corporation. We often locate the origin of the modern bureaucratic state in the Progressive Era or the New

Deal, but in fact the modern state was beginning its work in the 1870s by increasing its capacities, fragmenting its organizational style, and relying on a new class of white-collared experts and professionals. Just as rural areas had been the staging grounds for industrial capitalism, so did they (particularly in the West) become what Richard White calls the "kindergarten[s] of the American state." In the last three decades of the nineteenth century, the federal government expanded its power in land reclamation, irrigation, public education, Native American affairs, scientific agriculture, and forest management. Likewise, it created new centralized bureaucracies, staffed not by the political cronies of the Jacksonian era but by civil servants, professional government workers. Desperately in need of capital for development and practical information for survival, Americans on the frontier did not turn the government away. Instead, they began to imagine that they could potentially refashion the federal government into something they could recognize, something that would directly serve their interests and ideals. Until it did, however, they would continue to fear federal control of local affairs and scorn the intrusion of outsiders in their business.

Finally, between the end of the Civil War and the dawn of World War I, the dominant outlook of most Americans shifted from production to consumption. Again, this was not a trend that came out of the blue, or one in which rural people had not participated. Part of the currency crisis that led the United States into economic depression during and after the Revolutionary War was caused by the spending spree that Americans—settlers among them—went on to satisfy their pent-up demand for consumer products. In fact, there is evidence that ordinary colonists sought luxury items like fine china and fancy linens from Great Britain by the end of the seventeenth century. But after the Revolution, especially, farmers used consumption patterns as a way of demonstrating their status in the emerging American middle class. Late-eighteenth-century farmers' daughters increasingly understood the importance of including store-bought goods in their hope chests; farmers' sons understood the importance of obtaining manufactured implements for their farms. These needs and desires increased in the antebellum North as access to mass-produced goods improved. Pioneer families of the 1840s and 1850s set out on their overland journeys to California and Oregon in wagons overloaded with furniture, bedding, and clothing that their parents and grandparents would not even have imagined owning.

But a culture dedicated to consumption is more than a society of men and women who enjoy consumer products. It is one that begins to judge individual worth in terms of possessions and material goods rather than of work products. And this shift—among the most important in American history—took place first in the burgeoning cities of the nation in the late nineteenth century, not on its farms. As Robert McMath has put it, in the late nineteenth century farmers understood farming to be "more than a way of making money; it was still a way of life." Before the violent conflicts of the

1870s, 1880s, and 1890s, many urban artisans felt the same way and fought for the rights of workers to own the wealth that their labor created. But as the century wore on, the vacuum that meaningful work had occupied was increasingly filled with the activities of consumption: shopping, fashion, amusements, shows, professional sports, vaudeville. Urban and rural reformers and political organizers decried this trend, but to no avail. Like the children of immigrants, the children of farmers could see with their own eyes (thanks to the mass distribution of magazines, catalogs, and novels) that urban life was more exciting and more colorful than rural life. Back-country people thus increasingly felt, as David Danbom puts it, "that the nation was passing [them] by, leaving [them] behind, ignoring [them] at best and derogating [them] at worst."

Despite these changes and perhaps because of them too, rural people held more steadfastly to the dream of producerism in the late nineteenth century than they ever had before. When northerners traveled west, for example, they responded not only to the promise of free land but also to the corresponding vow of free labor. New Englanders on failing soil and sons of Ohio who had to move on believed that in the West it was still possible to be one's own boss, to control the affairs of the local community, and to maintain the age-old habits of mutuality associated with agrarian life. To the astonishment of some observers, this dream was strong enough to bring millions of immigrants from Europe as well. Swedes and Norwegians whose land could not sustain another generation; Germans in Russia experiencing persecution; Czechs, Bohemians, and Irishmen whose peasant villages were filled with the warmth of tradition and the cold of famine—all sent favorite sons and daughters to the American West. No matter where they hailed from, however, the new frontiersmen carried with them the same fervent desire for economic autonomy and personal liberty which had propelled British subjects into the wilderness two hundred years earlier.

The dream of rural producer radicalism survived the desolation of war in the American South as well—indeed it stretched its meaning to include many who had been disenfranchised before. For African American freedmen, the period between 1865 and 1890 was among the only times in African American history that such dreaming would be possible. On the Sea Islands off Georgia, for example, Union troops divided plantation lands among former slaves and watched as they learned to manage their own farms. Elsewhere, freedmen set up small farms and, with the arduous labors of their wives and many children, sometimes earned enough to profit from them. But African Americans did not seek simply to imitate white economic culture. Indeed, evidence suggests that freed slaves were more cautious and conservative about "safety first" agriculture, when they could afford to be, than whites were. Moreover, they maintained different crops, different management styles, and different leisure activities associated with the farm. Some of these, when seen through the eyes of whites, would be called lazy and used to demonstrate the futility of allowing African Americans economic or political independence. Nevertheless, some African Americans prospered and many learned to survive from year to year by conjoining producerist ideals and autonomous cultural patterns and traditions.

Whites in the Old South who did not own plantations were also determined to labor on the soil—despite the very small, even tiny size of their holdings. Eventually some would move to Texas and Kansas to find new lands. Those who stayed behind worked harder than ever to maintain productivity on their homesteads. Many switched all their acreage to production of King Cotton and gave up the safety net of self-sufficiency. In the Carolinas a new king was born of blue-flue tobacco. But surviving the economic turmoil of the period would prove nearly as difficult for small farmers in the South—sometimes called the "devastated generation"—as surviving the war had been. In time they would wonder whose lot in life they really shared—that of small farmers in other regions and even of different races, or that of the wealthy Democratic planters and politicians who seemed to have utterly forgotten them and their sacrifices.

None of these rural people—westerners, southerners, blacks, whites, Yankees, or Europeans—expected rural life to be easy. And after a few years, nearly all knew they had been right. The harsh plains environment taught new survival lessons by brute force: how to clean a house made of dirt; how to reach the barn in a blizzard and avoid freezing to death yards from shelter; how to clean grasshoppers inches deep from floors, cupboards, fields, and wells; how to endure illness, accident, and childbirth miles from medical care; how to maintain sanity in a one-room house with no trees, no water, and no neighbors anywhere in sight. In the South, drought, prairie fires, boll-weevil infestations, and unexpectedly early frosts could also mean the difference between food on the table or another year of hunger. Sometimes, when times were at their worst, farmers humbled themselves and requested aid from their local and state governments. Usually they were turned down by officials like Minnesota's Governor John Pillsbury, who worried that if he provided more than five dollars to a starving family of nine who had lost three years of crops to grasshoppers, they would be reduced to "habitual beggary" and "confirmed mendicancy."

As devastating as these natural disasters were and as much as rural people hoped that the government would help them, hard times were not by themselves sufficient cause for radicalism. Like Pillsbury, many rural people also felt that poverty was the result of personal failure like a lack of planning or enough hard work. For generations farmers had faced natural disasters of one kind or another and carried on in the hope that "next year" would be better. The kinds of disasters that rural people did not agree simply to endure were the peculiar economic problems of their time. These problems—a shortage of currency, a high rate of credit, a grossly inequitable system of rates on transcontinental railroads, the monopolization of industry, and the corruption of political parties—were anything but acts of God. They were, more and more farmers came to believe, the deliberate acts of greedy men, aided by an unresponsive and undemocratic government that had lost its concern for small producers. Before long, farmers in all sections would rise together to fight these man-made plagues and create an upheaval that, as one observer described it in 1890, could "hardly be diagnosed as a political campaign. It was a religious revival, a crusade . . . in which a tongue of flame sat upon every man, and each spake as the spirit gave him utterance."

The Populist movement was more than a political campaign, that much is certain. When it began it had little to do with institutionalized politics and a great deal to do with the anger and courage of ordinary men and women who had suffered too much for too long at the hands of wealthy men they had never met. These leaders combined commonsense economics with a vision of truly democratic politics to spark a cyclone of activity, education, and recruitment. As Lawrence Goodwyn has put it, Populism was a "spirit of egalitarian hope expressed . . . not in the prose of a platform, however creative, and not ultimately even in a third party, but in a self-generated culture of collective dignity and individual longing." Indeed, by the time the Populist movement waged a conventional political campaign within the two-party system in 1896, it had lost much of its initial radicalism. Nevertheless, the broad-based organizing strategies and nationwide programs developed by the Populists could never have been sustained—or even imagined—in the isolated settlements of colonial and revolutionary America.

In spite of all the things farmers were afraid they had lost to industrialization and modernization, they had gained some new resources that allowed them to work outside the two-party system but still on a nationwide scale. First and foremost, they had the voluntary association, a mainstay of American civic culture in the nineteenth century which brought isolated communities together through national organizations. Even in rural communities where neighbors customarily helped one another in the time-honored habits of mutuality, voluntarism thrived. Churches, schools, literary societies, secret clubs, and philanthropic organizations all brought self-interested Americans of the nineteenth century together in a new kind of community life. Every small town in the South and West was full of voluntary organizations like these. Webster, South Dakota, for example, whose population reached only a few thousand in the early twentieth century, hosted the Odd Fellows, Woodmen, Knights of Pythias, Catholic Order of Foresters, Royal Neighbors, and A.O.U.W.

Closely related to the growth of voluntary associations was the changing roles of women within the workplace and family. In urban areas where work and family life had become distinct, the ideology of separate spheres for men and women suggested to middle-class white women that their abilities, duties, and desires were also unique, defined by their capacity to nurture others and to understand moral issues with clarity. This role did not make women unimportant, however. Within the conventions of separate spheres women were free to acquire more education, to become more involved in their churches, and even to form associations with distinctly political orientations. Some urban women followed the logic of separate spheres all the way to radical abolitionism and feminism. In this way, the bonds of womanhood both kept women separate from and inherently unequal to men and also empowered women to achieve distinctly political acts of sisterhood.

The lives of nineteenth-century rural women were very different from those of urban women. As a very practical matter, they did not have, as Nancy Grey Osterud reveals, a separate sphere. They did not tend the home while men went to work in a factory or office or shop. They worked with men, sometimes even in the barns and fields with men, in a family-based business. Moreover, they were productive on their own terms, not only reproducing and training the farm's work force but also growing vegetables, selling dairy products, and running chicken and egg operations. Off the farm as well they sought to enact cross-gendered activities and to empower themselves through community-based habits of mutuality and reciprocity. At quilting bees, barn-raisings, and a host of other activities, rural women linked families and communities together and encouraged menfolk to do the same. Of course, they still did not own the value of their labor. Nevertheless, they actively pursued more egalitarianism within their activities. And yet the ideology of a separate sphere did not escape them entirely, especially by the end of the century. Rural women, too, formed voluntary associations at their churches and in their neighborhoods. Some were affiliated with men's groups, where they influenced men's activities, and some sought change strictly through a woman's perspective.

The first organizations that tried to modify the economic problems of the industrial age in rural America took the form of voluntary organizations that mimicked women's habits of mutuality and that included women and women's interests within their frameworks. The Patrons of Husbandry (more commonly referred to as the Grange) was founded in Ohio and Missouri in 1867 by Oliver Hudson Kelly as a social and educational club for farmers and their families whose lives were isolated and perhaps even a little bit dull. Kelly himself was a thirty-second-degree Mason, and it was in the Masonic tradition that he organized the club, leaving his job to recruit across the countryside. The growth in membership was slow, but the format was sure. As Kelly saw it, the Grange would have a men's and a women's division, have four ranks within each local division, and two more at the state and national levels. It would maintain secret initiation rites, rituals, and memberships. Its agenda would include monthly meetings, lectures on agricultural improvement, and picnics hosted by a women's auxiliary.

In many ways, however, women's lives were not merely auxiliary to the Grange's agenda. An early Grange credo read, "Woman was intended by our Creator to be the help meet, companion, and equal of man—the perfecting half added to his hemisphere—thus completing the fully globed orb of our common humanity." In 1893 the national headquarters of the Grange would announce what many state Granges had years earlier—that it was in full support of women's suffrage. Women and men who worked together on the farm were among the first to believe that they ought to vote together at the polls.

During the depression of 1873 the membership of the Grange began to accelerate—there were one and half million members by 1874—and its agenda began to include prescriptions for economic change. Reform of the railroads in particular came into its sights. Grangers complained that railroads had monopolies on their business, charged exorbitant rates, and charged the highest rates of all to farmers west of the Mississippi. Because railroads charged more per mile to westerners than to easterners, farmers in the West suffered simply because they lived in the West—where it was hard enough to live anyway. In 1890 it cost farmers as much to ship from Fargo, North Dakota, to Minneapolis as it did to ship from Minneapolis all the way to New York City. Likewise, farmers had to pay mileage to the farthest eastern point on the line, whether or not that was their destination. Other corporations, including creameries, processors, and banks, had comparable strangleholds on small producers and took huge bites from the profits the farmers saw as rightfully their own.

Grangers also complained about another vexing problem in rural America—the shortage of currency. Between 1865 and 1890 the supply of money in circulation in the United States remained the same, despite the increasing population and burgeoning business activity. The declining money supply meant that each dollar was worth more, and thus it became increasingly expensive for farmers to pay off their debts. A farmer who borrowed a thousand dollars in 1865 at 10-percent interest would have to pay back the equivalent of a hundred bushels of wheat. By 1880 he would have to produce twice as much to pay the same bill. And, like railroad rates, westerners paid higher interest rates than easterners did. In currency matters as in all economic affairs of the era, one historian notes that "the farmers' stick had two short ends." Grangers, like the members of the Greenback Party—a third party organized in the 1870s—encouraged the government to increase the supply of money either by returning to a bimetallic money system or by printing more paper money.

Antirailroad and soft-money factions existed as minorities in both major parties, but in a voluntary organization like the Grange, Republicans and Democrats found that they could come together and increase their influence. They succeeded in getting some regulation of the railroads when the Supreme Court upheld so-called Granger laws in *Munn v. Illinois* in 1876.

Despite a reversal in *Wabash v. Illinois* in 1886, the Interstate Commerce Act of 1887 made railroad regulation a lasting item on the American public-policy agenda. In the area of currency, however, the Grangers and their allies had significantly less success. When supplies of silver became scarce in 1873, the bimetallic money system was changed to a gold standard. But soon thereafter, much more silver became available through strikes in the Rocky Mountains and the Southwest. Still, wealthy businessmen and some urban laborers were resistant to increasing the money supply in any way. Not until 1890 would the Sherman Silver Purchase Act permit purchases of silver, and then only in very limited quantities. Meanwhile, the farm economy improved somewhat and most Grangers returned to the organization's social agenda. It would remain to another voluntary organization to bring farmers together in a sustained, nationwide, political program.

That organization was the Farmers' Alliance, begun in Texas in the mid-1880s when a severe drought and plummeting crop prices brought hard times back with a vengeance. A nonpartisan organization for a "farmer, farm laborer, a country mechanic, a country merchant, a country school teacher, a country physician, or a minister of the gospel," the Farmers' Alliance took on more than the railroads and developed into more than a club. It became a radical political organization dedicated to changing the direction of American capitalism toward sustained, cooperative producerism. Southern leaders Charles Macune and S. O. Daws focused on a host of economic problems, including railroad rates, credit rates, the monopolization of markets for their goods, and the high prices charged to them by retailers. Borrowing ideas and strategies from earlier organizations including the Agricultural Wheel and the Grange, they preached cooperation among farmers to overcome what Daws called the encroachments of monopolies. Soon Texas farmers began to do just that, by purchasing, selling, and distributing credit in their cooperative, nonprofit organization. Looking forward to the day when he too might be able to walk right past the local merchant's store, one Nebraska farmer wrote, "We'll have an Alliance Store too, at Hayes Center and back these merchants off the track. You just wait till we control things and we'll make you town leader hump yourselves."

"Alliance" was a good title for the new group, because it demonstrated the broad and inclusive attitude of its founders. As they were in the Grange, women were included in the Populist movement, and their experiences with community and kinship networking were reflected in the language of cooperation and reciprocity which defined the organization. Populists supported women's suffrage; many women were among its best-known and farthest-traveled leaders. Likewise, although whites debated over and over whether African American farmers should be allowed membership in white alliances, no one debated whether they should become part of the movement. Indeed, white recruiters were sent into African American communities to stress the commonality of economic problems which white and African

American farmers faced. The most radical believed that class interests transcended racial interests. In the end, African American farmers formed segregated "colored alliances." The fact that they existed at all, however, demonstrated the inclusiveness of Populism as well as the continuing relevance of radical producerism to freedmen and their children.

Ultimately Populists would also try to make alliances with industrial workers. Although their difference of opinion over free coinage of silver would make it difficult, the reality of a farmer-labor alliance seemed possible for a time. Populists believed that farm workers and industrial workers were caught in the same trap of exploitation and underrepresentation. They also did not necessarily equate rural with agrarian and urban with industrial work. There were, after all, burgeoning centers of industrial and especially extractive industry in both the West and South. The Knights of Labor recognized the importance of rural industry to their organization in the 1870s and 1880s. In the 1890s the Western Federation of Miners (WFM) would become one of the most radical unions in the country. Like farmers, miners were isolated from centers of economic and political power, and they did the most dangerous and difficult work in America. The WFM organized first to empower workers, and then to protect them. For example, the WFM created a network of union-supported, community-operated hospitals. They also attempted to negotiate issues of health and safety with corporations. To Populists, the twin ideals of workplace democracy and radical producerism were no different from the egalitarian and cooperative commonwealth for which they were struggling already.

After the St. Louis convention of 1889, which formally brought the northern and southern halves of the Alliance together, Populist leaders took on a specifically political, third-party agenda. They recruited new members, entered Alliance candidates in local, state, and national elections, and conceived of national programs. One of the most radical of these proposals was the subtreasury plan, whereby the federal government would buy farmers' crops and store them until the price was high, thus taking the middleman's profit out of the marketing process. This was one of the first articulations of an agricultural program whereby the federal government would essentially act as a low-cost lender to farmers and take away potential profits from large corporations. Equally original were the recommendations for a graduated income tax, a ban on land speculation, and the nationalization of the railroads. With leaders such as Ignatius Donnelly of Minnesota, Tom Watson of Georgia, and Mary Lease of Kansas, Populists also began to reimagine a political process that would be more responsive to the people. Direct election of senators and the initiative and referendum were two ways by which they believed the people's voices might better be heard and the party bosses', so often influenced by businesses and wealthy contributors, might be silenced.

Ironically, as the Populists sought to remake democratic politics, they also relied on its favorite out-of-doors rituals. It was difficult, terrible even, for some Populists to leave their political parties. Saying goodby to the party of their fathers, however, did not mean giving up the power or pleasure of partisanship. As they campaigned for state offices, Congress, and the presidency, Populists inherited the ability to organize politically and to make politics meaningful at the local level. In small towns and country fields, the rituals of conventional nineteenth-century politics were used in an attempt to overthrow what was left of conventional nineteenth-century politics. Speeches, parades, rituals, bands, glee clubs, picnics, orations, fireworks, banners, and unrestrained references to Thomas Jefferson, Andrew Jackson, Abraham Lincoln, the Declaration of Independence, the United States Constitution, and the Bible all evoked an older style of political community among people who believed—no, they knew—that they could think and vote and imagine a new day for America and help make it come true.

The rhetoric and ritual of the People's Party was powerful but its political success was short-lived. James Weaver won more than a million votes in his bid for the presidency in 1892, but nearly all of them came from voters in a handful of western states. In many of the same ways familiar to us today, third-party candidates in the late nineteenth century were limited by the structures of politics as usual. Thus some Populist leaders reluctantly came to believe that only fusion with a major political party would bring long-term success. In 1896 the Populists endorsed the candidacies of Democrat William Jennings Bryan for president and Populist Tom Watson of Georgia for vice president. While Watson stayed in the South, Bryan crisscrossed the Midwest by train traveling thirteen thousand miles and giving four hundred speeches. He warned crowds at every stop of the "cross of gold" upon which they were nailed. He also advocated the public ownership of the railroads, the free coinage of silver, the direct election of senators, and the imposition of a graduated income tax. But most of all he reminded rural voters of the eternal importance of farming and the high moral character of all producers. As Bryan told it, "There are but two sides in the conflict that is being waged in this country today. On the one side are the allied hosts of monopolies, the money power, great trusts and railroad corporations. . . . On the other are the farmers, laborers, merchants, and all other people who produce wealth and bear the burdens of taxation. . . . Between these two there is no middle ground."

Meanwhile, William McKinley sat on his back porch entertaining the press and giving interviews to prominent party leaders. He traveled nowhere, gave few speeches, and left most of the public-relations work to his assistant, Mark Hanna. When McKinley was elected, with a majority of 600,000 popular votes and nearly a hundred electoral votes, many observers believed that the distance between producer radicalism and industrial capitalism as well as that between participatory politics and modern consumer politics was measured by the miles between Bryan's train and McKinley's porch. Truth be told, however, the most radical of the Populists' ideals had been abandoned at the moment when the Alliance supporters had chosen to fuse with the Democrats. Democratic Party regulars and officials—even ordinary voters—cared a great deal more about the free-silver issue than they did about the transformative vision of an egalitarian and inclusive cooperative commonwealth. Thus the election was never really about the Populists' broader vision for America. In 1896 modern politics prevailed, as the modern industrial system had already. For another century the impact of the dual victories would be felt throughout rural America.

QUESTIONS TO CONSIDER

1. What was the significance for farmers of the transition of the American economy to an "advanced, centralized, and state-supported industrial-capitalist system" in the late nineteenth century?
2. Explain the split between rural and urban areas in terms of the transition from a production economy to a consumption economy.
3. Farmers had accepted the caprice of nature, or acts of God, as coming with the territory. What was different about the economic problems they faced in the late nineteenth century?
4. What was the Grange? What did it accomplish?
5. What was different about the Farmers' Alliance? What impact did it have?
6. What is Stock's assessment of the Populist movement?

5

The First Anti-Imperialists

BARBARA W. TUCHMAN

Reprinted with permission from
the September 20, 1965,
issue of *The Nation*.

In 1898 the United States fought the Spanish-American War, ostensibly to free Cuba from Spanish rule. In the aftermath of war, however, the nation found itself with colonial possessions (the Philippines, Puerto Rico, and Hawaii) and a paternalistic relationship to the newly independent Cuba. Furthermore, the Filipinos resisted the American takeover, and the United States fought a savage war to suppress the independence movement in the islands. This series of events caused a profound debate within the United States over the nature of the nation and its role in the world.

How, critics asked, could the United States, born in a revolution dedicated to self-rule, deny this same right to other peoples? What did it imply that the United States had acquired millions of ethnically alien subjects for whom citizenship was not a prospect? The American character, forged in a war for independence, became confused as the nation turned into what its ideals condemned—an imperial power. The debate would divide Americans often in the twentieth century, most passionately over Vietnam in the 1960s.

In 1965 the United States began bombing Vietnam and started the huge military buildup there. That same year *The Nation* magazine celebrated its hundredth anniversary with a special issue. In one of its articles, Barbara Tuchman explores in the impassioned words of the debaters the critical issues raised by the war in 1898 that had resurfaced in 1965. Tuchman (1912–1989) wrote several best-selling books during her career, including the Pulitzer Prize-winning *The Guns of August* (1962), a brilliant treatment of the opening month of World War I. *Stilwell and the American Experience in China, 1911–1945* (1970), acclaimed as her finest book, uses Stilwell as a vehicle for her discussion of Sino-American relations in the period. She was, in the best sense of the term, a "popular" historian.

Although in 1895 the name Anti-Imperialist had not yet come into use, President Cleveland was one in principle. Robustly opposed to expansion by America, he was no less ready to resist it by any other country. His Venezuela Message of 1895, emphatically asserting the Monroe Doctrine in defiance of Britain, touched off a burst of chauvinism and jingoism that revealed America in a mood of startling pugnacity. No question of gain, territorial or otherwise, was involved in Venezuela; it was simply a question, as it seemed to Cleveland, of asserting an American right.

The surge of militancy evoked by the Venezuela Message shocked people who still thought of the United States in the terms of its founders, as a nation opposed to militarism, conquest, standing armies and all the other bad habits associated with the monarchies of the old world. This tradition was strongest in New England and stronger among the older generation— roughly those who were over 50 in 1890—than among the new. They were closer to Jefferson who had said, "If there is one principle more deeply rooted in the mind of every American, it is that we should have nothing to do with conquest." They took seriously the Declaration of Independence and its principle of just power deriving from the consent of the governed. They regarded the extension of American rule over foreign soil and foreign peoples as a violation of this principle and a desecration of the American purpose. The original American democracy was to them a torch, an ideal, an example of a brave new world that had set its face against the old. They wanted nothing to do with titles of rank and nobility, knee breeches, orders or any of the other insidious trappings of monarchy and when in the Navy the title of Admiral was first proposed, an officer fumed, "Call them Admirals? Never! They will be wanting to be Dukes next."

First-generation immigrants who had come to the United States beckoned by the American dream were as deeply devoted to the founding principles as those in whom they had been bred for generations. Some came out of the balked revolution of 1848, seeking Liberty, like Governor Altgeld's father and like Carl Schurz, now 66, who as journalist, editor, cabinet minister and senator, had been a power and reformer ever since Lincoln's administration. Some came to escape oppression or poverty and to seek opportunity, like the Scottish weaver who arrived in 1848 with his twelve-year-old son, Andrew Carnegie, or like the Dutch-Jewish cigar maker who came from a London slum in 1863 with his thirteen-year-old son, Samuel Gompers. Some came like E. L. Godkin, editor of *The Nation* and the *New York Evening Post,* not as a refugee from oppression but as a voluntary exile from the old world, lured by America as a living demonstration of the democratic ideal. To them, as to men whose ancestors had come in the 1630s, America was a new principle and they saw the new militancy as its betrayal.

Godkin, filled with "anxiety about the country," determined to oppose the Cleveland message even at the risk of jeopardizing his paper with the "half-crazed public." Son of an English family settled since the 12th century in Ireland where he had been born and brought up, he had served as correspondent for English papers during the Crimean War and the American Civil War. He became editor of *The Nation* when it was founded in 1865 by a group of forty stockholders who supplied $100,000 with the stated purpose of championing the laboring class, the Negro, the cause of popular education and "true democratic principles in society and government." In 1883, while remaining at *The Nation,* he succeeded Carl Schurz as editor of the *Evening Post* and through the medium of these two organs made himself, as William James said, "a towering influence on all thought concerning public affairs."

He was a handsome, bearded, hot-tempered Celt, delighting in combat, brooding in melancholy, vivacious, pugnacious and a muckraker before Roosevelt invented the name. So unrelenting was his pursuit of corrupt practices by Tammany politicians that on one occasion they had him arrested for criminal libel three times in one day. James Russell Lowell agreed with the opinion of an English journalist that Godkin had made *The Nation* "the best periodical in the world" and James Bryce, already famous as the author of *The American Commonwealth,* declared the *Evening Post* to be "the best paper printed in the English language." Closer to home opinion was hotter. Governor Hill of New York said he did not care about "the handful of mugwumps" who read the *Post* in New York City. "The trouble with the damned sheet is that every editor in New York State reads it." This was what accounted for Godkin's pervasive influence; that other makers of opinion took their opinions from him—though not, to be sure, all. "What fearful mental degeneracy results from reading it or THE NATION as a steady thing," wrote Theodore Roosevelt to Captain Mahan in 1893. Roosevelt tended to confuse the desire for peace with physical cowardice and harped curiously on this subject: "I abhor men like [Edward Everett] Hale and papers like the *Evening Post* and *The Nation* in all of whom there exists absolute physical dread of danger and hardship and who therefore tend to hysterical denunciation and fear of war."

In 1895 Godkin was 64 and feared the future. The United States, he wrote to a friend, "finds itself in possession of enormous power and is eager to use it in brutal fashion against anyone who comes along without knowing how to do so and is therefore constantly on the brink of some frightful catastrophe." Indeed, as the United States had at this moment exactly one battleship in commission, Godkin was not unwarranted in thinking the Jingoes "absolutely crazy." He believed the new spirit of "ferocious optimism," as he strikingly described it, would lead to eventual disaster.

William James, Professor of Philosophy at Harvard, was equally disquieted. "It is instructive to find," he wrote apropos of Venezuela, "how near the surface in all of us the old fighting spirit lies and how slight an appeal will wake it up. Once really waked, there is no retreat." More outspoken was his colleague at Harvard, Charles Eliot Norton, Professor of Fine Arts and one of the forty stockholders who founded *The Nation*. Regarded as the exponent and arbiter of culture in American life, Norton protested the war spirit at a meeting in the Shepard Memorial Church in Cambridge. "The shout of brutal applause, which has gone up from every part of this nation," he said, makes every rational lover of his country feel the "greatest apprehension" for the future.

The white-haired, slender, stoop-shouldered figure, the husky yet musical voice speaking in its Boston Brahmin accent, the charm of that "supremely urbane and gentle presence" was never so at home as when against the herd. Born in 1827, only a year after Jefferson and John Adams died, Norton represented the puritan and militantly liberal conscience of an older generation. He was the son of Andrews Norton, "Unitarian Pope" of New England and Professor of Sacred Literature at Harvard, who had married Catherine Eliot, daughter of a wealthy Boston merchant, and was himself descended through a long line of ministers from John Norton, a Puritan divine who had emigrated to America in 1635.

Norton believed in the dominance of an aristocratic class which to him meant a class founded not in landowning but in a common background of culture, refinement, learning and manners. He saw it disappearing and protested regularly against encroaching vulgarity in his lectures. In parody of his manner a student said, "I propose this afternoon to make a few remarks on the hor-ri-ble vul-gar-ity of EVERYTHING." One of his students at Radcliffe in her diary for 1895 described him looking "so mildly happy and benignant . . . while he gently tells us it were better for us had we never been born in this degenerate and unhappy age."

Writing to Godkin about the Venezuela Message, Norton thought it made "a miserable end for this century" and had done much to increase the "worst spirit in our democracy . . . a barbaric spirit of arrogance and unreasonable self-assertion." What disturbed him more bitterly was the "deeper consideration" that the rise of democracy was not proving, after all, "a safeguard of peace and civilization" because it brought with it "the rise of the uncivilized whom no school education can suffice to provide with intelligence and reason." Norton felt the bitterness of a man who discovers his beloved to be not as beautiful—nor as pure—as he had believed. "I fear that America," he wrote to an English friend, "is beginning a long course of error and wrong and is likely to become more and more a power for disturbance and barbarism. . . . It looks as if the world were entering on a new stage of experience in which there must be a new discipline of suffering to fit men for the new conditions."

Occasionally, however, Norton would allow himself moments of optimism when he suspected that the loss of the values he loved might be the cost of a compensating gain in human welfare. "There are far more human beings materially well off today than ever before in the history of the world," he wrote in 1896 and he could not resist the thought, "How interesting our times have been and still are!"

Thomas B. Reed of Maine, formerly Speaker of the House and now Republican Minority Leader, belonged to the same tradition. During the Venezuela crisis he said little publicly, kept the Republicans in the House under firm control and trusted to Cleveland's basic antipathy for foreign adventure which he shared, to withstand the Jingoes' eagerness to annex this and that. Reed believed that American greatness lay at home and was to be achieved by improving living conditions and raising political intelligence among Americans rather than by extending American rule over half-civilized peoples difficult to assimilate. To him the Republican Party was the guardian of this principle and expansion was "a policy no Republican ought to excuse much less adopt."

Following the Republican victory and election of McKinley, supported by *The Nation,* in 1896, "Czar" Reed resumed the Speakership. Still firm in command of the Republican members, he could subdue any unhealthy lust among them for annexation but as Speaker he was bound to pilot Administration policy through the House. The question was, what *was* Administration policy: the soft reluctance of McKinley or the "outward" drive of Lodge and Roosevelt powered by the ideas of Mahan and the persuasions of the Sugar Trust? The answer came in June when a treaty of annexation was concluded with the Hawaiian Government, signed by McKinley and sent to the Senate for ratification. Although there was little likelihood of assembling two-thirds of the Senate in favor of it, the anti-expansionists were worried. Carl Schurz, whom McKinley, always anxious to please, had earlier assured of his lack of interest in Hawaii, faced him with the issue after dinner in the White House, over cigars. Very uncomfortable, McKinley pleaded that he had sent the treaty to the Senate only to get an expression of opinion. Nevertheless Schurz left with a heart "heavy with evil forebodings." In England the *Spectator* said somewhat nervously that the treaty marked "an end to the historic policy of the Republic since its foundation . . . and will mean its gradual evolution into a less peaceful and possibly militant power."

With the shrieks of the newspapers mounting over the "butcheries" of Spain and over the spirit of '76 reborn in the cry *Cuba Libre!,* the country was becoming increasingly excited. Reed regarded the Hearst-fabricated furor over Spain's oppression of Cuba with contempt and Republican espousal of Cuba's cause as hypocrisy. He saw his party losing its moral integrity and becoming a party of political expediency in response to the ignorant clamor of the mob. Without compunction he suppressed a resolution recognizing the belligerence of the "Republic" of Cuba. He took to the magazines to argue against expansion in an article whose title, "Empire Can Wait," became a rallying cry for the opponents of Hawaii's annexation. It spoke the awful name; as yet the outright words "empire" and "imperialism," which connoted the scramble for Africa then at its peak among the European powers, were not being used in the United States. James Bryce, perhaps the only Englishman who could have been allowed to give advice, urged Americans to have nothing to do with a policy of annexation. America's remote position and immense power, he wrote in the *Forum,* freed her from the burden of armaments crushing the European powers. Her mission in the world was "to show the older peoples and states an example of abstention from the quarrels and wars and conquests that make up so large and lamentable a part of the annals of Europe." To yield to the "earth-hunger" now raging among the European states would be "a complete departure from the maxims of the illustrious founders of the republic."

On February 15, 1898, the United States armored cruiser *Maine* blew up and sank in the harbor of Havana with the loss of 260 lives. Although the cause of the explosion was never ascertained, it was impossible in the mood of the time to assume other than a dastardly Spanish plot. The proponents of war burst into hysteria; the peace-minded were outshouted. McKinley hung back, but fearful of a split in his party, soon gave way to clamor. Speaker Reed did not. During the two months while negotiations aimed at forcing Spain into war were being pursued, he did his best to hold back the wave, limiting time for debate and quashing resolutions recognizing Cuban independence. When Senator Proctor who owned marble quarries in Vermont made a strong speech for war, Speaker Reed commented, "Proctor's position might have been expected. A war will make a large market for gravestones." He was attacked by the pro-war press and his rulings aroused resentment in the House which, on the whole, like the country, wanted war. "Ambition, interest, land-hunger, pride, the mere joy of fighting, whatever it may be," acknowledged the *Washington Post*, "we are animated by a new sensation. . . . The taste of Empire is in the mouth of the people even as the taste of blood in the jungle." War on Spain was declared on April 25.

On April 30 Admiral Dewey's squadron of four cruisers and two gunboats steamed into Manila Bay and with a day's bombardment, loosed by the classic order, "You may fire when ready, Gridley," destroyed or put out of action all ten ships of the Spanish squadron as well as the shore batteries. Never had the country felt such a thrill of pride. "Greatest Naval Engagement of Modern Times" was one headline. People went wild with excitement and hero-worship.

A new problem suddenly faced the country which none but a few had thought of: what to do about the Philippines. The American people on the whole, as Mr. Dooley said, did not know whether they were islands or canned goods and even McKinley confessed "he could not have told where those darned islands were within 2,000 miles." The disciples of Mahan knew well enough where they were and what must become of them. Within four days of Dewey's victory Lodge wrote, "We must on no account let the islands go. . . . The American flag is up and it must stay." Since there had been a Filipino independence movement in existence for thirty years for which many had fought and suffered prison, exile and death, Senator Lodge's simple solution took little account of the consent of the governed.

In America the outbreak of a war to be carried to the enemy and posing no danger to the homeland did not silence but galvanized the war's opponents. Suddenly they became an entity with a name: the Anti-Imperialists. Professor Norton, now over 70, brought upon himself torrents of abuse and threats of violence to his house and person by urging his students not to enlist in a war in which "we jettison all that was most precious of our national cargo." Although an Irish politician of Boston proposed to send a lynching party for him and the press called him a "traitor" and even Senator Hoar denounced him, Norton's grief at his country's course was too great to be contained. At a meeting of the Congregational Church in Cambridge he spoke of how bitter it was that now, at the end of a century which had seen the greatest advance in knowledge and the hope of peace, America should be turning against her ideals and "plunging into an unrighteous war."

Others in Boston spoke out. Moorfield Storey, President of the Massachusetts Reform Club and Civil Service Reform League, and a former President of the American Bar Association, was one; Gamaliel Bradford, a rampant critic of government known for his one-man crusades through a flow of letters to newspapers, was another. The first Story (minus the "e") had settled in Massachusetts in 1635 and Bradford was descended from the first Governor of the Plymouth Colony. Together they assembled a meeting of protest at Faneuil Hall and here on June 15, 1898, three days after Aguinaldo in the Philippines issued a declaration of independence, the Anti-Imperialist League was founded. Its president was the 80-year-old Republican George S. Boutwell, former Senator from Massachusetts and former Secretary of the Treasury under President Grant. Its stated purpose was not to oppose the war as such but to insist that having been undertaken as a war of liberation, it not be turned into one for empire. The quest for power, money and glory abroad, the League maintained, would distract from reform at home and bring in its train a strong central government destructive of traditional states' rights and local liberties. Americans had enough to do to solve the problems of municipal corruption, war between capital and labor, disordered currency, unjust taxation, the use of public office for spoils, the rights of the colored people in the South and of the Indians in the West, before taking alien peoples under their rule.

These were the problems that absorbed reformers many of whom, together with independents and dissenters of various kinds and distinguished Democrats who had perforce become the anti-expansion party, now banded together under the banner of the League. Its 41 vice-presidents soon included ex-President Cleveland, his former Secretary of War William Endicott and former Secretary of the Treasury, Speaker Carlisle, Senator "Pitchfork Ben" Tillman, President David Starr Jordan of Stanford, President James B. Angell of the University of Michigan, Jane Addams, Andrew Carnegie, William James, Samuel Gompers, president of the American Federation of Labor, and numbers of other congressmen, clergymen, professors, lawyers and writers. The novelist William Dean Howells thought the war "an abominable business" and when his friend Mark Twain came home from an extended trip abroad, he became a member of the league.

On the side of the Anti-Imperialists was a strong sentiment, growing out of the troubles with the Negroes after the Civil War, of reluctance to take on new colored populations. Nothing but more trouble would accrue, said Godkin harshly in *The Nation*, from "dependencies inhabited by ignorant and inferior races" with whom Americans had no union "other than would be necessary for purposes of carpet-baggery and corruption." Carl Schurz used the same argument against the Isthmian Canal, saying that "once fairly started on a career of aggrandizement" the imperialists would insist that the canal be bordered on both sides by American territory and would want to annex countries "with a population of 13,000,000 Spanish-Americans mixed with Indian blood" who would flood Congress with 20 Senators and 50 or 60 Representatives. Hawaii, where orientals greatly outnumbered the whites, posed the same threat.

The anti-imperialists did not sweep up with them the Populists and followers of William Jennings Bryan and those soon to be known as Progressives. While these groups opposed standing armies, big navies and foreign entanglements and were in theory anti-imperialist, anti-militarist and anti-European, they were simultaneously imbued with a fever to fight Spain as a cruel European tyrant stamping out liberty at America's doorstep. Bryan called for war as loudly as Theodore Roosevelt and in sincere flattery, if less promptly, had himself appointed Colonel of the Third Nebraska Volunteers, too late to see action in Cuba.

The Battle of Santiago in July brought the war in Cuba to an end. Since it had been undertaken with the stated purpose of "liberating" the Cubans from Spanish rule, annexation would have been awkward. But as fruit of conquest Puerto Rico, at least, was available. Required to renounce Cuba and cede the smaller neighbor, Spain was eliminated from the Western Hemisphere. Preliminary peace terms were signed in Washington on August 12 leaving the more troublesome question of the Philippines to be negotiated by peace commissioners who were to meet in Paris to conclude a final settlement.

At home the Anti-Imperialists through meetings, protests, speeches, articles, petitions and public conferences were attempting to hold their country back from plucking the archipelago in the Pacific which seemed to glow with the fatal evil of the apple in the Garden of Eden. Carl Schurz urged McKinley to turn the Philippines over as a mandate to a small power such as Belgium or Holland so that the United States could remain "the great neutral power of the world." In France it was the "Dreyfus summer" and Americans, too, in those months felt that their country had reached a moment critical for its character and future. In public and private the debate raged whether to keep the Philippines or turn them back to self-government by the Filipinos. A three-day conference on foreign policy to consider "some of the most momentous problems in the history of the Republic" was convened at Saratoga in August by leaders in public life both for and against expansion. The favored theme of the expansionists which called forth their most energetic arguments was a vision of the vast untapped markets of the Orient with their limitless opportunities for American enterprise. Speaking for the Anti-Imperialists, Henry Wade Rogers, President of Northwestern University and Chairman of the Conferences on opening day forcefully made the point that it was not necessary to annex territory in order to trade with it. But he could not summon passion equal to Judge Grosscup, notorious as the man who had issued the injunction in the Pullman strike, who delivered an exuberant paean to "the new career of commercial activity upon which I trust we are about to enter." The Philippines must be retained, in addition to Puerto Rico and Hawaii, so that the United States would have "clear across the Pacific a line of naval stations and home ports in every sense our own," leading to Asia, a whole continent with "doors swinging inward that will lead us to one half the desirable territory and one third the population of the earth." Samuel Gompers spoke against conquest of foreign lands not only as a betrayal of American principles but as a danger to the standards of American wage-earners. Strange combinations were wrought in the cause of Anti-Imperialism. When at a later meeting in Chicago Gompers declared that retention of the Philippines would show that "our war was without just cause," Andrew Carnegie sent him a telegram of congratulations saying, "Let us stand together to save the Republic."

The annexationist tide was too strong. At Paris the United States demanded "cession of the whole Archipelago," coupled with offer of a token payment to Spain of $20,000,000 to grease the acceptance of the inevitable. On December 10 the Treaty of Paris was signed transferring sovereignty of the Philippines to the United States with the $20,000,000 to follow upon ratification. "We have bought ten million Malays at $2.00 a head unpicked," remarked Reed acidly, and in the most prescient comment made by anyone at the time, he added, "and nobody knows what it will cost to pick them."

That winter in the Senate's battle over ratification of the Treaty of Paris, the Republicans needed every vote they could collect to muster the necessary two-thirds majority. In the delicate balance that prevailed, the most important issue since Secession depended on the votes of one or two vacillating Senators. Suddenly Bryan arrived in Washington and to the amazement of his followers urged them to vote *for* the treaty. Preparing to run again for President in 1900 he realized he could not win on a repetition of the silver issue and was perfectly prepared to give it up in favor of Imperialism, a new crown of thorns. To make acquisition of the Philippines a raging issue, it had to be consummated first. Consequently, he told his party, it would not do to defeat the treaty. Besides, he argued comfortingly, to ratify the treaty would end the war.

At this moment the Filipinos rose in their own war of independence. Their forces attacked the American lines outside Manila on the night of February 4. In Washington the news intensified the frenzied speculation over the vote on the treaty but no one could be certain what effect it would have. A last-minute petition signed by ex-President Cleveland, President Eliot of Harvard and twenty-two other men of national prominence was addressed to the Senate, protesting the treaty unless it included a provision against annexing the Philippines and Puerto Rico. "In accordance with the principles upon which our Republic was founded we are in duty bound to recognize the rights of the inhabitants . . . to independence and self-government," it said, and pointed out that if, as McKinley had once declared, the forcible annexation of Cuba would be "criminal aggression by our code of morals, annexation of the Philippines would be no less so."

When the Senate voted on February 6 Bryan's work told: the treaty won by a one-vote margin. "The way the country puked up its ancient principles at the first touch of temptation was sickening," wrote William James in a private letter. The saddest thing for such men was the parting with the American dream. "We are false to all we have believed in," wrote Moorfield Storey. "This great free land which for more than a century has been a refuge to the oppressed of every land, has now turned to oppression."

Hearing the sound of "ignoble battle" coming "sullenly over the Pacific seas," William Vaughn Moody wrote his "Ode in a Time of Hesitation" which appeared in the *Atlantic Monthly* in May, 1900. Are we still the "eagle nation" he asked, or

> *Shall some less lordly bird be set apart?*
> *Some gross-billed wader where the swamps are fat?*
> *Some gorger in the sun? Some prowler with the bat?*

This was the conscience of the few, felt too by Godkin who in his disillusion said a strange and clairvoyant thing at this time. "The military spirit," he wrote to Moorfield Storey in January, 1900, "has taken possession of the masses to whom power has passed."

In the election of 1900 the Anti-Imperialists were caught in an agonizing dilemma. McKinley represented the party of imperialism; Bryan, in Carl Schurz's words, was "the evil genius of the anti-imperialist cause." Nevertheless his reasoning had succeeded and as he was necessarily the champion of the Philippine cause, the Anti-Imperialists had nowhere else to go. They were called the "Hold-your-nose-and-vote" group but even by this technique Bryan could not be made acceptable to *The Nation*. Opposed to McKinley because of imperialism and to Bryan as irresponsible, it scolded both and supported neither.

The campaign represented the zenith of the Anti-Imperialists' effort but they were hampered by a tarnished candidate and a cause out of joint with the time. What a people thinks at any given time can best be measured by what they do. McKinley and Roosevelt were elected by 53 percent of the votes cast and with a greater margin over Bryan than in 1896. Expansion and conquest were accepted and the break with the American past confirmed. Still at war in the Philippines, America moved into the 20th century.

Professor Norton voiced the elegy of the Anti-Imperialists. "I reach one conclusion," he wrote to a friend, "that I have been too much of an idealist about America, had set my hopes too high, had formed too fair an image of what she might become. Never had a nation such an opportunity; she was the hope of the world. Never again will any nation have her chance to raise the standard of civilization."

QUESTIONS TO CONSIDER

1. What were the sources of the anti-imperial tradition?
2. Why did Thomas Reed and other Republicans oppose imperialism in early 1898?
3. What was the stated purpose of the Anti-Imperial League?
4. How did race prejudice contribute to the anti-imperial cause?
5. Why did William Jennings Bryan support the Treaty of Paris? What effect did his stand have? Was he wise?
6. What do *you* think of the Anti-Imperial League's allegation that the United States betrayed its principles by acquiring colonies?

6

Citizen Ford

DAVID HALBERSTAM

Reprinted from *American Heritage,*
Oct./Nov. 1986, by permission
of the author.

By 1920 the United States had been transformed from a production economy, designed to increase production as the key to increasing wealth, to a consumption economy, with workers increasingly being able to consume the fruits of their labor and broadening the base of American prosperity. Probably no person played as great a role in this change as Henry Ford. By introducing the mass-produced Model T in 1908 and the assembly line in 1913, and by doubling his workers' wages to $5 a day, Ford moved toward his dream of a car for every man. His importance was such that in Aldous Huxley's 1932 classic *Brave New World,* the calendar was dated not from Christ's birth (A.D.) but from the introduction of the Model T (A.F.).

But Ford was ambivalent about the changes he wrought. Even though he boasted that "I invented the modern age," he believed in hard work as the ultimate virtue and was dismayed by the emergence of a leisure culture. He had hated his farm upbringing, but he looked fondly back on his roots and recreated them in the nostalgic "Greenfield Village." He didn't like urban sprawl, but the Model T helped make it possible.

Perhaps more than anything Ford shows how difficult it is to sustain the vision and genius of youth. As David Halberstam so powerfully demonstrates in this 1986 article, Ford realized all his dreams by the early 1920s, but his flexibility and mental acuity then declined to the point that he destroyed his very capable son Edsel and almost ruined his company before finally stepping down under pressure.

David Halberstam (1934–) burst into the public's consciousness in 1972 with his smash bestseller about the Kennedy and Johnson leadership, *The Best and the Brightest*, which explored the ways in which such talent could lead the country into the Vietnam quagmire. He has since published numerous volumes to widespread acclaim, including sports books (*The Summer of 1949, October 1964*, and *Playing for Keeps*), period pieces (*The Fifties*), inside accounts of the world of journalism (*The Powers That Be*), and in 2001 an analysis of foreign policy under Clinton entitled *War in a Time of Peace*.

PART ONE: THE CREATOR

Late in the life of the first Henry Ford, a boy named John Dahlinger, who more than likely was Ford's illegitimate son, had a discussion with the old man about education and found himself frustrated by Ford's very narrow view of what schooling should be. "But, sir," Dahlinger told Ford, "these are different times, this is the modern age and—" Ford cut him off. "Young man," he said, "I invented the modern age."

The American century had indeed begun in Detroit, created by a man of simple agrarian principles. He had started with scarcely a dollar in his pocket. When he died, in 1947, his worth was placed at $600 million. Of his most famous car, the Model T, he sold 15,456,868. Mass production, he once said, was the "new messiah," and indeed it was almost God to him. When he began producing the Model T, it took twelve and a half hours to make one car. His dream was to make one car every minute. It took him only twelve years to achieve that goal, and five years after that, in 1925, he was making one every ten seconds. His name was attached not just to cars but to a way of life, and it became a verb—to *fordize* meant to standardize a product and manufacture it by mass means at a price so low that the common man could afford to buy it.

When Ford entered the scene, automobiles were for the rich. But he wanted none of that; he was interested in transportation for men like himself, especially for farmers. The secret lay in mass production. "Every time I reduce the charge for our car by one dollar," he said early in the production of the T, "I get a thousand new buyers," and he ruthlessly brought the price down, seeking—as the Japanese would some sixty years later—size of market rather than maximum profit per piece. He also knew in a shrewd, intuitive way what few others did in that era, that as a manufacturer and employer he was part of a critical cycle that expanded the buying power of the common man. One year his advertising people brought him a new slogan that said, "Buy a Ford—save the difference," and he quickly changed it to "Buy a Ford—SPEND the difference," for though he was innately thrifty himself, he believed that the key to prosperity lay not in saving but in spending and turning money over. When one of the children of his friend

Harvey Firestone boasted that he had some savings, Ford lectured the child. Money in banks was idle money. What he should do, Ford said, was spend it on tools. "Make something," he admonished, "create something."

For better or worse Ford's values were absolutely the values of the common man of his day. Yet, though he shared the principles, yearnings, and prejudices of his countrymen, he vastly altered their world. What he wrought reconstituted the nature of work and began a profound change in the relationship of man to his job. Near the end of this century it was clear that he had played a major part in creating a new kind of society in which man thought as much about leisure time as about his work. Ironically, the idea of leisure itself, or even worse, a leisure culture, was anathema to him. He was never entirely comfortable with the fruits of his success, even though he lived in a magnificent fifty-six-room house. "I still like boiled potatoes with the skins on," he said, "and I do not want a man standing back of my chair at table laughing up his sleeve at me while I am taking the potatoes' jackets off." Of pleasure and material things he was wary: "I have never known what to do with money after my expenses were paid," he said, "I can't squander it on myself without hurting myself, and nobody wants to do that."

Only work gave purpose: "Thinking men know that work is the salvation of the race, morally, physically, socially. Work does more than get us our living; it gets us our life."

As a good farm boy should, he hated alcohol and tobacco, and he once said that alcohol was the real cause of World War I—the beer-drinking German taking after the wine-drinking Frenchman. His strength, in his early years—which were also his good years—was in the purity of his technical instincts. "We go forward without facts, and we learn the facts as we go along," he once said. Having helped create an urbanized world where millions of God-fearing young men left the farm and went to the cities, he was profoundly uneasy with his own handiwork, preferring the simpler, slower America he had aided in diminishing. For all his romanticizing of farm life, however, the truth was that he had always been bored by farm work and could not wait to leave the farm and play with machines. They were his real love.

When Ford was born, in 1863, on a farm in Dearborn, Michigan, the Civil War was still on. His mother died at the age of thirty-seven delivering her eighth child. Henry was almost thirteen at the time. He had idolized her, and her death was a bitter blow. "I thought a great wrong had been done to me," he said. Later in his life he not only moved the house in which he grew up to Greenfield Village, and tracked down the Ford family's very own stove, whose serial number he had memorized, he also had a cousin who resembled his mother dress up in an exact imitation of the way she had and wear her hair in just the same style.

His father's people were new Americans. When the great potato blight had struck Ireland in 1846, ruining the nation's most important crop, that country had been devastated. Of a population of eight million, one million had died, and one million had emigrated to America. Among the migrants was William Ford, who had set off to the magic land with two borrowed pounds and his set of tools. He was a skilled carpenter, and when he arrived, he moved quickly to Michigan, where some of his uncles had already settled, and found work laying railroad track. With his savings he bought some land and built a house, in awe of an America that had so readily allowed him to do so. To William Ford, Ireland was a place where a man was a tenant on the land, and America was a place where he owned it.

Henry Ford started school when he was seven. The basic books were the McGuffey Reader; they stressed moral values but included sections from Dickens, Washington Irving, and other major writers, which enticed many children into a genuine appreciation of literature. Although Ford loved McGuffey, he did not like books or the alien ideas they sometimes transmitted. "We read to escape thinking. Reading can become a dope habit. . . . Book-sickness is a modern ailment." By that he meant reading that was neither technical nor functional, reading as an end in itself, as a pleasure without a practical purpose. But he was wary even of practical volumes. "If it is in a book, it is at least four years old, and I don't have any use for it," he told one of his designers.

What he truly loved was machinery. From the start, he had a gift for looking at a machine and quickly understanding it, not only to repair it but to make it work better. "My toys were all tools," he wrote years later. "They still are!" In his early teens he designed a machine that allowed his father to close the farm gate without leaving his wagon. Watches fascinated him. When he was given a watch at thirteen, he immediately took it apart and put it back together. He soon started repairing watches for his friends. His father complained that he should get paid for this, but he never listened, for it was a labor of love.

His father wanted him to become a farmer, but it was a vain hope. Henry Ford hated the drudgery of the farm. In 1879 he entered his seventeenth year, which in those days was considered maturity. On the first day of December of that year, he left for Detroit, a most consequential departure. He walked to the city, half a day's journey.

Detroit was a town of 116,000, a place of foundries and machine shops and carriage makers. There were some nine hundred manufacturing and mechanical businesses, many of them one-room operations but some of them large. It was an industrial city in the making. Ten railroads ran through it. As New York City, in the next century, would be a mecca for young Americans interested in the arts, Detroit was just becoming a city with a pull for young men who wanted to work with machines. The surge in small industries was beginning, and a young man who was good with his hands could always find a job.

Ford went to work at James Flower & Brothers, a machine shop with an exceptional reputation for quality and diversity of product. As an apprentice there, Ford was immersed in the world of machinery, working among men who, like himself, thought only of the future applications of machines. He made $2.50 a week, boarded at a house that charged him $3.50 a week, and walked to work. His salary left him a dollar a week short, and as a good, enterprising young man, he set out to make up the difference. Hearing that the McGill Jewelry Store had just gotten a large supply of clocks from another store, Ford offered to clean and check them. That job added another two dollars to his weekly salary, so he was now a dollar a week ahead.

His fascination with watches led him to what he was sure was a brilliant idea. He would invent a watch so elementary in design that it could be mass-produced. Two thousand of them a day would cost only thirty cents apiece to make. He was absolutely certain he could design and produce the watch; the only problem, he decided, was in marketing 600,000 watches a year. It was not a challenge that appealed to him, so he dropped the project. The basic idea, however, of simplifying the product in order to mass-produce it, stayed with him.

He went from Flower & Brothers to a company called Detroit Dry Dock, which specialized in building steamboats, barges, tugs, and ferries. His job was to work on the engines, and he gloried in it, staying there two years. There was, he later said, nothing to do every day but learn. In 1882, however, at the age of nineteen, he returned to the farm, and his father offered him eighty acres of land to stay there. William Ford did that to rescue his wayward son from the city and his damnable machines; Henry Ford took it because he momentarily needed security—he was about to marry Clara Bryant. Nothing convinced him more of his love of machines than the drudgery of the farm. Again he spent every spare minute tinkering and trying to invent and reading every technical magazine he could. He experimented with the sawmill on the farm; he tried to invent a steam engine for a plow. Crude stationary gasoline engines had been developed, and Ford was sure a new world of efficient gasoline-powered machines was about to arrive. He wanted to be part of it. In 1891, with all the timber on the farm cut, he asked Clara to go back to Detroit with him. "He just doesn't seem to settle down," his father said to friends. "I don't know what will become of him."

The last thing Henry Ford was interested in was settling down. He intended, he told his wife, to invent a horseless carriage. But first he needed to know a good deal more about electricity. So he took a job with Detroit Edison at forty-five dollars a month. The city had grown dramatically in the few years since he had first arrived; its population was now more than 205,000. The railroads had begun to open up the country, and, except for Chicago, no town in America had grown as quickly. Detroit now had streetlights. There were more machine shops than ever before. In this city the age of coal and steam was about to end.

By 1896, at the age of thirty-two, Ford finally had his first car on the street. He was so excited by the prospect of his inaugural ride that he barely slept for the forty-eight hours before it. He had been so obsessed and pre-occupied during the creation of the car that not until it was time for the test drive did he find that the door of the garage was too small for it to exit. So he simply took an ax and knocked down some of the brick wall to let the automobile out. A friend rode ahead on a bike to warn off traffic. A spring in the car broke during the ride, but they fixed it quickly. Then Henry Ford went home so he could sleep for a few hours before going to work. Later he drove the car out to his father's farm, but William Ford refused to ride in it. Why, he asked, should he risk his life for a brief thrill?

Henry Ford sold that first car for $200 and used the money to start work immediately on his next. It was considerably heavier than the first, and he persuaded a lumber merchant named William Murphy to invest in the project by giving him a ride. "Well," said Murphy when he reached home safely, "now we will organize a company." In August 1899 Murphy brought together a consortium of men who put up $15,000 to finance Ford's Detroit Automobile Company. Ford thereupon left Detroit Edison to work full time on his car.

In February 1900, at the threshold of the twentieth century, Ford was ready to take a reporter from the *Detroit News Tribune* for a ride. The car, he said, would go twenty-five miles an hour. The reporter sensed that he was witness to the dawn of a new era. Steam, he later wrote, had been the "compelling power of civilization," but now the shriek of the steam whistle was about to yield to a new noise, the noise of the auto. "What kind of a noise is it?" the reporter asked. "That is difficult to set down on paper. It is not like any other sound ever heard in this world. It was not like the puff! puff! of the exhaust of gasoline in a river launch; neither is it like the cry! cry! of a working steam engine; but a long, quick, mellow gurgling sound, not harsh, not unmusical, not distressing; a note that falls with pleasure on the ear. It must be heard to be appreciated. And the sooner you hear its newest chuck! chuck! the sooner you will be in touch with civilization's latest lisp, its newest voice." On the trip, Ford and the reporter passed a harness shop. "His trade is doomed," Ford said.

Ford, however, was not satisfied. The cars he was making at the Detroit Automobile Company were not far behind the quality of the cars being made by Duryea or Olds, but they remained too expensive for his vision. Ford desperately wanted to make a cheaper car. His stockholders were unenthusiastic. By November 1900 the company had died. But Ford was as determined as ever to make his basic car, and he decided that the way to call attention to himself and pull ahead of the more than fifty competing auto makers was to go into racing. In 1901 he entered a race to be held in Grosse Pointe. He won and became, in that small, new mechanical world, something of a celebrity. That propelled him ahead of his competitors.

Two years later, in 1903, he set out to start the Ford Motor Company. He was forty years old and had, he felt, been apprenticing long enough. There were 800 cars in the city at that time, and some owners even had what were called motor houses to keep them in. Ford soon worked up his plan for his ideal, inexpensive new car, but he needed money—$3,000, he thought, for the supplies for the prototype (the actual cost was $4,000). He got the financing from a coal dealer named Alexander Malcomson. Ford and Malcomson capitalized their original company for $150,000, with 15,000 shares. Some of the early investors were not very confident. John Gray, Malcomson's uncle, made a 500 percent return on his early investment but went around saying that he could not really ask his friends to buy into the company. "This business cannot last," he said. James Couzens, Malcomson's assistant, debated at great length with his sister, a schoolteacher, on how much of her savings of $250 she should risk in this fledging operation. They decided on $100. From that she made roughly $355,000. Couzens himself managed to put together $2,400 to invest, and from that, when he finally sold out to Ford in 1919, he made $29 million.

This time Ford was ready. He was experienced, he hired good men, and he knew the car he would build. "The way to make automobiles," he told one of his backers in 1903, "is to make one automobile like another automobile . . . just as one pin is like another pin when it comes from a pin factory, or one match is like another match when it comes from a match factory." He wanted to make many cars at a low price. "Better and cheaper," he would say. "We'll build more of them, and cheaper." That was his complete vision of manufacturing. "Shoemakers," he once said, "ought to settle on one shoe, stove makers on one stove. Me, I like specialists."

But he and Malcomson soon split over the direction of the company: Malcomson, like Ford's prior backers, argued that fancy cars costing $2,275 to $4,775 were what would sell. At the time, nearly half the cars being sold in America fell into this category; a decade later, largely because of Ford, those cars would represent only 2 percent of the market. Malcomson wanted a car for the rich; Ford, one for the multitude. Though the early models were successful—the company sold an amazing total of 1,700 cars in its first 15 months—it was the coming of the Model T in 1908 that sent Ford's career rocketing.

It was the car that Henry Ford had always wanted to build because it was the car that he had always wanted to drive—simple, durable, absolutely without frills, one that the farmer could use and, more important, afford. He was an agrarian populist, and his own people were farmers, simple people; if he could make their lives easier, it would give him pleasure. He planned to have a car whose engine was detachable so the farmer could also use it to saw wood, pump water, and run farm machinery.

The Model T was tough, compact, and light, and in its creation Ford was helped by breakthroughs in steel technology. The first vanadium steel, a lighter, stronger form developed in Britain, had been poured in the United States a year before the planning of the Model T. It had a tensile strength nearly three times that of the steel then available in America, yet it weighed less and could be machined more readily. Ford instantly understood what the new steel signified. He told one of his top men, Charles Sorensen, that it permitted them to have a lighter, cheaper car.

The T was a brilliantly simple machine: when something went wrong, the average owner could get out and fix it. Unimproved dirt tracks built for horses, which made up most of the nation's roads and which defeated fancier cars, posed no problem for it. Its chassis was high, and it could ride right over serious bumps. It was, wrote Keith Sward, a biographer of Ford, all bone and muscle with no fat. Soon the Ford company's biggest difficulty was in keeping up with orders.

Because the Model T was so successful, Ford's attention now turned to manufacturing. The factory and, even more, the process of manufacturing, became his real passions. Even before the T, he had been concerned about the production process. In 1906 he had hired an industrial efficiency expert named Walter Flanders and offered him a whopping bonus of $20,000 if he could make the plant produce 10,000 cars in 12 months. Flanders completely reorganized the factory and beat the deadline by two days. He also helped convince Ford that they needed a larger space. Flanders understood that the increasing mechanization meant that the days of the garage-shop car maker were over. There was a process now, a *line*, and the process was going to demand more and more money and employees. Flanders understood that every small success on the line, each increment that permitted greater speed of production (and cut the cost of the car), mandated as well an inevitable increase in the size of the company. "Henceforth the history of the industry will be the history of the conflict of giants," he told a Detroit reporter.

Ford thereupon bought his Highland Park grounds. Here he intended to employ the most modern ideas about production, particularly those of Frederic Winslow Taylor, the first authority on scientific industrial management. Taylor had promised to bring an absolute rationality to the industrial process. The idea was to break each function down into much smaller units so that each could be mechanized and speeded up and eventually flow into a straight-line production of little pieces becoming steadily larger. Continuity above all. What Ford wanted and what he soon got, was a mechanized process that, in the words of Ken Sward, was "like a river and its tributaries," with the subassembly tributaries merging to produce an ever-more-assembled car.

The process began to change in the spring of 1913. The first piece created on the modern assembly line was the magneto coil. In the past a worker—and he had to be skilled—had made a fly-wheel magneto from start to finish. An employee could make 35 or 40 a day. Now, however, there was an assembly line for magnetos. It was divided into 29 different operations performed by 29 different men. In the old system it took twenty minutes to make a magneto; now it took thirteen.

Ford and his men quickly imposed a comparable system on the assembly of engines and transmissions. Then, in the summer of 1913, they took on the final assembly, which, as the rest of the process had speeded up, had become the great bottleneck. Until then the workers had moved quickly around a stationary metal object, the car they were putting together. Now the men were to remain stationary as the semifinished car moved up the line through them.

One day in the summer of 1913, Charles Sorensen, who had become one of Ford's top production people, had a Model T chassis pulled slowly by a windlass across 250 feet of factory floor, timing the process all the while. Behind him walked six workers, picking up parts from carefully spaced piles on the floor and fitting them to the chassis. It was an experiment, but the possibilities for the future were self-evident. This was the birth of the assembly line, the very essence of what would become America's industrial revolution. Before, it had taken some thirteen hours to make a car chassis; now they had cut the time of assembly in half, to five hours and fifty minutes. Not satisfied, they pushed even harder, lengthening the line and bringing in more specialized workers for the final assembly. Within weeks they could complete a chassis in only two hours and thirty-eight minutes.

Now the breakthroughs came even more rapidly. In January of 1914 Ford installed his first automatic conveyor belt. It was, he said, the first moving line ever used in an industrial plant, and it was inspired by the overhead trolley that the Chicago meat-packers employed to move beef. Within two months of that innovation, Ford could assemble a chassis in an hour and a half. It was a stunning accomplishment, but it merely whetted his zeal. Everything now had to be timed, rationalized, broken down into smaller pieces, and speeded up. Just a few years before, in the days of stationary chassis assembly, the best record for putting a car together had been 728 minutes of one man's work; with the new moving line it required only 93 minutes. Ford's top executives celebrated their victory with a dinner at Detroit's Pontchartrain Hotel. Fittingly, they rigged a simple conveyor belt to a five-horse-power engine with a bicycle chain and used the conveyor to serve the food around the table. It typified the spirit, camaraderie, and confidence of the early days.

Henry Ford could now mass-produce his cars, and as he did so, he cut prices dramatically. In 1909 the average profit on a car had been $220.11; by 1913, with the coming of the new, speeded-up line, it was only $99.34. But the total profits to the company were ascending rapidly because he was selling so many more cars. When the company began making the Model T, its cash balance was slightly greater than $2 million. Nineteen years and more than 15 million cars later, when Ford reluctantly came to the conclusion that he had to stop making the T, the company balance was $673 million. But this was not the kind of success that merely made a company richer; it was the beginning of a social revolution. Ford himself knew exactly what he had achieved—a breakthrough for the common man. "Mass production," he wrote later, "precedes mass consumption, and makes it possible by reducing costs and thus permitting both greater use-convenience and price-convenience." The price of the Model T touring car continued to come down, from $780 in the fiscal year 1910–11 to $690 the following year, to $600, to $550, to, on the eve of World War I, $360. At that price he sold 730,041 cars. He was outproducing everyone in the world.

In 1913 the Ford Motor Company, with 13,000 employees, produced 260,720 cars; the other 299 American auto companies, with 66,350 employees, produced only 286,770. Cutting his price as his production soared, he saw his share of the market surge—9.4 percent in 1908, 20.3 in 1911, 39.6 in 1913, and with the full benefits of his mechanization, 48 percent in 1914. By 1915 the company was making $100 million in annual sales; by 1920 the average monthly earning after taxes was $6 million. The world had never seen anything remotely like it. The cars simply poured off the line. An early illuminated sign in Cadillac Square said, "Watch the Fords Go By." Ford's dreams, in a startlingly brief time, had all come true. He had lived his own prophecy.

There was a moment, however, in 1909 when Ford almost sold the entire company. William C. Durant, the entrepreneur who put General Motors together from several fledgling companies, felt him out about selling the company. An earlier offer of $3 million had fallen through because Ford wanted cash. This time, his company more successful, Ford demanded $8 million. But again he wanted what he called "gold on the table."

Durant couldn't get the financing.

Ford's timing in holding on to his company, it turned out, had been exquisite. There was no point in designing an Everyman's Car unless the average man could buy fuel cheaply as well. The coming of Ford was almost perfectly synchronized with the discovery in the American Southwest of vast new reserves of oil.

If, as has been said, the American century and the oil century were one and the same thing, then that century began on January 10, 1901, in a field just outside of Beaumont, Texas. The name of the field was Spindletop, so called because of the spindly pines that grew there. For years local children had tossed lighted matches into the field; as the flames hit the strong petroleum vapors seeping up through the soil, there would be a satisfying bang. But anyone who believed that there was real oil beneath the ground was thought an eccentric. Oil was not found in Texas; it was found in places like Pennsylvania, West Virginia, and Ohio. Those states were all Standard Oil territory, and the Rockefeller people had no interest in the Southwest. "I will drink any drop of oil west of the Mississippi," boasted John D. Archbold of Standard.

It was Patillo Higgins, a Beaumont man, who had insisted that there was oil underneath Spindletop, and he had been trying to tap it for several years. It had cost him $30,000 of his own money, and he owed friends an additional $17,000. As each attempt had failed and he had been forced to go to others for financial help in order to continue drilling, his own share of the operation shrank. Higgins's faith had never flagged, but he had become more and more a figure of ridicule in his hometown. "Millionaire," his neighbors nicknamed him. The drilling had gotten harder and harder; just before New Year's Day they had gone through 140 feet of solid rock. That had taken them to a level of 1,020 feet. On January 10 it happened. A geyser of oil roared out of the ground and shot a hundred feet above the derrick. No one had ever seen anything like it before; with it, the word *gusher* came into use.

At first no one could figure out how much oil the field was producing. Some said 30,000 barrels a day, some said 40,000. Capt. Anthony Lucas, who had become a partner of Higgins, said 6,000, because he had never heard of a larger hole in America. In fact, that one gusher was producing 100,000 barrels a day, roughly 60 percent of the total American production. One new well at Spindletop produced as much as the total from all the 37,000 wells back East in the Rockefeller territory. Within a short time there were five more hits. Eventually analysts found that the oil from the first six holes, some 136 million barrels annually, more than twice surpassed what Russia, then the world's leading petroleum producer, could generate.

Spindletop changed the nature of the American economy and, indeed, the American future. Before the strike, oil was used for illumination, not for energy. (Until 1911 the sales of kerosene were greater than the sales of gasoline.) Spindletop inaugurated the liquid-fuel age in America. The energy of the new age was to be oil, and America suddenly was rich in it.

Texas was providing the gas; Henry Ford was providing the cars. The only limits on him were those imposed by production, and he continued to be obsessed by it. He wanted to put as much of his money as he could back into the factory. He hated bankers and financial people anyway, and he did not want to waste the company's money on stockholders. They were, to his mind, parasites, men who lived off other men's labor. In 1917 the Dodge brothers, who had manufactured many of the early components for Ford and who had been rewarded with sizable amounts of stock, sued him for withholding stock dividends. Some $75 million was at stake. During the trial, Ford testified that putting money back into the plant was the real fun he got from being in business. Fun, the opposing attorney retorted, "at Ford Motor Company expense." Retorted Ford, "There wouldn't be any fun if we didn't try things people said we can't do."

That was the trial in which he referred to the profits he was making as "awful," and when questioned about that by attorneys for the other side, he replied, with absolute sincerity, "We don't seem to be able to keep the profits down." Ford lost the suit, and the court ordered him to pay $19 million in dividends, $11 million of which went to him. The decision probably persuaded him to take as complete control of the company's stock as he could, so that as little money would be wasted as possible. Money to stockholders was a waste, money gone idle; money for the factory was not.

Out of that suit came both the means and the determination to build the River Rouge plant, his great industrial masterpiece, a totally independent industrial city-state. Nothing in the period that followed was too good for the Rouge: it had the best blast furnaces, the best machine tools, the best metal labs, the best electrical systems, the most efficient efficiency experts. Dissatisfied with the supply and quality of the steel he was getting, Ford decided to find out how much it would cost to build a steel plant within the Rouge. About $35 million, Sorensen told him. "What are you waiting for?" asked Ford. Equally dissatisfied with both the availability and the quality of glass, he built a glass factory at the Rouge as well. The price of glass had been roughly thirty cents a square foot early in the life of the T; soon it had soared to $1.50 a foot. With the glass plant at the Rouge, the price came down to twenty cents a foot.

At the Rouge, barges carrying iron ore would steam into the inland docks, and even as they were tying up, huge cranes would be swinging out to start the unloading. Some sixty years later Toyota would be credited for its just-in-time theory of manufacturing, in which parts arrived from suppliers just in time to be part of the final assembly. But in any real sense that process had begun at the Rouge. As Eiji Toyoda, of the Toyota family said in toasting Philip Caldwell, the head of Ford, who in 1982 was visiting Japan: "There is no secret to how we learned to do what we do, Mr. Caldwell. We learned it at the Rouge."

All of this, the creation of the Rouge as the ultimate modern plant, speeded up production even more. Before the opening of the Rouge as an auto plant in 1920 (it had produced submarine chasers for World War I in 1918), it had taken 21 days from the receipt of raw material to the production of the finished car. The Rouge cut that time to 14 days. With the opening of the Rouge steel plant in 1925, it took only 4 days.

The Rouge was Henry Ford's greatest triumph, and with its completion he stood alone as the dominant figure in America and the entire developed world. He had brought the process of manufacture to its ultimate moment; he had given the world the first people's car and by dint of his inventive genius had become America's first billionaire. He was an immensely popular man as well, the man who had lived the American dream. But even then, forces he had helped set in motion would begin to summon forth the darkness in his character.

PART TWO: THE DESTROYER

Henry Ford's strengths eventually became his weaknesses. One notorious example was staying with his basic car far too long, ignoring technological change in the cars themselves while obsessively pursuing technological change in their manufacture. From the very start he fought off every attempt to perfect the Model T. In 1912, while he was off on a trip to Europe, his top engineers made some changes intended to improve the car. Their version of the T was lower and some twelve inches longer. It was a better, smoother-riding vehicle, and his associates hoped to surprise and please him. When he returned, they showed it to him. He walked around it several times, finally approaching the left-hand door and ripping it off. Then he ripped off the other door. Then he smashed the windshield and bashed in the roof of the car with his shoe. During all this he said nothing. There was no doubt whose car the T was and no doubt who was the only man permitted to change it. For years anyone wanting to improve a Ford car ran into a stone wall.

What had been another Ford strength, his use of manpower, also turned sour. The early workers at Ford had been skilled artisans, tinkering with designs as they worked. A job at Ford's, as it was known, had been desirable because Henry Ford was at the cutting edge of technology, always trying to do things better, and men who cared about quality wanted to be a part of his operation. In the early days he had his pick of the best men in Detroit. But the mechanized line changed the workplace. These new jobs demanded much less skill and offered much less satisfaction. The pressure to maximize production was relentless. Men who had prided themselves on their skills and had loved working with machines found themselves slaves to those machines, their skills unsummoned. The machines, they discovered to their rage, were more important than they were. The more the plant was mechanized, the more the work force began to unravel. Men began walking out of the Ford plant.

The turnover in the labor force in 1913, the year of the great mechanization, was 380 percent. It soon became even worse. In order to keep one hundred men working, Ford had to hire nearly a thousand. Ford and his principal business partner, James Couzens, realized they had to stabilize the work force. So they came up with the idea of the five-dollar day—that is, of doubling the existing pay. There were some who thought it was Couzens's idea, though Ford later took credit for it. Perceived by many observers as an act of generosity, it was also an act of desperation. Ford calculated that a five-dollar day would attract the best workers, diminish labor unrest, and thus bring him even greater profits. Besides, he believed, it was a mistake to spend money on the finest machinery and then put those precious machines into the hands of disgruntled, unreliable, perhaps incompetent men.

Ford's instincts were right. Not only did the decision solidify the work force; it was so successful a public relations gesture that it allowed Ford to cut back sharply on his advertising. He liked to refer to it as one of the finest cost-cutting moves he had ever made and insisted that he had no philanthropic intent. This denial of altruism, a young Detroit theologian named Reinhold Niebuhr said later, was "like the assurance of an old spinster that her reputation as a flirt has been grossly exaggerated." Indeed in 1914, 1915, and 1916, the first three years of the five-dollar wage, the Ford Motor Company's profits after taxes were $30 million, $20 million, and $60 million.

To workingmen, the five-dollar day was electrifying. Ford had also instituted an eight-hour workday and with it a third shift, and the day after his announcement of the new wage, 10,000 men turned up at the gates of the plant looking for work. Ford had wanted the pick of workers; the pick he now had. For days the crowds grew, and policemen were needed to keep them under control. It was probably the first time that the fruits of the oil-fueled industrial age had reached down to the average worker. A worker had a grim and thankless job that rarely let him get ahead. He would end his life as he began it, and his children were doomed to the same existence. Now, however, with cheap oil and mass production, the industrial cycle was different. It was more dynamic; it generated much more profit and many more goods, which required customers with money to buy them. The worker became the consumer in an ever-widening circle of affluence.

Ford became perhaps the greatest celebrity of his time. Reporters hung out at his office, and his every word was quoted. That both helped and hurt him, because although he was a certifiable genius in manufacturing and perhaps a semi-genius for a long time in business, much of what he said was nonsense, albeit highly quotable nonsense. On cigarettes: "Study the history of almost any criminal, and you will find an inveterate cigarette smoker." On Jews: "When there is something wrong in this country, you'll find Jews." The Jews, he thought, were particularly unproductive people, and he once vowed to pay a thousand dollars to anyone who would bring him a Jewish farmer, dead or alive. He hated the diet of Americans of his generation—"Most people dig their graves with their teeth," he once said. He was prophetic about the nutritional uses of the soybean and intuitive about the value of whole wheat bread, and he wanted his friends to eat no bread but whole wheat. He felt that people who wore glasses were making a serious mistake; they should throw away their glasses and exercise their eyes. For almost all his adult life, he used unadulterated kerosene as a hair cream. He did this because he had observed, he said, that men who worked in the oil fields always had good heads of hair. "They get their hands filled with the oil, and they are always rubbing their hands through their hair," he said, "and that is the reason they have good hair." One of the jobs of

E. G. Liebold, his private secretary, was to keep a gallon of No. 10 light kerosene on hand for Ford's hair and constantly to watch that it did not turn rancid.

On one occasion someone noticed that his shoes did not match; he replied that every year on his birthday he put on one old shoe to remind himself that he had once been poor and might be poor again.

He was in some ways a shy man. In the old Ford factory his office had a window through which he used to crawl in order to escape visitors. Nonetheless he was acutely aware that his name was the company name and that his personal publicity generally helped the company. All news from the Ford Motor Company was about him. He was also a hard man, and he became harder as he became older. He distrusted friendship and thought it made him vulnerable: friends might want something from him. He used a company group called the Sociological Department—allegedly started to help workers with personal problems in finances or health—to check up on employees and find out whether they drank at home or had union sympathies. If they were guilty of either, they were fired. For all his populism, he always took a dim view of the average employee. Men worked for two reasons, he said. "One is for wages, and one is for fear of losing their jobs." He thought of labor in the simplest terms—discipline. He once told a journalist named William Richards, "I have a thousand men who, if I say, 'Be at the northeast corner of the building at 4:00 A.M.,' will be there at 4:00 A.M. That's what we want—obedience."

Even in the days before he became isolated and eccentric, he liked playing cruel tricks on his top people. He loved pitting them against one another. A favorite ploy was to give the identical title to two men without telling either about the other. He enjoyed watching the ensuing struggle. The weaker man, he said, would always back down. He liked the idea of keeping even his highest aides anxious about their jobs. It was good for them, he said. His idea of harmony, his colleague Charles Sorensen wrote, "was constant turmoil." The same sort of thing was going on in the factories. The foremen, the men who ruled the factory floor, were once chosen for their ability; now, increasingly, they were chosen for physical strength. If a worker seemed to be loitering, a foreman simply knocked him down. The rules against workers talking to each other on the job were strict. Making a worker insecure was of the essence. "A great business is really too big to be human," Ford himself once told the historian Allan Nevins.

Slowly, steadily, in the twenties, Henry Ford began to lose touch. He had played a critical role in breeding new attitudes in both workers and customers. But as they changed, he did not, and he became more and more a caricature of himself. "The isolation of Henry Ford's mind is about as near perfect as it is possible to make it," said Samuel Marquis, a Detroit minister who had headed the Sociological Department when its purpose had been to help the employees and who later became its harshest critic.

The Ford Motor Company was no longer a creative operation focused on an exciting new idea and headed by an ingenious leader. For its engineers and designers, the company, only a decade earlier the most exciting place to work in America, was professionally a backwater. Sycophants rose, and men of integrity were harassed. Rival companies were pushing ahead with technological developments, and Ford was standing pat with the Tin Lizzie. His own best people became restless under his narrow, frequently arbitrary, even ignorant, policies. He cut off anyone who disagreed with him. Anyone who might be a threat within the company because of superior leadership ability was scorned as often and as publicly as possible.

Eventually he drove out Big Bill Knudsen, the Danish immigrant who was largely responsible for gearing up the Ford plants during World War I and was widely considered the ablest man in the company. Knudsen was a formidable production man who had been in charge of organizing and outfitting the Model T assembly plants; he had set up fourteen of them in two years. But his prodigious work during World War I made him a target of perverse attacks by Henry Ford. Knudsen was a big, burly man, six foot three and 230 pounds, and he drank, smoked, and cursed, all of which annoyed the puritanical Ford. Worse, Knudsen was clearly becoming something of an independent figure within the company. He was also drawing closer to Ford's son, Edsel, believing him a young man of talent, vision, and, most remarkable of all, sanity. Together they talked of trying to improve the Model T. All of this merely infuriated the senior Ford and convinced him that Knudsen was an intriguer and becoming too big for his place. Ford took his revenge by making a great show of constantly countermanding Knudsen's production decisions. Knudsen became frustrated with these public humiliations and with the company's failure to move ahead technologically. He finally told his wife that he did not think he could work there any longer. He was sure he was going to have a major confrontation with Henry Ford.

"I can't avoid it if I stay," he said, "and I can't stay and keep my self-respect. I just can't stand the jealousy of the place any more."

"Then get out," she said.

"But I'm making $50,000 a year. That's more money than we can make anywhere else."

"We'll get along," she said. "We did before you went to work there."

In 1921 he quit, virtually forced out. "I let him go not because he wasn't good, but because he was too good—for me," Ford later said.

Knudsen went to General Motors for a starting salary of $30,000, but GM soon put him in charge of its sluggish Chevrolet division. It was the perfect time to join GM. Alfred P. Sloan, Jr., was putting together a modern automotive giant, building on Ford's advances in simplifying the means of production and bringing to that manufacturing success the best of modern business practices. Within three years of Knudsen's arrival, GM became a serious challenger to Ford.

By the early twenties the rumblings from Ford's dealers were mounting. They begged him to make changes in the Model T, but he had become so egocentric that criticism of his car struck him as criticism of himself. Ford defiantly stayed with the Model T. Perhaps 1922 can be considered the highwater mark of Ford's domination of the market. The company's sales were never higher, and with an average profit of $50 a car, it netted more than $100 million. From then on it was downhill. As Chevy made its challenge, the traditional Ford response—simply cutting back on the price—no longer worked. The success of that maneuver had been based on volume sales, and the volume was peaking. From 1920 to 1924 Ford cut its price eight times, but the thinner margins were beginning to undermine Ford's success. The signs got worse and worse. For the calendar year ending February 1924, the Ford company's net profit was $82 million; of that only $41 million came from new cars, and $29 million came from the sales of spare parts. If anything reflected the stagnation of the company, it was that figure.

In 1926 Ford's sales dropped from 1.87 million to 1.67. At the same time, Chevy nearly doubled its sales, from 280,000 to 400,000. America's roads were getting better, and people wanted speed and comfort. In the face of GM's continuing challenge, Henry Ford's only response was once again to cut prices—twice in that year. The Model T was beginning to die. Finally, in May of 1927, on the eve of the manufacture of the fifteenth million Model T, Henry Ford announced that his company would build a new car. The T was dead. His domination over a market that he himself had created was over. With that he closed his factories for retooling, laying off his workers (many of them permanently).

The new car was the Model A. It had shock absorbers, a standard gearshift, a gas gauge, and a speedometer, all things that Chevy had been moving ahead on and that Ford himself had resisted installing. In all ways it seemed better than its predecessor, more comfortable, twice as powerful, and faster. When it was finally ready to be revealed, huge crowds thronged every showplace. In Detroit one hundred thousand people turned up at the dealerships to see the unveiling. In order to accommodate the mob in New York City, the manager moved the car to Madison Square Garden. Editorials ranked the arrival of the Model A along with Lindbergh's solo transatlantic flight as the top news story of the decade. The car was an immense success. Even before it was available, there were 727,000 orders on hand. Yet its success was relatively short-lived, for once again Henry Ford froze his technology. Even the brief triumph of the Model A did not halt the downward spiral of the company. Henry Ford remained locked into the past. The twenties and thirties and early forties at Ford were years of ignorance and ruffianism. Henry Ford grew more erratic and finally senile. At the end of his life he believed that World War II did not exist, that it was simply a ploy made up by the newspapers to help the munitions industry. No one could reach the old man any more. His became a performance of spectacular self-destructiveness, one that would never again be matched in a giant American corporation. It was as if the old man, having made the company, felt he had a right to destroy it.

With Knudsen's departure, the burden of trying to deal with Ford fell on his son, Edsel. Gentle and intelligent, Edsel Ford reflected the contradictions in his father's life. He had been born while the Fords were still poor. (As a little boy, Edsel had written Santa Claus a letter complaining: "I haven't had a Christmas tree in four years and I have broken all my trimmings and I want some more.") By the time he entered manhood, his father was the richest man in the country, unsettled by the material part of his success and ambivalent about the more privileged life to which his son was being introduced. Henry Ford wanted to bestow on his son all possible advantages and to spare him all hardship, but, having done that, he became convinced that Edsel was too soft to deal with the harsh, brutal world of industry, symbolized by nothing better than the Ford Motor Company.

Edsel was not a mechanical tinkerer himself, but he had spent his life in the auto business, and he knew who in the company was good and who was not; he was comfortable with the engineers and the designers. Edsel knew times were changing and that the Ford Motor Company was dying. During his father's worst years, Edsel became a magnet for the most talented men in the company, who came to regard his defeats as their defeats. He was a capable executive, and an exceptionally well-trained one: his apprenticeship was full and thorough—and it lasted thirty years. Absolutely confident in his own judgment about both people and cars, Edsel Ford was beloved by his friends and yet respected in the automobile business for his obvious good judgment. "Henry," John Dodge, Henry Ford's early partner and later his rival, once said, "I don't envy you a damn thing except that boy of yours."

Edsel was the first scion of the automotive world. He married Eleanor Clay, a member of the Hudson family that ran Detroit's most famous department store. They were society, and the marriage was a great event, the two worlds of Detroit merging, the old and the new, a Ford and a Clay. Henry Ford hated the fact that Edsel had married into the Detroit elite and had moved to Grosse Pointe. He knew that Edsel went to parties and on occasion took a drink with his friends, not all of whom were manufacturing people and some of whom were upper class—worse, upper-class citified people—and was sure all this had corrupted him. It was as if Edsel, by marrying Eleanor, had confuted one of Henry Ford's favorite sayings: "A Ford will take you anywhere except into society."

On top of all his other burdens, it was Edsel's unfortunate duty to represent the future to a father now absolutely locked in a dying past. Genuinely loyal to his father, Edsel patiently and lovingly tried to talk Henry Ford into modernizing the company, but the old man regarded his son's loyalty as weakness and spurned him and his advice.

When everyone else in the company agreed that a particular issue had to be brought before the old man, Edsel became the designated spokesman. With Knudsen now gone, he usually stood alone. He was probably the only person who told the truth to his father. Others, such as Sorensen, were supposed to come to Edsel's defense during meetings with Henry, but they never did. Sorensen, brutal with everyone else in the company but the complete toady with the founder, always turned tail in the face of Henry Ford's opposition.

All the while the competition was getting better faster. Chevy had hydraulic brakes in 1924; Ford added them fourteen years later. Because Chevy had already gone to a six-cylinder car, Edsel pleaded even more passionately with his father to modernize the Ford engine. A six, his father retorted, could never be a balanced car. "I've no use for an engine," he said, "that has more spark plugs than a cow has teats." After all, he had built one back in 1909, and he had not liked it.

The six-cylinder engine, more than any other issue, stood between the two Fords. The quintessential story about Henry Ford and the six-cylinder engine—for it reflects not just his hatred of the new but his contempt for his son as well—concerns a project that Edsel and Laurence Sheldrick, the company's chief engineer, had been working on. It was a new engine, a six, and Edsel believed he had gotten paternal permission to start experimenting with it. He and Sheldrick labored for about six months and they were delighted with the prototype. One day when they were just about ready to test it, Sheldrick got a call from Henry Ford.

"Sheldrick," he said, "I've got a new scrap conveyor that I'm very proud of. It goes right to the cupola at the top of the plant. I'd like you to come and take a look at it. I'm really proud of it."

Sheldrick joined Ford for the demonstration at the top of the cupola, where they could watch the conveyor work. To Sheldrick's surprise, Edsel was there too. Soon the conveyor started. The first thing riding up in it, on its way to becoming junk, was Edsel Ford's and Larry Sheldrick's engine.

"Now," said the old man, "don't you try anything like that again. Don't you ever, do you hear?"

In 1936, his company under mounting pressure, Henry Ford reluctantly built a six-cylinder engine. It went into production a year later. But moves like this were too late. By 1933, *Fortune*, reflecting the growing scorn and indeed the contempt of the business community that Henry Ford had once dazzled, called him "the world's worst salesman."

He became more and more distant from the reality of his own company. As he became more senile and more threatened by growing pressure from a restive labor force, he began to cut back on the power of Charlie Sorensen and grant it instead to Harry Bennett, who was head of the company's security forces. Sorensen had been a savage man, hated by many, capable of great cruelty, eager to settle most disputes with his fists, but at least he knew something about production. Bennett was worse. An ex-seaman who had boxed professionally under the name of Sailor Reese, he had come to power in the post–World War I days, when his assignment was to hire bullies and ex-cons and wrestlers and boxers to help control the plant and keep the union out. Bennett was well suited for that role. His was an empire within an empire, and that inner empire was built on fear. He padded his pockets with Ford money—the finances of the company were in chaos. He built at least four houses with his appropriated wealth. His rise exactly paralleled the decline of the old man, and he played on all the fears the old man had, especially fear of labor and fear of kidnapping. Ford was convinced that Bennett, with his connections in the underworld, could stop any attempt to kidnap his son or grandchildren. Ford loved the fact that Bennett used force to intimidate people. "Harry gets things done in a hurry," he liked to say.

To the distress of Ford's family, Bennett's power over Henry grew almost without check in the 1930s, when the founder was in his seventies. Board meetings were a travesty. Often Ford did not show up. Or he would walk in at the last minute with Bennett and after a few minutes say, "Come on, Harry, let's get the hell out of here. We'll probably change everything they do anyway." Once a magazine writer was in a car with Ford and Bennett, and he asked Ford who was the greatest man he had ever known—after all, in so rich and varied a career he had known quite a few exceptional people. Ford simply pointed at Bennett.

At the very end he used Bennett as his principal weapon against his son. The last years were truly ugly. Sure that he was protected by Ford, Bennett harassed Edsel mercilessly. The old man took obvious pleasure in Edsel's humiliations. Already emotionally beaten down by his father, Edsel had become a sick man. He had remained loyal to his father and endured his humiliations while healthy. Now, battling stomach cancer, he had less and less to fight back with. Edsel's last years were very difficult, as he struggled to expedite the war-production work his father hated while at the same time resisting his illnesses. In 1942 Edsel got undulant fever from drinking milk from his father's dairy; Ford disapproved of pasteurization. The old man blamed it on Edsel's bad habits. In 1943 Edsel died. He was only forty-nine. Almost everyone who knew both Henry and Edsel Ford thought the son had really died of a broken heart.

This was the final, malevolent chapter in Henry Ford's own life. Not only had he destroyed his son, he had all but ruined a once-great industrial empire. By the middle of the war, the Ford Motor Company was in such poor shape that high government officials pondered whether to take it over, for the government had to keep the giant going. Without the stimulus of the war and the work it eventually brought the company, it is possible that Ford might have failed completely. As the government debated, two women stepped forward. Clara Bryant Ford and Eleanor Clay Ford, one Henry Ford's wife and the other Edsel's widow, had watched it all with dismay—the old man's senility, the crushing of Edsel, the rise of Bennett—but with a certain helplessness. "Who is this man Bennett who has such power over my husband and my son?" Clara Ford once asked. She had hated the fact that Bennett and Sorensen had both taken it upon themselves to speak for Henry against Edsel and had participated in and encouraged his destruction. Now both women feared that the same forces might prevent young Henry, Edsel's son, from ascending and assuming power.

Henry Ford II had been serving in the Navy during the war, enjoying a taste of personal freedom. But in August 1943, thanks to intervention by his mother and grandmother, he got orders sending him back to Detroit; the nation's highest officials feared that, after Edsel's death, Harry Bennett might actually take over the company. Young Henry returned reluctantly, but he was the firstborn of Edsel Ford, and familial obligation demanded it. He had no illusions about the challenge ahead. He was well aware that, except for a very few men, the Ford Motor Company was a corrupt and corrupting place.

Bennett and Sorensen immediately began belittling him, Bennett by undoing what Henry was attempting to do each day and Sorensen by demeaning him in front of other people and by always calling him "young man." "He might just as well have called me Sonny," Henry later told friends. Henry Ford II might have titular power—he was named vice president in December 1943—and the power of blood, but unless his grandfather moved aside and Bennett left the company, he would never be able to take control. Even Sorensen was in the process of being destroyed by Bennett, and young Henry seemed very vulnerable. Again Eleanor Clay Ford put her foot down and forced an issue. Widowhood had stirred in her the kind of indignation her husband had always lacked. He had been too loyal to challenge his father, but now Edsel's company stock was hers to vote. She threatened to sell it unless old Henry moved aside in favor of his grandson. Her son would not be destroyed as her husband had been. Clara Bryant Ford backed her completely. They fought off the old man's excuses and his delaying ploys. With that threat, and a sense that these women were intensely serious, Henry Ford finally, furiously, gave up, and Henry Ford II took control.

The young man—he was just twenty-eight—had not served the long apprenticeship his father had, and he had only the scantest knowledge of the vast and complicated world he inherited. But it soon became clear that he was shrewd and tough. Through the most unsparing work he mastered the business; and he got rid of Harry Bennett. "You're taking over a billion-dollar organization here that you haven't contributed a thing to!" Bennett yelled. But, having no other recourse, he left.

In the end Henry Ford II broke all of Bennett's cronies and put an end to the bad old era. But there was no way to escape the complex legacy of the founder.

Once a popular figure with the average man, Henry Ford had become known as one of the nation's leading labor baiters. He had helped usher in a new age of economic dignity for the common man, but he could not deal with the consequences. His public statements during the Depression were perhaps the most pitiless ever uttered by any capitalist. He repeatedly said that the Depression was good for the country and the only problem was that it might not last long enough, in which case people might not learn enough from it. "If there is unemployment in America," he said, "it is because the unemployed do not want to work." His workers, embittered by his labor policies, marched against him and were put down by Bennett's truncheons and guns. His security people were so vicious that when Ford's workers marched against the company, the workers wore masks over their faces to hide their identities—something rare in America. Nothing could have spoken more eloquently of tyrannical employment practices.

In business Henry Ford was overtaken by General Motors, which relentlessly modernized its design, its production, and its marketing. GM fed the appetites Ford had helped create. In addition, GM inaugurated a dynamic that haunted the Ford company for the next fifty years; buyers started out driving Fords when they were young and had little money, but slowly, as their earnings rose, they graduated to more expensive GM cars. As a workingman's hero, Ford was replaced by FDR. What had once been charming about his eccentricity now became contemptible.

Nothing reflected his failures more tellingly than the fate of the River Rouge manufacturing complex. It was an industrial masterpiece, and it should have stood long after his death as a beacon to the genius of its founder. But the treatment of human beings there had been so mean and violent, the reputation of the Rouge so scurrilous, that in the postwar era it stood as an embarrassment to the new men running Ford, a reputation that had to be undone.

The bequeathment had other unfortunate aspects. By fighting the unions so unalterably for so long, Ford and the other Detroit industrialists had ensured that, when the unions finally won power, they would be as strong as the companies themselves, and that there would be a carry-over of distrust and hatred. There were other, more concrete, burdens as well. Because he had been locked in the past and had frozen his technology, the company was on the verge of bankruptcy.

Probably no major industrial company in America's history was ever run so poorly for so long. By the beginning of 1946, it was estimated, Ford was losing $10 million a month. The chaos was remarkable, but some of it, at least, was deliberate. The old Henry Ford hated the government and in particular the federal income tax, and by creating utter clerical confusion he hoped to baffle the IRS. He also hated bookkeepers and accountants; as far as he was concerned, they were parasitical. When Arjay Miller, who later became president of the company, joined Ford in 1946, he was told to get the profit forecast for the next month. Miller went down to the Rotunda, where the financial operations were centralized, or at least supposed to be. There he found a long table with a lot of older men, who looked to him like stereotypes of the old-fashioned bookkeeper. These men were confronted by bills, thousands of bills, and they were dividing them into categories—A, B, C, D. The piles were immense, some several feet high. To Miller's amazement the bookkeepers were actually estimating how many million dollars there were per foot of paper. That was the system.

Miller asked what the estimates for the following month's profits were. One of the men working there looked at him and asked, "What do you want them to be?"

"What?" asked Miller.

"I can make them anything you want."

He meant it, Miller decided. It was truly a never-never land.

It was not surprising, then, that the young Henry Ford, seeking to bring sense to the madness he found all around him, turned to an entirely new breed of executive—the professional managers, the bright, young financial experts who knew, if not automobiles and manufacturing plants, then systems and bottom lines. To them Henry Ford II gave nearly unlimited power. And they, in turn, would in the years to come visit their own kind of devastation on the company. The legacy of what the old man had done in his last thirty years left a strain of tragic unreason in the inner workings of the company. So, once again did the past influence the future. For the past was always present.

QUESTIONS TO CONSIDER

1. What was Henry Ford's vision from his early days?
2. What factors account for the great success of the Model T?
3. How did the mass-produced Model T fit with another key phenomenon to usher in the century of the automobile?
4. Which of Ford's virtues became liabilities for him after 1922?
5. What noteworthy signs indicated that Ford was losing his grip on reality after the early 1920s? Which had been seen earlier in his career as weaknesses?
6. How was Henry Ford finally removed from power?

7

Woodrow Wilson, Ethnicity, and the Myth of American Unity

HANS VOUGHT

Reprinted by permission of Transaction Publishers.
"Woodrow Wilson, Ethnicity, and the Myth of American
Unity" by Hans Vought, *Journal of American Ethnic
History*, Spring 1994. © 1994 by Transaction Publishers.

The industrialization and urbanization of the United States was accompanied by a change in the sources of immigration. Around 1890 the dominant northwestern European regions gave way to southern and eastern European countries as the largest sources of new Americans. These new regions tended to be less Anglo and Protestant and more Catholic, Jewish, and Orthodox, of Slavic or Mediterranean ethnicity. As the number of immigrants increased to over one million in 1907, opposition to them became more and more strident.

Milton Gordon argued in his 1962 *Assimilation in America* that visions of assimilation had historically taken three different forms. He believed that Anglo-conformity dominated, with immigrants expected to take on the language, religion, and ideals of Anglo-Americans to fit into American society. A second ideal, the melting pot, got its name from a 1908 play and its champion in Woodrow Wilson; all cultures were to melt together in the United States and form a new breed by drawing on all their characteristics. The third vision was cultural pluralism, or what today is dubbed multiculturalism. In this view, immigrant peoples should retain much of their own ways and make the nation more like a stew than a melting pot, with each ethnicity enriching the stewpot. This idea has become much more prevalent since the 1965 Immigration and Naturalization Act opened up the country to greatly increased immigration from Asia and Latin America, people that Wilson considered much more difficult to assimilate.

In this article, Hans Vought, a young scholar teaching at Central Connecticut State University, explores the vision of Woodrow Wilson and how it differed from others in his time and in our own era. He raises the question of how our ideals may differ from reality and what the implications of such a discrepancy might be.

Historians have examined Thomas Woodrow Wilson perhaps more closely than any other United States president. Sixty-five volumes of his papers have now been edited and published, numerous books analyzing his character, administration, and relationship to his times have been written. One would think that nothing remains to be said about the man. But surprisingly, very little attention has been paid to President Wilson's attitude towards immigration. Historians have given passing notice only to his two vetoes of the Burnett Immigration Restriction Bill, without bothering to question why [one] so clearly racist towards blacks and Asians would reject a literacy test to keep ignorant, non-Teutonic foreigners out of the United States. Not only was the bill popular, the very concept of the literacy test was one that he endorsed in his native South to keep blacks disfranchised. Clearly, there is an issue here that needs to be examined.

This essay addresses the issue, and seeks to place Wilson's attitude towards immigration not only in the context of his overall character, but in the larger context of traditional American political attitudes. Specifically, Wilson is pictured in this study as embodying the American political ideal of complete homogeneity. He was upset by the fierce class and ethnic conflict that raged in America in the latter half of the nineteenth and the first two decades of the twentieth century, a struggle that he viewed as a second Civil War and Reconstruction. Wilson saw himself as taking over the role of his hero, Grover Cleveland, the Democrat who, in Wilson's opinion, reunited the sections and brought peace and prosperity to the United States.

Wilson was representative of a moderate progressivism that existed in the latter part of the nineteenth century and the early part of this one. He was reacting negatively to the new, industrialist class, but maintaining a strong belief in the triumph of American ideals and progress. In general, moderate progressives believed that ethnic and class conflict resulted from valuing private interests over the public interest. This in turn led to widespread corruption of the spoils system by political machines. Immigrants living in the major cities had too often been the cogs that kept the machines running. The solution, according to the moderate progressives, was to unify all classes and ethnic groups into a homogeneous middle class. They believed that the majority of Americans, including themselves, belonged to this middle class. Not only did the classes need to be unified, they also needed to be socialized through education to accept the American political, social, and economic ideals. Only with a common basis of belief could the body politic agree upon the national interest.

Wilson, like most progressives, moderate or otherwise, abhorred not only the anarchist and socialist beliefs of some of the foreign born, he failed completely to understand their conception of politics as an exchange of favors. Wilson's heroes were great statesmen, who selflessly served their country's commonweal while rallying the people to patriotic endeavors. Wilson saw himself as another Pitt, another Bismarck who could create an efficient, honest government to which all people would rally.

In all of this, the underlying political idealism was that strange mixture of the Enlightenment and Protestant Christianity, which the founding fathers had incorporated into American political structure and thought. Wilson championed the belief in society as a collection of rational, autonomous men who, given the right education, would always agree as to what was the commonweal and then act upon it. Furthermore, he believed in the inevitability of progress, because he believed in a God who was active in history. His own deep, personal faith in Jesus Christ led him to temper his belief in autonomous reason with the realization that some truths could only be revealed by the Holy Spirit. But this mattered little, for God's will, in Wilson's mind, was the same as American national interest.

Hyphenated immigrants were unacceptable to Wilson and most progressives because they acted as groups, and put selfish group interests blindly above the national interest, which, in Wilson's thought, was naturally all of humanity's interest. Moderate progressives sought reforms to improve the lives of immigrants, the urban poor, and the working class, but they sought reforms designed scientifically to meet objectively the needs of society as a whole. Hyphenates, suffragettes, unions, and those demanding welfare legislation were thus all grouped together as selfish special interests to Wilson. Later on, he would become more sympathetic to some of these groups, but only when he began to see their special interest as the national interest. The hyphenate groups never fell into this category. Their disloyalty was bad enough in times of peace; in times of war, it was intolerable.

Note, however, that Wilson opposed hyphenate groups, not immigrants in general. Although he was racist towards blacks and Asians, he was only mildly paternalistic towards the former residents of southern and eastern Europe. Wilson thought the literacy test indeed served a valid purpose in preventing the unassimilable blacks and Asians from voting, but it was invalid to deny admittance to people on the basis of ignorance. For Wilson, illiteracy did not equate with unassimilability, despite the great stock that he placed in education. After all, one could hardly expect southern and eastern Europeans to have received a decent education in their homelands. The point was that they were capable of being educated and assimilated into American culture because they shared a similar enough moral and cultural background as well as a similar shade of skin. More importantly, the United States had to allow the "poor, huddled masses, yearning to breathe free" to enter in order to fulfill God's purpose in creating the "land of the free and the home of the brave." . . .

The insistence of hyphenates upon retaining their national loyalty stood directly in the way of the triumphal American century that Wilson envisioned. He had no quarrel with those who wished to remember fondly their heritage. Wilson often referred proudly to his Scotch-Irish background. But he firmly believed that it was background, and that all American citizens, whether naturalized or native born, should think and act in the foreground. After all, the United States was the last, best hope of mankind, and hence far more deserving of loyalty than any lesser land. In a 1902 speech, Wilson defined patriotism as not merely a sentiment, but a principle of action: the Biblical command—to "love thy neighbor as thyself." And who was one's neighbor? He answered, "Patriotism comes when a man is of big enough range of affection to take the country in. It is friendship writ large. It is fellowship with many sides, which expends itself in service to all mankind joined in the same citizenship, and who are bound up in the same principles of civilization."

Note once again the theme of unity, a brotherhood of servants of God. In Wilson's view, to take the oath of citizenship was to join this lay order. Immigrants who then insisted on hyphens in their name, and tried to fight out Old World battles in the New World, had broken their vows, and quite literally broken faith with America. He probably remembered his father pronouncing the judgement of Jesus from the pulpit: "No one who puts his hand to the plow and looks back is fit for service in the Kingdom of God." He used similar language when addressing a crowd of several thousand newly naturalized citizens in Philadelphia in 1915:

> You have just taken an oath of allegiance to the United States. Of allegiance to whom? Of allegiance to no one, unless it be God—certainly not of allegiance to those who temporarily represent this great Government. You have taken an oath of allegiance to a great ideal, to a great body of principles, to a great hope of the human race. . . . And while you bring all countries with you, you come with a promise of leaving all other countries behind you—bringing what is best of their spirit, but not looking over your shoulder and seeking to perpetuate what you intended to leave behind in them. I certainly would not be one even to suggest that a man cease to love the home of his birth and the nation of his origin—these things are very sacred and ought not to be put out of our hearts—but it is one thing to love the place where you were born and it is another thing to dedicate yourself to the place to which you go. You cannot dedicate yourself to America unless you become in every respect and with every purpose of your will thorough Americans. *You cannot become thorough Americans if you think of yourselves in groups. America does not consist of groups.* A man who thinks of himself as belonging to a particular national group in America has not yet become an American.

The fate of immigrants who continued to look to the past would be that of Lot's wife, according to Wilson. Of course, he desired unity of American spirit at all times. But the efforts of hyphenated Americans, whether Irish, German, Italian, or English, to draw the United States into World War I on behalf of their homelands particularly infuriated Wilson, violating as it did his proclamation of neutrality. It is not by accident that in the same speech quoted above, Wilson made his famous declaration that America was "too proud to fight."

Joe Tumulty, Wilson's Irish Catholic secretary (who today would be called chief of staff), recorded Wilson's anger at Irish Americans who wanted the United States to support Germany in order to force Great Britain to give Ireland her freedom, an anger which Tumulty claims to have shared. When Irish agitator Jeremiah O'Leary wrote to Wilson in 1916, threatening the loss of the Irish vote, Wilson replied angrily in a published letter, "I would feel deeply mortified to have you or anybody like you vote for me. Since you have access to many disloyal Americans and I have not, I will ask you to convey this message to them." Although he thus repudiated the hyphenate vote in 1916, Wilson was not ready to silence all disloyal opposition completely, as Roosevelt was. That would come with the United States' entry into the war, one year later.

Wilson most clearly enunciated his views on this subject when giving an address at the unveiling of a statue of Irish-American Commodore John Barry:

> John Barry was an Irishman, but his heart crossed the Atlantic with him. He did not leave it in Ireland. And the test of all of us—for all of us had our origins on the other side of the sea—is whether we will assist in enabling America to live her separate and independent life, retaining our ancient affections, indeed, but determining everything that we do by the interests that exist on this side of the sea. Some Americans need hyphens in their names, because only part of them has come over, but when the whole man has come over, heart and thought and all, the hyphen drops of its own weight out of his name. This man was not an Irish-American; he was an Irishman who became an American. I venture to say that if he voted he voted with regard to the questions as they looked on this side of the water and not as they affected the other side; and that is my infallible test of a genuine American.

Wilson had indeed long supported the Irish nationalists in their struggle for independence, but it must not come at the expense of United States neutrality or interests.

His campaign against hyphenism coincided with ever-present nativism and the growing pro-Allied war movement to produce a backlash against immigration. This backlash led to the Burnett Immigration Restriction Bill passing Congress in 1915 and 1917, and becoming law in 1917 over the president's veto.

Wilson was genuinely opposed to nativism, and he viewed the unions' position as merely selfish interest, which he could not tolerate. To assuage the fears of average Americans, he portrayed the hyphenates as a minor faction, comparable in their disloyalty to the most outspoken Allied supporters, such as Theodore Roosevelt. In a stump speech on preparedness in 1916, Wilson said of the immigrants, "Their intimate sympathies are with some of the places now most affected by this titanic struggle. You can not [sic] wonder—I do not wonder—that their affections are stirred, old memories awakened and old passions rekindled. The majority of them are steadfast Americans, nevertheless." He noted that by contrast, many nativist Americans had been disloyal in seeking to draw the United States into the war on the Allied side, and concluded that all disloyal favoritism must be put down.

Again, in an address to the Daughters of the American Revolution (an organization that was notoriously nativist) in 1915, entitled, "Be Not Afraid of Our Foreign-Born Citizens," Wilson cautioned them, "There is too general an impression, I fear, that very large numbers of our fellow-citizens born in other lands have not entertained with sufficient intensity and affection the American ideal. But the number is, I am sure, not large. Those who would seek to represent them are very vocal, but they are not very influential." He went on to remind these ancestor-worshipping women that "Some of the best stuff in America has come out of foreign lands, and some of the best stuff in America is in the men who are naturalized citizens. . . . The vast majority of them came here because they believed in America, and their belief in America has made them better citizens than some people who were born in America."

The fact that Wilson equated his struggle to bring unity to warring ethnic groups with Abraham Lincoln's struggle to bring unity to the warring states was made explicit in Wilson's Flag Day address of 1916. By an earlier proclamation, he had made Flag Day an official, nationwide celebration, seeking to use this obvious patriotic symbol to end the "influences which have seemed to threaten to divide us in interest and sympathy," by saying to his "fellow countrymen," "Let us on that day rededicate ourselves to our Nation, 'one and inseparable,' from which every thought that is not worthy of our fathers' first vows of independence, liberty, and right shall be excluded and in which we shall stand with united hearts, for an America which no man can corrupt, . . . no force divide against itself." Here was an obvious reference to Lincoln's immortal maxim, "A house divided against itself cannot stand." In the June 14 address itself, Wilson explicitly compared the current test of unity to that of the Civil War, and stated, "There is disloyalty active in the United States, and it must be absolutely crushed." Unfortunately, all dissent was indeed to be crushed under the weight of George Creel's Committee on Public Information and other wartime measures.

All of these themes came together in Wilson's decision to veto the Burnett Immigration Restriction Bill in 1915 and 1917. The bill's main feature was a literacy test, designed to exclude those who threatened the health and morals of the United States, as Wilson had asked for. He followed the example of Cleveland and Taft in vetoing the bill. In the process, he was standing up to the growing nativist hysteria brought on by the war. The vote to override failed narrowly in 1915; in 1917 the override passed and the Burnett Bill became law.

The movement to restrict immigration had caught Congress's attention in the 1880s, and produced the Chinese Exclusion Act, as well as the later "Gentlemen's Agreement" with Japan. President Cleveland's position was, not surprisingly, very close to that of his protégé's thirty years later. In 1886, Cleveland stated in his annual message to Congress, "In opening our vast domains to alien elements, the purpose of our law-givers was to invite assimilation, and not to provide an arena for endless antagonisms. The paramount duty of maintaining public order and defending the interests of our own people, may require . . . restriction, but they should not tolerate the oppression of individuals of a special race." In his second term, Cleveland did call for legislation to check the "growing evil" of the padrone system, and he voiced concern over the rising illiteracy rates among immigrants. Nevertheless, he vetoed Sen. Henry Cabot Lodge's literacy test bill as too restrictive in 1897. Taft likewise vetoed a similar bill in 1913.

The earliest champion of the literacy test was [Henry Cabot] Lodge, the Massachusetts Brahmin who became Wilson's nemesis. Wilson and Lodge both held an idealistic, optimistic view of America's past and future greatness, and both upheld the Puritan ideal of a public-spirited, homogeneous society as the only salvation for the morass of self-serving urban politics. Where the infamous antagonism existed between the two leaders was over *how* to achieve that homogeneity. Wilson sought American strength through unity, blending together the best characteristics of every nationality to create the ideal citizenry. Lodge, on the other hand, sought strength through purity, convinced that only the Anglo-American "race" could succeed. Lodge believed in assimilation and Americanization, to be sure, but it could only be successful when immigrants abandoned their ethnic heritage entirely and became Anglo Americans. Where Wilson wanted only for the immigrants to share a common vision, Lodge wanted them to share a common history, common language, and common customs. This subtle contrast between amalgamation and isolation was, of course, also at the heart of the battle over the League of Nations.

Lodge argued for the literacy test bill almost as soon as he was elected to the House of Representatives. As a senator in 1896, he recommended the literacy test to his colleagues precisely because it would discriminate against undesirable Italians, Poles, Hungarians, Greeks, and Asians, while allowing British, German, Scandinavian, and French immigrants to come in. He declared that "illiteracy runs parallel with the slum population, with criminals, paupers, juvenile delinquents of foreign birth or parentage ... [and] those who bring the least money to the country and come most quickly upon private or public charity for support." Furthermore, the new immigrants were dangerous because they were "changing the quality of our race and citizenship through the wholesale infusion of races whose traditions and inheritances, whose thoughts and whose beliefs are wholly alien to ours." For Lodge, citizenship was directly tied to ethnicity. He could not see Wilson's argument that the American spirit could transcend ethnicity.

The G.O.P. platform of 1896 called for a literacy test, and Roosevelt pressed Congress to ban all anarchists after McKinley's assassination. Roosevelt tried to maintain a balanced position on immigration, however, despite favoring the literacy test. In his 1903 message to Congress, he sounded the theme of Wilson's National Liberal Immigration League (NLIL) which sought to break up the urban slums and spread the immigrants across the nation. "The need is to devise some system by which undesirable immigrants shall be kept out entirely, while desirable immigrants are properly distributed throughout the country." Again in 1905 he called for distribution, suggesting the banning of immigration only in the big Northern cities. It was only during World War I that Roosevelt became the champion of the rabid nationalists.

The Southerners were violently opposed to any immigrants being distributed around Dixie, and it is not surprising to find that most of the literacy test's supporters were Southern Democrats such as Oscar Underwood and John Burnett. They wanted an end to all immigration of non-"Teutonic" foreigners, and thought that the literacy test could accomplish this as well as it kept blacks from voting in their home states. Immigration restriction was also a golden opportunity for Southern Democrats to win back the farmers and unions that had bolted the party for the Populists in the 1890s.

The theme of racial superiority dominated Congressional debates quite as much as economic concerns about wages and jobs. Congressman Everis A. Hayes of California made a motion in 1914 to amend the Burnett Bill by excluding all "Hindoos [sic] and all persons of the Mongolian or yellow race, the Malay or brown race, the African or black race," but it was defeated handily. Sen. James A. Reed of Missouri did get an amendment excluding all blacks (carefully worded so as to bar even black United States citizens who travelled abroad from returning!) to pass the Senate, but it was dropped in conference committee in 1915. The 1917 bill that finally passed over Wilson's veto did include an "Asiatic Barred Zone" that restricted immigration by longitude and latitude.

While Wilson saw the Southerners and the unions as guilty of promoting selfish special interests, Congressman John L. Burnett of Alabama attacked the foes of his bill as special interests: the "Ship Trust," the "Brewer's Trust." He argued that his bill did exactly what Wilson had called for in his address to the foreign-language editors during the campaign: restricting immigration to maintain American ideals. (However, he contradicted himself immediately by quoting a *Boston Transcript* editorial claiming that the literacy test was *not* a test of character.) Burnett made sure to fill his speeches with the social science statistics that made progressives' ears perk up, and quoted experts such as New York Police Commissioner Bingham: "You will notice that these particular crimes [against women and children] are done by fellows who can't talk the English language; . . . [who] don't know what liberty means, and don't care; don't know our customs; . . . and are in general the scum of Europe." While Burnett was definitely a white supremacist, he urged the House to vote down the amendment restricting all blacks—but only because the amendment would insure the bill's defeat.

The most outspoken opponent of the Burnett Bill was Congressmen James A. Gallivan of Massachusetts. He joined Washington Gladden in denouncing the new "holy wars" between Catholics and Protestants that the debate on immigration was engendering. He also pointed out the hypocrisy of the bill's supporters, noting that the majority of white Southerners, let alone blacks, were as poor as the immigrants, and had much higher rates of illiteracy. He observed, too, that wealth and education had grown in the North along with immigration. Gallivan reminded his colleagues that the twelve Apostles were mostly illiterate when Jesus called them, and that their own colonial ancestors, of whom they were so proud, were largely illiterate, too. As he said: "Then, as now, the men who faced the hazards of the tempestuous ocean and the perils of the savage continent were usually the bravest and most enterprising of their class; they had courage, strength, common sense, native ability, and a willingness to work out their own salvation in a new country . . . ," but not a good education. Gallivan pleaded always for a true test of character, noting that anarchists and socialists were almost always well-educated, and so a literacy test would not keep them out. He concluded that "we have grown fat and foolish in our progress; we forgot our origins; we imagine that the eternal verities will change and that the letters and scripts that man has made have, by some curious alchemy, become greater and more worthy than the gifts God has given us."

In Wilson's first veto message, he called the bill, "a radical departure from the traditional and long-established policy of this country . . . in which our people have conceived the very character of their government to be expressed, the very mission and spirit of the Nation . . ." because it greatly curtailed the right to political asylum in the United States. In addition, the bill was unsound because it would, "turn away from tests of character and of quality and impose tests which exclude and restrict; for the new tests are . . . tests of opportunity. Those who come seeking opportunity are not to be admitted unless they have already had one of the chief opportunities they seek, the opportunity of education." Wilson's second veto message basically reiterated the first. Ironically, however, he criticized an amendment put in to answer his objections about the elimination of asylum, saying that it would lead to diplomatic difficulties. The ever-approaching war no doubt contributed to this seeming about-face.

Wilson did not desire the severe repression of the wartime years, although he did condone it. The Burnett Immigration Restriction Bill, on the other hand, was a measure that he opposed from the start. Not only did Wilson deem it unnecessary (as he remained confident that the majority of immigrants were loyal Americans) but more importantly, it violated the foundational principles of America. Wilson consistently saw America as more of a spiritual concept than a physical reality, a mental device used by most Americans to reconcile the image of America that they have been socialized to accept with the far-from-perfect reality which they can plainly see. Wilson recognized that it was vital to keep the spiritual concept of America, symbolized by the Statue of Liberty, not too far out of line with the reality of Ellis Island.

This spiritual concept called America was in reality the old Puritan dream of the New World as the new Jerusalem, the "city set on a hill" of which Jesus spoke, and of the American people as the new Israel, a people set apart by God to be an example and inspiration to all the world. The biblical texts and the writings of Calvinist preachers were all familiar to the son of a Presbyterian minister and a devout Christian in his own right, and his allusions clearly drew on them. In a Thanksgiving Day address to the Har Sinai Temple of Trenton, New Jersey in 1910, he quoted the old New England divine William Stoughton on the subject of God sifting the nations of the world to plant the choicest seed in America, and he went on to say, "And so, apparently God is sifting the nations yet to plant seed in America." He described the American people as a "conglomerate," with each ethnic group contributing necessary characteristics, "I will not say, out of alien stocks, for these stocks are bound by adoption, by mixture and by union." One can hear St. Paul saying, "Theirs is the adoption as sons; theirs the divine glory, the covenants, the receiving of the law, the temple worship and the promises." Wilson then said, "I don't regard these national elements, that is, race elements, that make up American life as something outside America for they have come in and been identified with her. They are all instantly recognizable as Americans and America is enriched with the variety of their gifts and the variety of their national characterization."

His campaign speeches in 1912 emphasize this spiritual concept as the force which motivated most immigrants to come to the United States. In part, this was because Wilson was trying to mollify hyphenate groups who were outraged over the infamous passage in Wilson's *History* by arguing that the quote was taken out of context, and that he referred only to those immigrants who were "forced" to come over as contract labor. By contrast, the majority of immigrants came over voluntarily, literally "moved by the spirit."

But this defense merged in Wilson's mind with what he considered to be the more important reason to emphasize the spiritual concept of America: the unity of believers that it implied. Wilson believed that he could reunite the divided American people by teaching them that the past no longer mattered, save to teach them the necessity and inevitability of their being all as one now in the American spirit. It is as if Wilson was paraphrasing St. Paul again: "Here there is no Greek or Jew, immigrant or native, Pole, Italian, slave or free, but America is all, and is in all." It also calls to mind the motto of King Louis XVIII of France after the French Revolution: "L'union et l'oublie" ("Union and Forgetfulness").

We can hear this cry in Wilson's address to a Polish-American crowd in Chicago's South Side:

> When we speak of America, we speak not of race; but of a people. After we have enumerated the Irish-Americans, the Jewish-Americans, the German-Americans, and the Polish-Americans who will be left? Settlers and descendants of settlers constitute the minority in America, and the people of all the races of Europe a majority. The term America is bigger than the continent. America lives in the hearts of every man everywhere who wishes to find a region somewhere where he will be free to work out his destiny as he chooses.

Wilson, indeed, began to protest wherever he spoke against the very hyphenated terms with which the immigrants were labelled. He realized that the use of such terms fostered the lack of unity felt by Americans of different ethnic backgrounds, and prevented the full flowering of united American power that he predicted for this century. He declared, "I am looking forward to an era of unprecedented national action. We are now coming to an era where there will be but one single expression and but one common thought." In order for this era to be brought about, the usages of thought and expression had to be changed, however. Thus he went on, "I protest against speaking of German-Americans, or Irish-Americans or Jewish-Americans, for these nationalities are becoming indistinguishable in the general body of Americans. Drop out the first words, cut out the hyphens and call them all Americans."

The importance of language in communicating this spiritual concept of America was stressed to a group of approximately one hundred editors of foreign-language newspapers in 1912. Wilson explained to them his view of America, and stated that immigrants should only be restricted to exclude those who did not have the spirit of American idealism which caused people to voluntarily emigrate. He then protested against their designation as foreign-language editors, arguing that whatever language was used to convey American ideals was the language of America: "All my interest is that you shouldn't regard the language in which you print your periodicals as a foreign language when printed in America for the conveyance of American thinking." This was indeed a radical statement of the American spirit of unity erasing even the most obvious ethnic divisions.

True American faith was limited to the elect, however. There were certain languages that simply could not convey the American spirit. Wilson thought that the key to a successful immigration policy was assimilation. Indeed, it was on this basis that Wilson supported the Chinese Exclusion Act. Oriental people, like the blacks in the South, were simply incapable of conforming to the ideal, Wilson believed. Therefore, they were obviously heathen intruders in the Kingdom of God, who should be tolerated, but kept in their place.

Despite the fact that Europeans emigrated to the United States because they were already Americans at heart, assimilation was not an automatic experience. Immigrants needed to work out their salvation with fear and trembling, and it was up to the "native" citizens to aid them in the assimilation process. The key was education. Wilson heartily approved the naturalization classes and night school movements started by progressive social workers during this time period. But, he believed that "the chief school that these people must attend after they get here is the school which all of us attend, which is furnished by the life of the communities in which we live and the Nation to which we belong. . . . It is easy . . . to communicate physical lessons, but it is very difficult to communicate spiritual lessons." The ideal American community (i.e., small and rural) was the best school for instilling American ideals, not crowded cities where those ideals had been corrupted.

The chief spiritual lessons which immigrants needed to learn were American political ideals. Wilson was very upset that the immigrants kept the urban political machines running by exchanging votes for jobs and other favors. This process corrupted Wilson's, and America's, ideals of both the statesmen and the electorate. His views on the ideal statesman have been discussed above. It needs to be pointed out here that although Wilson saw the party as a powerful tool, he demanded that elected officials act as individually responsible trustees, and not as mere delegates, blindly following party dictates. As early as 1876 he wrote:

> Although there are principles of duty to his party and to the cause he has espoused, still no statesman should allow party feeling to bias his opinions on any point which involves truth or falsehood, justice or injustice. He should search for truth with the full determination to find it, and in that search he should most earnestly seek aid from God, who will surely hold him responsible for the course he pursues.

In a 1912 campaign speech, Wilson cautioned his audience to, "always distinguish a boss from a political leader. Party organization is absolutely legitimate and absolutely necessary," but only when the political leader uses the party to serve the commonweal. "A boss is a man who uses this splendid open force for the secret processes of selfish control."

Voters must vote for the good of the nation as a whole, and politicians must serve that greater good. In Wilson's speech accepting the Democratic nomination in 1912, the man who had defeated the bosses in New Jersey called on his party to do the same nationwide: "We are servants of the people, the whole people. *The nation has been unnecessarily, unreasonably at war within itself.* Interest has clashed with interest when there were common principles of right and of fair dealing which . . . should have bound them all together. . . . As servants of all, we are bound to undertake the great duty of accommodation and adjustment." Thus the call once more to end the civil war and unite in patriotic homogeneity of belief and practice.

Wilson explicitly linked this homogeneity of American idealism to the assimilation of immigrants during the campaign. He argued that America had always opened its doors and extended hospitality to all the "modern civilized peoples," that they might share in our ideals and enrich our melting pot. America must be careful to live up to the ideals which persuaded the immigrants to come here, the vision of "a place of close knit communities, where men think in terms of the common interest, where men do not organize selfish groups to dominate the fortunes of their fellow men, but where, on the contrary, they, by common conference, conceive the policies which are for the common benefit." Once more, the image of special interest groups as an evil, divisive force emerges, as well as the image of small-town community life as the ideal force to Americanize and unify the diverse elements of the population.

Although he believed that Americans came with, and because of, this ideal vision, they did not always realize it. Often they continued to act politically in the manner that they learned in the Old World, giving loyalty on the basis of debts owed and blood ties. Wilson saw a need to educate immigrants to accept that in the United States, the people, and not the State, were sovereign. He told the Conference on Americanization, "When you ask a man to be loyal to a government, if he comes from some foreign countries, his idea is that he is expected to be loyal to a certain set of persons like a ruler or a body set in authority over him. . . . Our idea is that he is to be loyal to certain objects in life." Not only must they be taught that idealism is allowed in the United States, they must be taught that idealism is mandatory in the United States.

> Loyalty means nothing unless it has at its heart the absolute principle of self-sacrifice. Loyalty means that you ought to be ready to sacrifice every interest that you have, and your life itself, if your country calls upon you to do so, and that is the sort of loyalty which ought to be inculcated into these newcomers, . . . that, having once entered this sacred relationship, they are bound to be loyal whether they are pleased or not; and

that loyalty which is merely self-pleasing is only self-indulgence and selfishness.

Education was necessary for assimilation. But, as noted above, Wilson believed that the best education came from everyday community life. The healthiest communities were naturally the rural ones. Wilson therefore supported efforts to get the immigrants out of the crowded, squalid cities in which most of the immigrants stayed, and spread them out in the great expanse of American country. To this end he became a director of the National Liberal Immigration League. In fact, he asked for legislation to facilitate such assimilation by dilution instead of the Burnett Bill in 1915.

Seen now in the context of Wilson's overall attitude towards immigration, these two vetoes make much more sense. Wilson saw himself as another Lincoln or Cleveland, trying to heal the divisions of civil war and reunify the country to carry on its God-ordained mission. The literacy test may have been useful in keeping blacks and Asians out of American political life, because they were patently unassimilable to Wilson. However, it constituted an arbitrary restriction on thousands of European immigrants, who had the spirit of America in their hearts, and could only help build the glorious empire of the United States in the twentieth century, and spread the gospel of political freedom to all the world.

More importantly, the rhetoric of Woodrow Wilson reveals several foundational myths in American life. The myth of America as the chosen people of God, building His Kingdom on Earth, rings forth in Wilson's religious imagery. This myth requires logically the myth of homogeneity, that all cultural differences must blend away in the melting pot, and that education will lead all rational men to recognize and strive only for the commonweal. "E pluribus, unum," thundered Wilson from the classroom and the bully pulpit of the Presidency. And the people responded by silencing all opposition to the war, by staging race riots, by abandoning the very ideals which Wilson had said unity would serve.

In this decade of the 1990s, when "multiculturalism" is the watchword of the universities, and cultural pluralism continues to increase rather than decrease, America needs to examine closely her foundational myths. Can, or should, the divided Puritan ideal be reunified? Does the concept of a nation still require a set of shared values and cultural experiences? The message of Woodrow Wilson is therefore a challenge to our society to redefine our national character, and examine anew our complex reactions to immigration. We can harshly suppress all differences, and thus destroy the very ideals we seek to preserve. We can abandon all hope of cultural cohesiveness, and either Balkanize our society or water down our ideals to meaninglessness. Or we can try to follow the middle road that Wilson attempted to lay down: teaching immigrants what it means to be Americans, but at the same time learning and adopting from them what their cultures have to offer.

QUESTIONS TO CONSIDER

1. What was the difference to Woodrow Wilson between blacks and Asians, on the one hand, and southern and eastern Europeans, on the other? How did this view affect his policies?

2. Why did Wilson define as un-American those who thought of themselves as groups?

3. Explain the difference between Lodge's and Wilson's visions of homogeneity. Which of Gordon's three models did each represent?

4. What does Vought mean when he says that Wilson saw America as more a spiritual concept than a physical reality? To what extent do *you* agree?

5. How does Vought relate Wilson's ideas to the "multiculturalism" of twenty-first-century America? How does the article affect *your* thinking on assimilation today?

8

Women in Politics Between the Wars

ELISABETH PERRY

"Why Suffrage for American Women Was
Not Enough," by Elisabeth Perry.
Reprinted by permission of
History Today, Sept. 1993.

In 1920, following a seventy-two-year struggle, American women finally won the right to vote in national elections. For a very few years after that the political parties took women seriously, catering to them with positions on committees, with women's divisions, and by considering their views. But it quickly became evident that women voted not as a block but rather like men, divided in their opinions. Not until the 1980 election would a gender gap, a significant difference in the way women and men voted, emerge. Women's failure to vote as a block should not have been surprising. Over the past century, women have been among the strongest voices on *both* sides of major women's issues (not to mention nongender issues), including the vote, protective legislation, the equal rights amendment, and abortion.

Elisabeth Perry explores the restricted options, external obstacles, and self-imposed limitations that characterized the political careers of four capable women in the 1920s. Belle Moskowitz, Eleanor Roosevelt, Frances Perkins, and Molly Dewson achieved a great deal politically, but the idea of running for political office themselves was unthinkable in the 1920s. Women today have far more opportunity to win elective office, as Hillary Clinton demonstrated by her election to the U.S. Senate in 2000. Yet a strong, capable, outspoken woman like Clinton polarizes public opinion even in the twenty-first century. No wonder women were not much tempted by elective races eighty years ago.

Elisabeth Perry, a specialist in women in politics, is in a unique professional position. Since 2000 she and her husband, Lewis, have shared the John Francis Bannon, S. J., Endowed Chair in History and American Studies at Saint Louis University. Her most recent book, coauthored with Kathryn Kish Sklar, is *Belle Moskowitz: Feminine Politics and the Exercise of Power in the Age of Alfred E. Smith* (2000).

A s a result of the autumn elections in 1992, a year the American media billed as "The Year of the Woman," the numbers of women holding elective office in the United States rose to unprecedented heights. The percentage of women office holders at state level climbed to 22.2 per cent for state-wide elected executives and 20.4 per cent for legislators. At the national level, the number of female US Senators tripled (from two to six), while the number in the House of Representatives rose from twenty-eight to forty-seven (there is a forty-eighth, who represents the District of Columbia, but she has no vote). Even with this impressive progress, however, women's share of elective office in the United States remains relatively small.

It is not hard to explain why. Deeply ingrained global traditions have long kept women out of public, authoritative roles. But why have these traditions remained so entrenched in the United States, ostensibly one of the most advanced, modernised countries of the world? A close look at American women's political history in the immediate post-suffrage era might provide a few clues.

American women won the vote in 1920 with the ratification of the Nineteenth Amendment to the federal Constitution. Women had worked for this goal since 1848, when Elizabeth Cady Stanton, a reformer active in the campaigns to abolish slavery and also a temperance advocate, organised a public meeting in Seneca Falls, New York, to discuss women's rights. Many observers ridiculed her demand for the vote. By the turn of the century, this demand had become the focal point of the entire women's movement. Suffrage for women was eventually won in a number of the states, and then nationwide in August, 1920.

By the time this event occurred, women were no longer political novices. For decades they had been organising conventions, giving public speeches, writing editorials, campaigning door-to-door, petitioning and marching. These activities gave them vast political expertise, as well as access to wide networks of other women activists and of male political leaders. This combination of expertise and contacts ought to have placed them at the centre of American political life. It did not.

The winning of female suffrage did not mark the end of prejudice and discrimination against women in public life. Women still lacked equal access with men to those professions, especially the law, which provide the chief routes to political power. Further, when women ran for office—and many did in the immediate post-suffrage era—they often lacked major party backing, hard to come by for any newcomer but for women almost impossible unless she belonged to a prominent political family. Even if successful in winning backing, when women ran for office they usually had to oppose incumbents. When, as was often the case, they lost their first attempts, their reputation as "losers" made re-endorsement impossible.

American political parties did try to integrate women into their power structures after suffrage. They courted women's votes, especially in the early 1920s, when a "woman's voting bloc" seemed real. In addition, the parties formed "women's divisions" or created a committee system of equal numbers of committee women and committee men (with the latter usually choosing the former). But when party leaders sought a candidate for preferment, they tended to look for "a good man," seldom imagining that a woman might qualify. In short, in the years immediately after suffrage most party leaders confined women to auxiliary, service roles. They expected women to help elect men but not seek office themselves. That party men in the early 1920s held to such an expectation is hardly surprising. That many of the most politically "savvy" American women went along with them is more difficult to understand.

In the post-suffrage United States, although there were many strong, executive-type women with considerable political expertise, none of them became the vanguard of a new, office-seeking female political leadership. Because of women's long exclusion from the vote and political parties, these women had worked for change only in a nonpartisan fashion from within their own gender sphere. After suffrage, in part because men kept them there, they accepted the notion that separate roles for women in politics ought to continue.

The reasons for this acceptance are complex, and probably differ from woman to woman. Some women felt most comfortable operating from within their own sphere. In single-sex groups, they made lifelong friendships with women who shared their interests and problems. In addition, in women's groups they did not have to compete with men for positions of authority. A deep suspicion of electoral politics was yet another important factor. Political women distrusted the world of electoral politics. It was a man's world, a world filled with "dirty games" that men had been trained to play, and indeed were forced to play, if they wanted to "get ahead." For these women, it held few allures. Educated and middle-class, they had not been brought up to be career-orientated or personally ambitious. Rather, they had been taught that their proper role was to serve others and to work for idealistic causes. The winning of the vote did little to change this socialisation.

These were some of the views of women's role in politics held by both men and women in the 1920s. The careers of four suffragists, all politically active in the post-suffrage era and all of whom could have held elective office had circumstances differed, serve to illustrate how these views affected individual lives. The four do not comprise a balanced "sample," for they were all based in New York City and were all active in the Democratic Party. They are exemplars, however, because they thrived in a hotbed of women's activism in the post-suffrage era. If any woman could have risen into electoral political prominence during that era, she would have been a New York City Democrat.

My first example is Belle Lindner Moskowitz (1877–1933). A shopkeeper's daughter born in Harlem, New York, she spent her early career as a social worker on the city's Lower East Side. After her marriage in 1903, while her children were growing up, she did volunteer work until, by the 1910s, she had developed a city-wide reputation as an effective social and industrial reformer. Although considering herself an independent Republican, in 1918, the first year New York State women voted, because of Democrat Alfred E. Smith's reputation as an advocate for labour, she supported him for governor.

After organising the women's vote for him, Moskowitz proposed that Governor-elect Smith establish a "Reconstruction Commission" to identify and propose solutions for the state's administrative, social, and economic problems. Smith not only formed the Commission but appointed her its executive director. During the one year of its existence (1919–20), it outlined Smith's legislative programme and launched Moskowitz's career as his closest political advisor. From 1923 on, she ran his state re-election campaigns and guided the legislative enactment of his policies, all the while preparing the ground for his nomination by the Democratic Party as presidential candidate in 1928. In that year, she directed national publicity for the campaign and served as the only woman on the national Democratic Party executive committee.

Al Smith lost that election to Herbert Hoover. But because Belle Moskowitz had played such a central role in his career throughout the 1920s, by the time of his presidential race she was a nationally known political figure. Still, her fame depended on his. Smith had offered her a number of government posts but she had refused them. She believed, and rightly so, that her work from behind the scenes would in the end give her more power than the holding of any bureaucratic, appointive office. Thanks to her, Smith, a man whose formal education had ended at the age of thirteen, was able to pursue his legislative programme with enough success to become a viable presidential candidate. But because of her self-effacement, when Smith failed to win the presidency and then lost his party leadership role to Franklin Delano Roosevelt, her career was eclipsed along with his. Future generations of political women would not see her example as an inspiration or model for their own careers.

More famous than Moskowitz, Anna Eleanor Roosevelt (1884–1962) became known worldwide for the role she played as the wife of Franklin Roosevelt, four-term president during the Great Depression and Second

World War. Most portraits of Eleanor focus on her activities after 1933, when Franklin became president, until his death in 1945, when she became a United Nations delegate and moral force in world politics. What is less well known is that, before FDR became president, even before he became governor of New York, she had accumulated a vast amount of political experience and influence in her own right.

Unlike Moskowitz, Eleanor Roosevelt was born into wealth and privilege, but endured an unhappy childhood. A measure of fulfillment came to her through her education and volunteer social work. She married Franklin in 1905, bore him several children, and fostered her husband's promising political career. In 1920, this career reached its first culmination when he ran, unsuccessfully, for vice-president. By then their marriage was on shaky ground. Although in 1918 Eleanor had discovered Franklin's affair with Lucy Mercer, the couple had resolved to keep the marriage together. In 1921, Franklin was stricken with polio and withdrew from politics. Franklin's political manager and publicist, Louis Howe, convinced Eleanor to keep her husband's name alive by becoming active herself in women's organisations. Once involved in this work, Eleanor confirmed what she had discovered during her husband's earlier campaigns. She liked politics.

But primarily from within her own sphere. She took up volunteer work for four New York City women's groups: the League of Women Voters and Women's City Club, the Women's Trade Union League, and the Women's Division of the State Democratic Party. For this latter group, from 1925 to 1928 she developed and edited a newspaper that, in bridging the gap between upstate and downstate Democrats, formed a critical base for Al Smith and her husband's future support. Through her other groups she worked for legislation on a variety of important issues: public housing for low-income workers; the dissemination of birth control information, the reorganisation of the state government, and shorter hours and minimum wages for women workers.

To accomplish her goals, she gave talks on the radio and published articles. Journalists interviewed her. She travelled all around the state during and in between campaigns to keep local party leaders connected with one another. She ran the women's campaigns for the Democrats at the state level in 1924 and national level in 1928. As a result, she became a well known figure, almost as well known as her husband, at both state and national level. But when her husband won the governorship in 1928, she gave up all activity. She knew where her duty lay—to become Albany's First Lady, not to hold office herself.

By 1928, in the crucible of New York women's politics, Eleanor Roosevelt had forged for herself acute political skills. These would serve her well as she continued until her husband's death to support his political agendas and afterwards to pursue more directly her own. By 1928, however, she herself had become so prominent that had she wanted she could have run for office and probably won. It did not even occur to her to do so. That was not what women did, especially not women married to ambitious men.

The first woman in the United States to hold cabinet rank was Frances Perkins (1880–1965). Even though she held public office my argument holds true for her as well: her post was appointive, not elective, and she asserted to the end of her life that she had never been interested in a political career. Better educated than either Moskowitz or Roosevelt (she graduated from Mt. Holyoke College), Perkins had a background similar to theirs. After working as a teacher and in a social settlement, she became secretary of the New York Consumers' League, a group seeking labour legislation to improve factory safety and health conditions for all workers. Although always known as "Miss" Perkins, she was married and bore one child, but her husband suffered from mental illness and was later unable to earn a living. This circumstance gave her a keen interest in finding well paid jobs. Like Moskowitz, she came to admire Al Smith and in 1918 worked for his election as governor. Unlike Moskowitz, when Smith offered her a job as a State Industrial Commissioner, she accepted. This post became the launching pad from which she entered Roosevelt's cabinet in 1933.

Still, when she reflected on her career years later, she denied being a "career woman" with political ambitions. Doors had opened for her and she had gone through them. She had never dreamed of being Secretary of Labor or Industrial Commissioner, she said. A "series of circumstances" and her "own energies" had thrown her into "situations" where she had assumed responsibility and then was asked to assume more. Before she knew it she "had a career."

Here again is an accomplished, talented woman who had matured through social reform and suffrage politics in the 1910s and then moved into appointive office. As she plied her way, although she wanted and needed to work, ideas of personal advancement or career ambition were seldom at the forefront of her thinking. Convinced even at the moment of Roosevelt's elevation of her that she was probably unworthy, she accepted the offer as a "call to service." Once she attained office, fearful that men would resist answering to her, she took on the look, dress, and behaviour of a schoolmarm so as to appear less threatening to them. Despite all of her accomplishments, the gender stereotypes and constraints of her time prevailed.

My last example from the period is Mary W. (Molly) Dewson (1874–1962). Like Perkins, Dewson was well educated. After graduating from Wellesley College and holding some research jobs, she became Superintendent of Probation at the nation's first reform school for girls and then executive secretary of the Massachusetts Commission on the

Minimum Wage. Never married, she maintained a lifelong partnership with a friend, Polly Porter, with whom she farmed in Massachusetts and did suffrage and war work. Eventually, under the mentorship of Eleanor Roosevelt, Dewson moved into Democratic state and then national politics. Her personal ambitions remained severely limited, however.

When Dewson assessed women's political progress since suffrage, she confessed that their opportunities had barely expanded, usually on the basis of their "looks, money," or a "late husband's service to the party," they had received only ceremonial party positions. In these circumstances, Dewson decided that the only way to build women's political strength was through separate women's divisions. As head of the Women's Division of the Democratic National Committee, she organised women workers for FDR's campaigns and co-ordinated support for his programmes between elections. In so doing, she played roles essential to the success of the Democratic Party during the New Deal initiative. Like Perkins, Dewson followed a cautious philosophy in working with men: she took on a maternal or "aunty" pose and disclaimed any relationship to feminism. She also turned down posts when they threatened her partnership with Polly Porter. Only in her old age did she finally enter a political race in her own right. But the race she chose was in a solidly-Republican district where she had no chance of winning.

Among the most politically adept of their generation, all four of these women pursued political goals in the 1920s but none as a man would have done. Moskowitz achieved an important advisory role but lost all her power at the fall of her mentor. Roosevelt sacrificed her own needs to those of her husband. Perkins reached high office but masked her strength and denied personal ambition. Dewson often put domestic happiness before career fulfilment and, like Perkins, downplayed her feminism. Others of their generation who had been leaders in the suffrage struggle acted similarly.

When younger women growing up in the 1920s and 30s looked at their political forbears, Belle Moskowitz, Eleanor Roosevelt, Frances Perkins, and Molly Dewson were among the few successful ones they saw. But younger women wanted real careers, not roles as an amanuensis to a man or as a behind-the-scenes campaigner. But "real careers" were denied them. Either men discriminated against them and kept them out of the central circles of power, or when they married they discovered that domestic life and a political career just did not mix.

The door was open to women in politics in the 1920s. But, as Molly Dewson once said, the battle was uphill and most women got quickly discouraged. By accommodating themselves to a reality they could not control, they participated in the perpetuation of a "separate spheres ideology" long after it had outlived its relevance. Looking back at them from the standpoint of 1993 we might judge these women as "old fashioned." But we ought not reject them as important role models. As smart, wily, and skilled political strategists, they have much to teach us. We must reject not them but the constraints that held them back.

Some of those constraints are still with us. Throughout the 1992 campaign, questions about women's appropriate roles in politics continued to surface. They dominated the controversies that swirled around Hillary Clinton, wife of Democratic presidential candidate, Bill Clinton. What role had she played in his years as governor of Arkansas? Why did she keep her maiden name when they were married? What was the quality of their married life together? Had she been a good mother or was she one of those career-orientated, ambitious feminists?

At its national convention in August, the Republican Party exploited popular doubts about Hillary Clinton's ability to operate in the traditional mode of the political wife. In an unprecedented move, convention organisers asked the wives of its candidates, Barbara Bush and Marilyn Quayle, to speak. The shared theme of the women's speeches, "traditional" family values, sent out a clear message: political wives must adhere strictly to giving priority to their husbands' careers.

The Democratic Party response disturbed many feminists, but it was probably essential to victory. Hillary Clinton got a makeover. She baked cookies and, in response to rumours that she was childless, trotted out her daughter Chelsea at every possible occasion. Still, when Bill Clinton and his running mate, Albert Gore, Jr., made their victory speeches on election night, women heard some new words on national television. In describing their future government, for the first time in history both president and vice-president-elect included the category of "gender" as an important test of the diversity they envisioned.

Despite their personal openness to women in government, Hillary Clinton remained vulnerable to further attacks. As a lawyer with a distinguished record of accomplishment concerning the rights of children, she took active part in her husband's transition team discussions. Later, she received an appointment as unpaid head of a task force addressing one of the nation's most pressing problems, the lack of a national health insurance system. In response to a query by the press as to how reporters should refer to her, she asked them to use all three of her names, Hillary Rodham Clinton. The charges flew. Ambitious feminist. Power mad. Who is in charge here? In March 1993, on a flight over Washington DC, an airline pilot joked over the loudspeaker, "Down below you can see the White House, where the president and her husband live."

If, on the brink of the twenty-first century, the wife of the President of the United States still cannot perform in an authoritative role without questions being raised about the appropriateness of her behaviour how could the women of the 1920s have stood a chance? Today's "Hillary factor" shows just how far we have come and how far we have to go before women can at last take up citizenship roles equal to those of men.

QUESTIONS TO CONSIDER

1. What factors blocked women's entrance into public life once they won the right to vote?
2. According to Perry, why did women acquiesce to separate roles in politics? Are these reasons still valid today?
3. What factors did the four women have in common? What distinguished them from one another?
4. What has changed in the United States since the 1920s that gives women a better political chance? What factors continue to hold women back?
5. How does Hillary Clinton's 2000 election as senator relate to the article's thrust?

9

Depression

WILLIAM MANCHESTER

William Manchester (1922–   ) brought history alive for countless readers over the past generation. His best-selling histories include the controversial *The Death of a President* (1967); the colorful *American Caesar: Douglas MacArthur, 1880–1964* (1978); and the monumental narrative history of America from 1932 to 1972, *The Glory and the Dream* (1974), from which this selection was taken.

The Great Depression permeated all areas of American society in the 1930s and became the terrible nightmare underlying every thought of the people in that grim decade. The human mind possesses a remarkable talent, perhaps necessary for mental health, for filtering out the bad experiences of the past and remembering only the good. So it was with the astounding nostalgia craze of the 1970s that young Americans looked back on the Depression and saw primarily the positive things about it: jobs conscientiously done; neighbor helping neighbor; a nation united in its attempts to defeat the economic catastrophe. Despite their protective filters, however, those who had lived through it regarded such nostalgia as beyond belief. The searing misery of the 1930s had scarred their generation, molding its attitudes toward employment, credit, saving, and security in ways that made them incomprehensible to those Americans who grew up in the virtually nonstop prosperity after World War II. In this moving selection, Manchester gives younger readers a chance to understand how the Depression shaped the character of a generation.

In June 1932, Ivy League seniors joined 21,974 other alumni hunting for jobs. By then New York department stores were requiring bachelor degrees for all elevator operators, and that was the best many of them could do, but twenty-year-old Sylvia Field Porter, Hunter '32, was an exception. She switched her major from English to economics because of what she later called "an overwhelming curiosity to know why everything was crashing around me and why people were losing their jobs" and talked her way into an investment counsel firm. At the same time she began a systematic study of the financial world, with the thought that one day she might write a column about it. She then discovered that she was in the middle of a crisis without historical precedent.

Ever since the fiasco of England's South Sea Company in 1720, the phrase "South Sea bubble" had been used to describe a doomed business venture. The bubble had certainly burst; South Sea stock had plunged to 13.5 percent of its highest quotation. Yet it subsequently rallied, and the firm continued to do business for eighty years. By the time of Miss Porter's commencement, however, United States Steel and General Motors had dropped to 8 percent of their pre-Crash prices. Overall, stocks listed on the Big Board were worth 11 percent of their 1929 value. Investors had lost 74 billion dollars, three times the cost of the World War. More than 5,000 American banks had failed—in Iowa City, just across the county line from [President Herbert] Hoover's native West Branch, all five banks were shut—and 86,000 businesses had closed their doors. The country's Gross National Product had fallen from 104 billion dollars to 41 billion (in 1973 it would be 2,177 billion). In 1932, 273,000 families were evicted from their homes, and the average weekly wage of those who had jobs was $16.21.

Some enterprises flourished. The contraceptive business was netting a quarter-billion dollars a year, a fact which the youth of that day conveniently forgot after they had become parents. Over half the population was going to the movies once a week (admission was a quarter for adults, a dime for children), and each year saw an increase in the number of cigarette smokers, none of them aware that the habit might be harmful. Kelvinator refrigerators and Atwater Kent radios were moving briskly. Miniature golf courses and circulation libraries were booming. Alfred C. Fuller was doing very nicely with his corps of door-to-door brush salesmen; in the grim month of August 1932 his sales leaped from $15,000 to $50,000 and grew thereafter at the rate of a million dollars a year. A prodigy named J. Paul Getty was quietly picking up cheap petroleum wells; that February he gained control of 520,000 of the Pacific Oil Corporation's one million shares. Here and there a venture was lucky. In Quincy, Massachusetts, the owner of a curious restaurant with a bright orange roof and pseudo-Colonial architecture was almost bankrupt when a stock company opened across the street. Its first play was Eugene O'Neill's nine-act *Strange Interlude*. Every evening there was an 8:30 intermission for supper, and the restauranteur, Howard Johnson, survived.

But these were exceptions. U.S. Steel, the key to heavy industry, was operating at 19.1 percent of capacity. The American Locomotive Company didn't need much steel. During the 1920s it had sold an average of 600 locomotives a year; in 1932 it sold one. Nor was the automotive industry the big steel customer it had been. Month by month its fine names were vanishing: the Stutz Motor Company, the Auburn, the Cord, and Edward Peerless, the Pierce Arrow, the Duesenberg, the Franklin, the Durant, the Locomobile. One rash man decided to challenge Ford with another low-priced car. He called it the Rockne, lost 21 million dollars, and killed himself. In January an inventive bacteriologist named Arthur G. Sherman had become the sensation of the Detroit Auto Show by exhibiting the first crude, handcarpentered, wooden trailer. In 1932 he sold just eighty of them. Air transport nose-dived. Airliners then had twelve seats, of which, the Department of Commerce reported, an average of seven were flying empty. And with the exception of the new talkies, most entertainers were foundering. In four years the jazz musician Eddie Condon landed four recording sessions; the phonograph recording industry had dwindled from 50 million dollars a year to a quarter-million. Sally Rand was making a precarious living with her celebrated fans; to a reporter who asked why she did it, she replied, "I never made any money till I took off my pants."

Because poverty was considered shameful, people tried to conceal destitution from neighbors, often with considerable success. One could never be sure about the family across the street. The smartly dressed young lawyer who always left home at the same time each morning may have been off to sell cheap neckties, magazines, vacuum cleaners, pressure cookers, or Two-in-One shoe polish door-to-door in a remote neighborhood. He may have changed his clothes and gone to another part of the city to beg. Or he may have been one of the millions who looked for work day after day, year after year, watching his children grow thinner and fighting despair in the night. There were certain skills developed by men who spent their days in the streets. You learned to pay for a nickel cup of coffee, to ask for another cup of hot water free, and, by mixing the hot water with the ketchup on the counter, to make a kind of tomato soup. In winter you stuffed newspapers under your shirt to ward off the cold; if you knew you would be standing for hours out-side an employment office, you wrapped burlap bags around your legs and tied them in place. Shoes were a special problem. Pasteboards could be used for inner soles, and some favored cotton in the heels to absorb the pounding of the concrete. But if a shoe was really gone, nothing worked. The pavement destroyed the cardboard and then the patch of sock next to it, snow leaked in and accumulated around your toes, and shoe nails stabbed your heels until you learned to walk with a peculiar gait.

It was remarkable how ingenious an impoverished, thrift-minded family could be. Men resharpened and reused old razor blades, rolled their own cigarettes or smoked Wings (ten cents a pack), and used twenty-five-watt light bulbs to save electricity. Children returned pop bottles for two cents or stood in line for day-old bread at the bakery. Women cut sheets lengthwise and resewed them to equalize wear, retailored their clothes for their daughters, and kept up a brave front with the wife next door—who may have been doing the same thing on the same meager budget. Families sorted Christmas cards so they could be sent to different friends next year. Sometimes a man would disappear for weeks. All the neighborhood knew was that he had gone on a "business trip." It was a considerate husband who withheld the details of such trips from his wife, for they were often more terrible than anything she could imagine.

He was, of course, looking for work. The legends of job hunting had become folklore by 1932, and some of the unbelievable stories were true. Men *did* wait all night outside Detroit employment offices so they would be first in line next morning. An Arkansas man did walk nine hundred miles looking for work. People *did* buy jobs. In Manhattan a Sixth Avenue employment agency *did* have five thousand applicants for three hundred jobs. It is a matter of record that a labor subcommittee of the 72nd Congress heard testimony about men setting forest fires in the state of Washington so they would be hired to put them out. *Business Week* verified the fact that a great many people who no longer loved America either left it or attempted to. Throughout the early Thirties the country's emigration exceeded its immigration. Amtorg, the Russian trading agency in New York, was getting 350 applications a day from Americans who wanted to settle in Russia. On one memorable occasion Amtorg advertised for six thousand skilled workers and a hundred thousand showed up, including plumbers, painters, mechanics, cooks, engineers, carpenters, electricians, salesmen, printers, chemists, shoemakers, librarians, teachers, dentists, a cleaner and dyer, an aviator, and an undertaker.

New York drew countless job seekers from surrounding states though the city had a million jobless men of its own. A few strangers joined Manhattan's seven thousand nickel shoeshine "boys" or found furtive roles in the bootleg coal racket—10 percent of the city's coal was being sneaked in by unemployed Pennsylvania miners—but most outsiders wound up on one of New York's eighty-two breadlines. If a man had a dime he could sleep in a flophouse reeking of sweat and Lysol. If he was broke he salvaged some newspapers and headed for Central Park, or the steps of a subway entrance, or the municipal incinerator. The incinerator's warmth drew hundreds of men on winter nights, even though they had to sleep on great dunes of garbage.

Returning from such an expedition in or under an empty freight car, a husband would review family assets with his wife and estimate how long they could keep going. Wedding rings would be sold, furniture pawned, life insurance borrowed upon, money begged from relatives. Often the next step was an attempt at a home business, with its implicit confession to the neighborhood that the pretense of solvency had been a hoax. The yard might be converted to a Tom Thumb miniature golf course. The husband might open a "parlor grocery." The wife might offer other wives a wash, set, and manicure for a dollar. In Massachusetts, idle textile workers erected looms in their living rooms; in Connecticut, households strung safety pins on wires, toiling long hours and earning a total of five dollars a week for an entire family.

These last-ditch efforts rarely succeeded; there were so few potential customers with money. Finally hope was abandoned. The father went to the city hall, declared himself penniless, and became a statistic. Because those figures were poorly kept, the precise extent of poverty is unknown. Somewhere between 15 million and 17 million men were unemployed, with most of them representing a family in want. *Fortune,* in September 1932, estimated that 34 million men, women, and children were without any income whatever. That was nearly 28 percent of the population, and like all other studies it omitted America's 11 million farm families, who were suffering in a rural Gethsemane of their own.

During the Nixon presidency, when America's farm population had shrunk to 5.2 percent of the population, it was hard to realize that only forty years earlier 25.1 percent had been living, or trying to live, on the land. They had not shared in New Era prosperity; the Crash merely worsened a situation which had already become a national scandal. By 1932 U.S. farmers had come to remind one reporter of Mongolian peasants seen in the rotogravure sections of Sunday newspapers, and the shadow of imminent famine fell across the plains. Agricultural prices hadn't been so low since the reign of Queen Elizabeth. Farmers were getting less than twenty-five cents for a bushel of wheat, seven cents for a bushel of corn, a dime for a bushel of oats, a nickel for a pound of cotton or wool. Sugar was bringing three cents a pound, hogs and beef two and a half cents a pound, and apples—provided they were flawless—forty cents for a box of two hundred.

Translated into the bitter sweat of rural life, this meant that a wagon of oats wouldn't buy a pair of four-dollar Thom McAn shoes. A wagon of wheat would just do it, but with mortgage interest running at $3.60 an acre, plus another $1.90 in taxes, the wheat farmer was losing $1.50 on every acre he reaped. In cotton fields the strongest and most agile man would toil from "can see" to "can't see"—fourteen hours of daylight—and receive sixty cents for the 300 pounds he had picked. It was cheaper to burn corn than sell it and buy coal. With meat bringing such ruinous prices, a man would spend $1.10 to ship a sheep to market, where it would return him less than $1.00. In Montana a rancher bought bullets on credit, spent two hours slaughtering a herd of livestock, and left it rotting in a canyon. It wasn't worth its feed. Turning away, he muttered to a reporter, "One way to beat the Depression, huh?"

As farm prices caved in, tens of thousands of mortgage foreclosure notices went up on gateposts and county courthouses. It has been estimated that one-fourth of the state of Mississippi was auctioned off. William Allen White, the Republican country editor who had pleaded with Hoover to come and see what was happening to the Middle West, wrote, "Every farmer, whether his farm is under mortgage or not, knows that with farm products priced as they are today, sooner or later he must go down." When the farmer did fail, unable to pay the small costs of binder twine, tool repair, and seed, the bank would take title as absentee landlord, and he would rent from it the land his family had owned for generations. Meantime, while ranchers fed mutton to buzzards and warmed their hands over corn fires, millions in the cities could not afford the low prices which were destroying farmers (butter at 39 cents a pound, prime rib roast at 21 cents, two dozen eggs for 41 cents) because so many were idle and those who had jobs were often earning what could only be called starvation wages.

There was no one to protect them. The President disapproved of wage cuts and said so, but he was equally opposed to wage-hour legislation, so that when U.S. Steel made its second big wage slash in the spring of 1932, the workers were helpless. The labor movement was almost extinct; AFL membership had dwindled from 4.1 million in 1920 to 2.2 million, about 6 percent of the work force. There were strikes of desperation in 1932. All were lost. Miners were paid $10.88 a month, were at the mercy of check-weight men, and were required to buy groceries at inflated prices in the company store; when they rebelled the protest was bloodily suppressed by armed strikebreakers backed by the National Guard. The United Mine Workers were too weak to offer the victims anything but sympathy.

In such New England mill towns as Lynn and Lowell, where only one worker in three was employed, men were treated like serfs; one of them left Manchester, New Hampshire, to apply for a job in New Haven, was arrested, brought before a judge on a charge of vagrancy, and ordered back to his Manchester mill. The immense pool of job seekers tempted employers to slash their wage bills again and again. Department stores paid clerks as little as five dollars a week. An investigation in Chicago disclosed that the majority of working girls were getting less than twenty-five cents an hour; for a fourth of them, it was less than a dime. In 1932 hourly rates had shrunk to ten cents in lumbering, seven-and-a-half cents in general contracting, six cents in brick and tile manufacturing, and five cents in sawmills. Before the Depression, Massachusetts textile mills rarely required skilled operators to be responsible for more than twenty looms eight hours a day. Then the mills introduced speed-ups and stretch-outs, and Louis Adamic saw teen-aged girls running thirty wide looms from before dawn until after sunset.

In the sweatshops of Brooklyn fifteen-year-olds were paid $2.78 a week. Women received as little as $2.39 for a fifty-hour week. In the summer of 1932 the Connecticut Commissioner of Labor reported that there were over a hundred shops in the state paying as little as sixty cents for a fifty-five-hour week. New York City was the worst sweat spot in that state, and its garment industry, employing fifty thousand women, was the most sweated trade. "Unscrupulous employers," *Time* reported, had "battered wages down to the Chinese coolie level." Hat makers crocheted hats for forty cents a dozen; in a week a worker could make two dozen. Apron girls were paid two-and-a-half cents an apron; they earned twenty cents a day. A slipper liner received twenty-one cents for lining seventy-two pairs; if she completed one slipper every forty-five seconds, she took home $1.05 after a nine-hour day. Girl cleaners in a pants factory were paid a half-cent for each garment they threaded and sponged. It was a five-minute operation; their income was six cents an hour. Honest employers could not survive that kind of competition. Welfare rolls grew longer and longer, the President continued to withhold federal help, and as the fourth Depression winter loomed the relief structure began to disintegrate.

When a senator declared the workers simply could not survive on one or two days' wages a week, President J. E. Edgerton of the National Association of Manufacturers said, "Why, I've never thought of paying men on the basis of what they need. I pay for efficiency. Personally, I attend to all those other things, social welfare stuff, in my church work." Doubtless he thought he did. As *Fortune* explained it, the theory was that now, as in the past, private charity and semipublic welfare groups could care for the old, the sick, and the indigent.

It wasn't working. The Depression, while multiplying the demands upon charities, had dried up their sources of contributions. By 1932, private help had dwindled to 6 percent of the money spent upon the needy, leaving some thirty million people to public welfare. Unfortunately, local governments couldn't handle the burden. State and city budgets had been in the red since 1930. About nine-tenths of municipal income came from taxation on real estate, which in terms of the Depression dollar was ludicrously overappraised. Landlords were liable to taxation if they held title to buildings; their inability to realize income from their houses was legally irrelevant, even when their tenants were on municipal relief, which never paid rentals. The landlords tried desperately to get their money. At first, in exasperation, they turned penniless occupants out. In New York there was hardly a block without a daily dispossession, and in Philadelphia so many families were put on the street that little girls invented a doll game called Eviction.

But empty tenements solved nothing; they merely contributed to the unpopularity of men of property while leaving tax bills unpaid. Eventually, as Professor Sumner H. Slichter of the Harvard Business School explained to the Senate Committee on Manufactures, there was "a more or less national moratorium on rents, insofar as the unemployed are concerned." Delinquent tax ratios hovered between 20 and 30 percent in metropolitan areas, and the cities, lacking this revenue, cut services. Roads were unpaved, sidewalks crumbled, streets blocked by winter snow were left unplowed. Chicago, deprived of two years' receipts by a taxpayers' strike, borrowed from the banks—and agonized over its unemployed population of 600,000.

Given the bankruptcy of public treasuries, and the widespread feeling that the poor were somehow responsible for their fate, it was inevitable that admittance to relief rolls would be made extremely difficult. Before applications were even considered, homes and possessions had to be sold, insurance canceled, credit exhausted, and evidence produced that all known relatives were broke. Even then, in many cities no assistance was granted to unmarried people or people without young children. Every possible stigma was attached to aid. In September 1932 Lewiston, Maine, voted to bar all welfare recipients from the polls, a goal already achieved by property requirements in the constitutions of ten states from Massachusetts to Oregon. West Virginia hospitals refused to admit patients unless payment for services was guaranteed; a referring physician suggested to one surgeon that he delay operating upon a child until the parents promised to pay $1000. Two doctors in Royce City, Texas, put the following advertisement in the local paper:

> TO WHOM IT MAY CONCERN: If you are expecting the stork to visit your home this year and he has to come by way of Royce City, he will have to bring a checkbook to pay his bill before delivery.

In some communities taxpayer associations tried to prevent welfare children from attending schools, and families receiving public assistance were known to have been excluded from churches.

Even those who surmounted all barriers found that the approval of a welfare application was exceptional. In mill towns, mining communities, and on sharecropper farms, *Fortune* reported, "relief is merely a name." In the cities only 25 percent of qualified families were getting some form of help. The mayor of Toledo said in 1932: "I have seen thousands of these defeated, discouraged, hopeless men and women, cringing and fawning as they come to ask for public aid. It is a spectacle of national degradation." Admittance to the rolls did not end the defeat, discouragement, and hopelessness. In Philadelphia a family of four was given $5.50 a week, which hardly encouraged the debauchery predicted by those who objected to the dole, and Philadelphia was munificent compared to New York ($2.39), Mississippi ($1.50) and Detroit ($0.60). At the most, assistance covered only food and fuel. Since welfare families had often been inadequately clothed before the Crash, their rags three winters later sometimes defied description. It was not uncommon to see the head of a family dressed like a vaudeville tramp, wearing a buttonless suit coat out at one elbow, a pair of trousers out at the knee and in the seat, an old summer cap that had hung for years in some furnace room, worn tennis shoes covered by patched rubbers, a pair of mismatched canvas gloves; the whole covered by a filthy old sheepskin.

Frequently public employees were almost indistinguishable from public wards, since money for both came from the same sources. As a rule community elders found a way to provide their policemen with decent uniforms, for it was a time of anxiety about public safety. This concern did not cover schoolteachers, who more than any other group were victims of local governments' inadequate tax base. At the beginning of the Depression they had been assessed part of their pay to finance soup kitchens. With the school population increasing by over two hundred thousand each year, further economies were inevitable. Desks were set up in corridors, in coal-heated portables, in tin shacks; courses in art and music were stricken from the curriculum; the same textbooks were handed down semester after semester, until they had become dog-eared, dirty, with pages defaced or missing. Classrooms became more and more crowded. Finally, the money to pay the teachers began to disappear.

By 1932, a third of a million children were out of school because of lack of funds. Teachers in Mississippi, northern Minnesota, Idaho, South Dakota, and Alabama managed to eat only by "boarding around" at the homes of parents. In Dayton, Ohio, schools were open only three days a week; in Arkansas over three hundred schools were closed ten months or more. In Kansas, twenty-five-cent wheat meant rural teachers were being paid $35 a month for an eight-month year—$280 a year. In Iowa they were receiving $40 a month, half the income Washington had said was necessary for industrial workers to exist. Akron owed its teachers $300,000, Youngstown $500,000, Detroit $800,000, and Chicago's debts to its teachers were more than 20 million dollars.

The story of the Chicago schools was a great Depression epic. Rather than see 500,000 children remain on the streets, the teachers hitchhiked to work, endured "payless paydays"—by 1932 they had received checks in only five of the last thirteen months—and accepted city scrip to be redeemed after the Depression, even though Chicago bankers would not accept it. Somehow the city found money to invest in its forthcoming World's Fair of 1933, when Sally Rand would gross $6000 a week, but it turned a deaf ear to the Board of Education. A thousand teachers were dismissed outright. Those who remained taught on at immense personal sacrifice. Collectively the 1400 teachers lost 759 homes. They borrowed $1,128,000 on their insurance policies and another $232,000 from loan sharks at annual interest rates of 42 percent, and although hungry themselves, they fed 11,000 pupils out of their thin pocketbooks.

Teachers, welfare workers, and policemen saw hardship at close range. Nobody called cops pigs in the early 1930s. Even when they were used to break strikes, it was widely acknowledged that they were as exploited as the workers. In New York, men on the beat had been distributing food in the most stricken neighborhoods since 1930. The money came from city employees, including themselves, who contributed 1 percent of their salaries; as Caroline Bird pointed out, this was "the first public confession of official responsibility for plain poverty, and it came, not from the top, but from the lowest civil servants, who worked down where the poor people were."

Once more the teachers bore witness to the worst, for the most heartbreaking Depression martyrs were in the classrooms. In October of that terrible year, a month before the presidential election, the New York City Health Department reported that over 20 percent of the pupils in the public schools were suffering from malnutrition. In the mining counties of Ohio, West Virginia, Illinois, Kentucky, and Pennsylvania, the secretary of the American Friends Service Committee told a congressional committee, the ratio was sometimes over 90 percent, with deprived children afflicted by "drowsiness, lethargy, and sleepiness," and "mental retardation." A teacher suggested that one little girl go home and eat something; the child replied, "I can't. This is my sister's day to eat." A little boy exhibited his pet rabbit to a visitor and the boy's sister whispered, "He thinks we aren't going to eat it, but we are." Lillian Wald, a social worker, asked in anguish, "Have you ever seen the uncontrolled trembling of parents who have starved themselves for weeks so that their children might not go hungry?" A bitter father said, "A worker's got no right to have kids any more," and a Massachusetts priest said, "One family I know has lived on lentils, nothing but lentils, all this year. They can't afford to buy bread. What is going to happen to our children?"

"Nobody is actually starving," President Hoover told reporters. "The hoboes, for example, are better fed than they have ever been. One hobo in New York got ten meals in one day." In September 1932 *Fortune* flatly called the President a liar and suggested that "twenty-five millions in want" might be a fairer description of the nation's economic health. Cases of starvation were being chronicled by *Fortune*, the *San Francisco Chronicle*, the *Atlantic*, the *New York Times*, and in congressional testimony. The New York City Welfare Council reported 29 victims of starvation and 110, mostly children, dead of malnutrition. Hoover simply hadn't seen the suffering, though he was not to be spared after his departure from the White House; on a fishing trip in the Rocky Mountains he was led by a native to a hut where one child had succumbed and seven others were dying of hunger.

Millions stayed alive by living like animals. In the Pennsylvania countryside they were eating wild weed-roots and dandelions; in Kentucky they chewed violet tops, wild onions, forget-me-nots, wild lettuce, and weeds which heretofore had been left to grazing cattle. City mothers hung around docks, waiting for spoiled produce to be discarded and then fighting homeless dogs for possession of it. After the vegetables had been loaded on trucks they would run alongside, ready to snatch up anything that fell off. A cook in a midwestern hotel put a pail of leftovers in the alley outside the kitchen; immediately a dozen men loomed out of the darkness to fight over it. In Long Beach, California, a sixty-six-year-old physician named Francis Everett Townsend glanced out his window while shaving and saw, among a group of refuse barrels, "three haggard very old women," as he later called them, "stooped with great age, bending over the barrels, clawing into the contents." Whole families were seen plunging into refuse dumps, gnawing at bones and watermelon rinds; a Chicago widow always removed her glasses so she wouldn't see the maggots. At night in New York Thomas Wolfe observed "the homeless men who prowled in the vicinity of restaurants, lifting the lids of garbage cans and searching around inside for morsels of rotten food." He saw them "everywhere, and noticed how their numbers increased during the hard and desperate days of 1932."

It was considered benevolent by well-to-do Americans that year to give your garbage to fellow countrymen who were famished. The Elks of Mount Kisco, New York, and the eating clubs of Princeton University instructed their servants to see that their leftovers reached the needy. The *Brooklyn Eagle* proposed a central depot where edible swill could be sent by charitable citizens and where the poor might apply for portions of it. In Oklahoma City John B. Nichlos, a gas company executive, worked out a plan under which restaurants, civic clubs, and hotel chefs would pack swill in "sanitary containers of five (5) gallons each," to be "labeled 'MEAT, BEANS, POTATOES, BREAD AND OTHER ITEMS.'" The Salvation Army would pick up the cans, the contents of which would then be distributed to jobless men who would first chop wood donated by—of all people—the farmers. "We expect a little trouble now and then from those who are not worthy of the support of the citizens," the gas man wrote Secretary of the Army Hurley, "but we must contend with such cases in order to take care of those who are worthy." Hurley thought it a marvelous idea, and urged the administration to adopt it. It was vetoed by the director of Hoover's Emergency Committee for Employment on the ground that the gesture might be misunderstood.

It never seems to have occurred to Nichlos, the *Eagle*, the Princetonians and the Elks that more dramatic solutions might lie ahead. But already there were those who pondered the contrast between the well-fed rich and the starving multitude, and who thought they saw the dark shadow of things to come. Thomas Wolfe would talk to the tragic men in New York's public toilets until he could not stand their anguish any more. Then he would mount the steps to the pavement twenty feet above and gaze out upon "the giant hackles of Manhattan shining coldly in the cruel brightness of the winter night. The Woolworth Building was not fifty yards away, and a little further down were the silvery spires and needles of Wall Street, great fortresses of stone and steel that housed enormous banks. The blind injustice of this . . . seemed the most brutal part of the whole experience, for there . . . in the cold moonlight, only a few blocks away from this abyss of human wretchedness and misery, blazed the pinnacles of power where a large section of the entire world's wealth was locked in mighty vaults."

QUESTIONS TO CONSIDER

1. What was the popular attitude toward poverty during the Depression?
2. What were some indications that people were eager to find work?
3. Who, according to prevailing theory, was supposed to take care of charity? What was wrong with this theory?
4. Do you see much evidence of attempts to cheat the welfare system?
5. What was President Hoover's response to public hunger?
6. Does the conclusion make you feel that you would have been interested in participating in some kind of revolt against the system in 1932? Why or why not? What actually happened in 1932?

10

The Achievement
of the New Deal

WILLIAM LEUCHTENBURG

Reprinted from Harvard Sitkoff, ed.,
*Fifty Years Later: The New Deal
Evaluated,* Knopf, 1985, by permission.

William Leuchtenburg (1922–   ), a longtime professor of history at the University of North Carolina, ranks as the top authority on Franklin Roosevelt's New Deal. His 1963 book, *Franklin D. Roosevelt and the New Deal, 1932–1940,* remains the finest one-volume treatment after forty years. *In the Shadow of FDR* (1983) traces the impact of that great president on his successors, down to Ronald Reagan, who paid tribute to him even while trying to undermine his legacy. Another of Leuchtenburg's books, *The Perils of Prosperity, 1914–1932,* has long been the most popular account of that period.

In this article, written in 1983 on the occasion of the fiftieth anniversary of the launching of the New Deal, Leuchtenburg takes issue both with radicals who denounce the New Deal for preserving the old capitalist system and with conservatives upset that FDR made the national government as powerful as he did. He argues that Roosevelt made substantial changes in the American system that greatly benefited the nation and its people. In particular, he notes that through the New Deal, the government took on responsibility for the downtrodden as never before. Its success at lifting workers into the middle class was, ironically, shown by New Deal Democrats who deserted their party for Ronald Reagan and the Republicans in the 1980s; they had "made it" and no longer needed as much help from Uncle Sam.

The New Deal revolutionized the two-party system in the United States. For the first time in a systematic way, the Democrats came to view the government as the solution to problems in society, especially economic problems, and took an active role in improving the lot of the common people. Republicans then and since have been more likely to see the government—big government—more as the problem than as the solution. The new attitudes were exemplified in the debate over New Deal relief programs. Herbert Hoover had resisted welfare, fearing that it would create dependence on the government that would be hard to overcome and would undermine people's character. Roosevelt argued that people were in need and should be helped, not least because the problems of the Depression were not of their making. He opposed handouts but instead proposed and implemented public works programs of bewildering variety to restore people's self-respect and productivity. Ever since, the Democrats have been the "big government" party and the Republicans have resisted that tendency. As you read about the programs of the New Deal, consider whether they were proper areas for government action or not. Has a stronger federal government, as Hoover feared, subverted the sense of personal responsibility so crucial to traditional conceptions of the national character? Your answer may say a lot about your political inclinations today.

The fiftieth anniversary of the New Deal, launched on March 4, 1933, comes at a time when it has been going altogether out of fashion. Writers on the left, convinced that the Roosevelt experiment was either worthless or pernicious, have assigned it to the dustbin of history. Commentators on the right, though far less conspicuous, see in the New Deal the origins of the centralized state they seek to dismantle. Indeed, the half-century of the age of Roosevelt is being commemorated in the presidency of Ronald Reagan, who, while never tiring of quoting FDR, insists that the New Deal derived from Italian fascism.

To be sure, the New Deal has always had its critics. In Roosevelt's own day Marxists said that the New Deal had not done anything for agriculture that an earthquake could not have done better at the same time that conservatives were saying that FDR was unprincipled. Hoover even called him "a chameleon on plaid." Most historians have long since accepted the fact that New Deal policies were sometimes inconsistent, that Roosevelt failed to grasp countercyclical fiscal theory, that recovery did not come until armaments orders fueled the economy, that the President was credited with certain reforms like insurance of bank deposits that he, in fact, opposed, that a number of New Deal programs, notably aid for the marginal farmer, were inadequately financed, and that some New Deal agencies discriminated against blacks.

During the 1960s historians not only dressed up these objections as though they were new revelations but carried their disappointment with contemporary liberalism to the point of arguing either that the New Deal was not just inadequate but actually malign or that the New Deal was so negligible as to constitute a meaningless episode. This estimate derived in large part from disaffection with the welfare state, which Herbert Marcuse in *One-Dimensional Man* characterized as "a state of unfreedom," and which, as one critic noted, some considered "the ultimate form of repressive super-ego." The New Deal was now perceived to be elitist, since it had neglected to consult the poor about what legislation they wanted, or to encourage the participation of ghetto-dwellers in decision-making. Roosevelt's policies, historians maintained, redounded to the benefit of those who already had advantages—wealthier staple farmers, organized workers, business corporations, the "deserving poor"—while displacing sharecroppers and neglecting the powerless. An "antirevolutionary response to a situation that had revolutionary potentialities," the New Deal, it was said, missed opportunities to nationalize the banks and restructure the social order. Even "providing assistance to the needy and . . . rescuing them from starvation" served conservative ends, historians complained, for these efforts "sapped organized radicalism of its waning strength and of its potential constituency among the unorganized and discontented." The Roosevelt Administration, it has been asserted, failed to achieve more than it did, not as a result of the strength of conservative opposition but because of the intellectual deficiencies of the New Dealers and because Roosevelt deliberately sought to save "large-scale corporate capitalism." In *Towards a New Past*, the New Left historian Barton Bernstein summed up this point of view: "The New Deal failed to solve the problem of depression, it failed to raise the impoverished, it failed to redistribute income, it failed to extend equality and generally countenanced racial discrimination and segregation."

Although the characterization of Bernstein as "New Left" suggests that he represents a deviant persuasion, the New Left perspective has, in fact, all but become the new orthodoxy, even though there is not yet any New Left survey of the domestic history of the United States in the 1930s. This emphasis has so permeated writing on the New Deal in the past generation that an instructor who wishes to assign the latest thought on the age of Roosevelt has a wide choice of articles and anthologies that document the errors of the New Deal but no assessment of recent vintage that explores its accomplishments.

The fiftieth anniversary of the New Deal provides the occasion for a modest proposal—that we reintroduce some tension into the argument over the interpretation of the Roosevelt years. If historians are to develop a credible synthesis, it is important to regain a sense of the achievement of the New Deal. As it now stands, we have a dialectic that is all antithesis with no thesis. The so-called "debate" about the New Deal is not truly a debate, for even some of the historians who dispute the New Left assertions agree that one can only take a melancholy view of the period. The single question asked is whether the failure of the New Deal was the fault of the Roosevelt Administration or the result of the strength of conservative forces beyond the government's control; the fact of failure is taken as the basic postulate. As a first step toward a more considered evaluation, one has to remind one's self not only of what the New Deal did not do but of what it achieved.

NEW DEAL CHANGES

Above all, one needs to recognize how markedly the New Deal altered the character of the State of America. Indeed, though for decades past European theorists had been talking about *der Staat,* there can hardly be said to have been a State in America in the full meaning of the term before the New Deal. If you had walked into any American town in 1932, you would have had a hard time detecting any sign of a federal presence, save perhaps for the post office and even many of today's post offices date from the 1930s. Washington rarely affected people's lives directly. There was no national old-age pension system, no federal unemployment compensation, no aid to dependent children, no federal housing, no regulation of the stock market, no withholding tax, no federal school lunch, no farm subsidy, no national minimum wage law, no welfare state. As late as Herbert Hoover's presidency, it was regarded as axiomatic that government activity should be minimal. In the pre-Roosevelt era, even organized labor and the National Conference of Social Workers opposed federal action on behalf of the unemployed. The New Deal sharply challenged these shibboleths. From 1933 to 1938, the government intervened in a myriad of ways from energizing the economy to fostering unionization.

In the First Hundred Days of 1933, the New Deal reversed the familiar assumptions in an electrifying manner. André Maurois has commented:

> One cannot help calling to mind, as one writes the history of these three crowded months, the Biblical account of the Creation. The first day, the Brain Trust put an embargo on gold; the second day, it peopled the forests; the third day, it created three point two beer; the fourth day, it broke the bonds that tied the dollar to gold; the fifth day, it set the farmers free; the sixth day, it created General Johnson, and then, looking upon what it had made of America, it saw that it was good.
>
> But it could not rest on the seventh day.

This vast expansion of government led inevitably to the concentration of much greater power in the presidency, whose authority was greatly augmented under FDR. Rexford Tugwell has written of Roosevelt: "No monarch, . . . unless it may have been Elizabeth or her magnificent Tudor father, or maybe Alexander or Augustus Caesar, can have given quite that sense of serene presiding, of gathering up into himself, of really representing, a whole people." The President became, in Sidney Hyman's words, "the chief economic engineer," to whom Congress naturally turned for the setting of economic policy. Roosevelt stimulated interest in public affairs by his fireside chats and freewheeling press conferences, shifted the balance between the White House and Capitol Hill by assuming the role of Chief Legislator, and eluded the routinized traditional departments by creating emergency agencies. In 1939 he established the Executive Office of the President, giving the Chief Executive a central staff office for the first time. "The verdict of history," wrote Clinton Rossiter, "will surely be that he left the Presidency a more splendid instrument of democracy than he found it."

To staff the national agencies, Roosevelt turned to a new class of people: the university-trained experts. Before FDR, professors had not had an important role in the national government, save briefly in World War I, but when Roosevelt ran for president in 1932, he recruited advisers, most of them from Columbia University, who supplied him with ideas and helped write his speeches. During the First Hundred Days, large numbers of professors, encouraged by FDR's reliance on the Brain Trust, flocked to Washington to draft New Deal legislation and to administer New Deal agencies. The radical literary critic Edmund Wilson wrote, "Everywhere in the streets and offices you run into old acquaintances: the editors and writers of the liberal press, the 'progressive' young instructors from the colleges, the intelligent foundation workers, the practical idealists of settlement houses." He added: "The bright boys of the Eastern universities, instead of being obliged to choose, as they were twenty years ago, between business, the bond-selling game and the field of foreign missions, can come on and get jobs in Washington."

The capital had hitherto thought of government workers largely as civil service employees awaiting the rise in grade that would permit them to buy a house in Chevy Chase and it scarcely knew what to make of the invasion of eager newcomers. Everybody wanted to know the professors, reported one magazine: "Office-seekers dog their footsteps. Hostesses vie to land them as guest of honor. Professors are the fad." "On a routine administration matter you go to a Cabinet member," observed a reporter, "but on matters of policy and the higher statesmanship you consult the professoriat." "All Washington is going to school to the professors," he noted. "Debutantes hang on their exposition of the quantitative theory of money, the law of diminishing returns, and the intricacies of foreign exchange. Bookstores are selling their books like hot cakes. Their works are not available at the Library of Congress, the volumes having been withdrawn by the Senators and Congressmen."

Some may doubt today whether it is always an unmitigated good to have "the best and the brightest" in seats of power, but in the 1930s this infusion of talent gave an élan to the national government that had been sorely missing in the past. The *New Republic* commented: "We have in Washington not a soggy and insensitive mass of dough, as in some previous administrations, but a nervous, alert and hard-working group who are doing their level best to effectuate a program." Friends of Roosevelt's, like Felix Frankfurter, sent to Washington a cadre of brilliant young lawyers—men like David Lilienthal and Jerome Frank—who, immensely confident of their ability, generated new ideas, tested novel methods, and conveyed an infectious enthusiasm for the possibilities of government.

This corps of administrators made it possible for Roosevelt to carry out a major change in the role of the federal government. Although the New Deal always operated within a capitalist matrix and the government sought to enhance profitmaking, Roosevelt and his lieutenants rejected the traditional view that government was the handmaiden of business or that government and business were coequal sovereigns. As a consequence, they adopted measures to discipline corporations, to require a sharing of authority with government and unions, and to hold businessmen accountable. In the early days of the National Recovery Administration, the novelist Sherwood Anderson wrote:

> I went to several code hearings. No one has quite got their significance. Here for the first time you see these men of business, little ones and big ones, . . . coming up on the platform to give an accounting. It does seem the death knell of the old idea that a man owning a factory, office or store has a right to run it in his own way.
> There is at least an effort to relate it now to the whole thing, man's relations with his fellow men etc. Of course it is crude and there will be no end to crookedness, objections, etc. but I do think an entire new principle in American life is being established.

Through a series of edicts and statutes, the administration invaded the realm of the banker by establishing control over the nation's money supply. The government clamped an embargo on gold, took the United States off the gold standard, and nullified the requirement for the payment of gold in private contracts. In 1935 a resentful Supreme Court sustained this authority, although a dissenting justice said that this was Nero at his worst. The Glass-Steagall Banking Act (1933) stripped commercial banks of the privilege of engaging in investment banking, and established federal insurance of bank deposits, an innovation which the leading monetary historians have called "the structural change most conducive to monetary stability since bank notes were taxed out of existence immediately after the Civil War." The Banking Act of 1935 gave the United States what other industrial nations had long had, but America lacked—central banking. This series of changes transformed the relationship between the government and the financial community from what it had been when Grover Cleveland had gone, hat in hand, to beseech J. P. Morgan for help. As Charles Beard observed: "Having lost their gold coins and bullion to the Federal Government and having filled their vaults with federal bonds and other paper, bankers have become in a large measure mere agents of the Government in Washington. No longer do these powerful interests stand, so to speak, 'outside the Government' and in a position to control or dictate to it."

A number of other enactments helped transfer authority from Wall Street to Washington. The Securities Act of 1933 established government supervision of the issue of securities, and made company directors civilly and criminally liable for misinformation on the statements they were required to file with each new issue. The Securities and Exchange Act of 1934 initiated federal supervision of the stock exchanges, which to this day operate under the lens of the Securities and Exchange Commission (SEC). The Holding Company Act of 1935 leveled some of the utility pyramids, dissolving all utility holding companies that were more than twice removed from their operating companies, and increased the regulatory powers of the SEC over public utilities. Robert Sobel has concluded that the 1934 law marked "a shift of economic power from the lower part of Manhattan, where it had been for over a century, to Washington." To be sure, financiers continued to make important policy choices, but they never again operated in the uninhibited universe of the Great Bull Market. By the spring of 1934, one writer was already reporting:

> Financial news no longer originates in Wall Street. . . . News of a financial nature in Wall Street now is merely an echo of events which take place in Washington. . . . The pace of the ticker is determined now in Washington not in company boardrooms or in brokerage offices. . . . In Wall Street it is no longer asked what some big trader is doing, what some important banker thinks, what opinion some eminent lawyer holds about some pressing question of the day. The query in Wall Street has become: "What's the news from Washington?"

The age of Roosevelt focused attention on Washington, too, by initiatives in fields that had been regarded as exclusively within the private orbit, notably in housing. The Home Owners' Loan Corporation, created in 1933, saved tens of thousands of homes from foreclosure by refinancing mortgages. In 1934 the Federal Housing Administration (FHA) began its program of insuring loans for the construction and renovation of private homes, and over the next generation more than 10 million FHA-financed units were built. Before the New Deal, the national government had never engaged in public housing, except for the World War I emergency, but agencies like the Public Works Administration now broke precedent. The Tennessee Valley Authority laid out the model town of Norris, the Federal Emergency Relief Administration (FERA) experimented with subsistence homesteads, and the Resettlement Administration created greenbelt communities, entirely new towns girdled by green countryside. When in 1937 the Wagner-Steagall Act created the U.S. Housing Authority, it assured public housing a permanent place in American life.

A NEW DEAL FOR THE COMMON MAN

The New Deal profoundly altered industrial relations by throwing the weight of government behind efforts to unionize workers. At the outset of the Great Depression, the American labor movement was "an anachronism in the world," for only a tiny minority of factory workers were unionized. Employers hired and fired and imposed punishments at will, used thugs as strikebreakers and private police, stockpiled industrial munitions, and ran company towns as feudal fiefs. In an astonishingly short period in the Roosevelt years a very different pattern emerged. Under the umbrella of Section 7(a) of the National Industrial Recovery Act of 1933 and of the far-reaching Wagner Act of 1935, union organizers gained millions of recruits in such open-shop strongholds as steel, automobiles, and textiles. Employees won wage rises, reductions in hours, greater job security, freedom from the tyranny of company guards, and protection against arbitrary punishment. Thanks to the National Recovery Administration and the Guffey acts, coal miners achieved the outlawing of compulsory company houses and stores. Steel workers, who in 1920 labored twelve-hour shifts seven days a week at the blast furnaces, were to become so powerful that in the postwar era they would win not merely paid vacations but sabbatical leaves. A British analyst has concluded: "From one of the most restrictive among industrially advanced nations, the labour code of the United States (insofar as it could be said to exist before 1933) was rapidly transformed into one of the most liberal," and these reforms, he adds, "were not the harvest of long-sustained agitation by trade unions, but were forced upon a partly skeptical labor movement by a government which led or carried it into maturity."

Years later, when David E. Lilienthal, the director of the Tennessee Valley Authority, was being driven to the airport to fly to Roosevelt's funeral, the TVA driver said to him:

> I won't forget what he did for me. . . . I spent the best years of my life working at the Appalachian Mills . . . and they didn't even treat us like humans. If you didn't do like they said, they always told you there was someone else to take your job. I had my mother and my sister to take care of. Sixteen cents an hour was what we got; a fellow can't live on that, and you had to get production even to get that, this Bedaux system; some fellows only got twelve cents. If you asked to get off on a Sunday, the foreman would say, "All right you stay away Sunday, but when you come back Monday someone else will have your job." No, sir, I won't forget what he done for us.

Helen Lynd has observed that the history of the United States is that of England fifty years later, and a half century after the welfare state had come to Western Europe, the New Deal brought it to America. The NRA wiped out sweatshops, and removed some 150,000 child laborers from factories.

The Walsh-Healey Act of 1936 and the Fair Labor Standards Act of 1938 established the principle of a federally imposed minimal level of working conditions, and added further sanctions against child labor. If the New Deal did not do enough for the "one-third of a nation" to whom Roosevelt called attention, it at least made a beginning, through agencies like the Farm Security Administration, toward helping sharecroppers, tenant farmers, and migrants like John Steinbeck's Joads. Most important, it originated a new system of social rights to replace the dependence on private charity. The Social Security Act of 1935 created America's first national system of old-age pensions and initiated a federal-state program of unemployment insurance. It also authorized grants for the blind, for the incapacitated, and for dependent children, a feature that would have unimaginable long-range consequences.

The veteran social worker Grace Abbott, in explaining why, as a lifelong Republican, she was voting for Roosevelt in 1936, said that greater progress had been made in security for children "during the past three years than the previous thirty years." She added: "The support of the Child Labor Amendment by the President and his cabinet, the raising of Child Labor standards under the N.R.A., the inclusion of the sugar beet children in the benefits of the Costigan Sugar Act and the President's own pet project—the C.C.C. Camps—now so largely filled by young men and boys are also concrete evidence that the President considers the welfare of children of national importance."

Roosevelt himself affirmed the newly assumed attitudes in Washington in his annual message to Congress in 1938 when he declared: "Government has a final responsibility for the well-being of its citizenship. If private cooperative endeavor fails to provide work for willing hands and relief for the unfortunate, those suffering hardship from no fault of their own have a right to call upon the Government for aid; and a government worthy of its name must make fitting response."

A NEW DEAL FOR THE UNEMPLOYED

Nothing revealed this approach so well as the New Deal's attention to the plight of the millions of unemployed. During the ten years between 1929 and 1939, one scholar has written, "more progress was made in public welfare and relief than in the three hundred years after this country was first settled." A series of alphabet agencies—the FERA, the CWA, the WPA—provided government work for the jobless, while the National Youth Administration (NYA) employed college students in museums, libraries, and laboratories, enabled high school students to remain in school, and set up a program of apprentice training. In Texas, the twenty-seven-year-old NYA director Lyndon Johnson put penniless young men like John Connally to work building roadside parks, and in North Carolina, the NYA employed, at 35 cents an hour, a Duke University law student, Richard Nixon.

In an address in Los Angeles in 1936, the head of FDR's relief operations, Harry Hopkins, conveyed the attitude of the New Deal toward those who were down and out:

> I am getting sick and tired of these people on the W.P.A. and local relief rolls being called chiselers and cheats. . . . These people . . . are just like the rest of us. They don't drink any more than us, they don't lie any more, they're no lazier than the rest of us—they're pretty much a cross section of the American people. . . . I have never believed that with our capitalistic system people have to be poor. I think it is an outrage that we should permit hundreds and hundreds of thousands of people to be ill clad, to live in miserable homes, not to have enough to eat; not to be able to send their children to school for the only reason that they are poor. I don't believe ever again in America we are going to permit the things to happen that have happened in the past to people. We are never going back . . . to the days of putting the old people in the alms houses, when a decent dignified pension at home will keep them there. We are coming to the day when we are going to have decent houses for the poor, when there is genuine and real security for everybody. I have gone all over the moral hurdles that people are poor because they are bad. I don't believe it. A system of government on that basis is fallacious.

Under the leadership of men like Hopkins, "Santa Claus incomparable and privy-builder without peer," projects of relief agencies and of the Public Works Administration (PWA) changed the face of the land. The PWA built thoroughfares like the Skyline Drive in Virginia and the Overseas Highway from Miami to Key West, constructed the Medical Center in Jersey City, burrowed Chicago's new subway, and gave Natchez, Mississippi, a new bridge, and Denver a modern water-supply system. Few New Yorkers today realize the long reach of the New Deal. If they cross the Triborough Bridge, they are driving on a bridge the PWA built. If they fly into La Guardia Airport, they are landing at an airfield laid out by the WPA. If they get caught in a traffic jam on the FDR Drive, they are using yet another artery built by the WPA. Even the animal cages in the Central Park Zoo were reconstructed by WPA workers. In New York City, the WPA built or renovated hundreds of school buildings; gave Orchard Beach a bathhouse, a mall, and a lagoon; landscaped Bryant Park and the campus of Hunter College in the Bronx; conducted examinations for venereal disease, filled teeth, operated pollen count stations, and performed puppet shows for disturbed children; it built dioramas for the Brooklyn Museum; ran street dances in Harlem and an open-air night club in Central Park; and, by combing neglected archives, turned up forgotten documents like the court proceedings in the Aaron Burr libel case and the marriage license issued to Captain Kidd. In New York City alone the WPA employed more people than the entire War Department.

Though much of the makework inevitably concentrated on operations like road building, the Roosevelt government proved ingenious in devising other activities. Years later, John Steinbeck recalled:

> When W.P.A. came, we were delighted, because it offered work. . . . I was given the project of taking a census of all the dogs on the Monterey Peninsula, their breeds, weight and characters. I did it very thoroughly and, since I knew my reports were not likely to get to the hands of the mighty, I wrote some pretty searching character studies of poodles, and beagles and hounds. If such records were kept, somewhere in Washington, there will be a complete dog record of the Monterey Peninsula in the early Thirties.

The New Deal showed unusual sensitivity toward jobless white-collar workers, notably those in aesthetic fields. The Public Works of Art Project gave an opportunity to muralists eager for a chance to work in the style of Rivera, Orozco, and Siqueiros. The Federal Art Project fostered the careers of painters like Stuart Davis, Raphael Soyer, Yasuo Kuniyoshi, and Jackson Pollock. Out of the same project came a network of community art centers and the notable *Index of American Design*. A generation later the sculptor Louise Nevelson, summed it up what it meant:

> When I came back from Germany where I studied with Hans Hoffman . . . I got on the WPA. Now that gave me a certain kind of freedom and I think that our great artists like Rothko, de Kooning, Franz Kline, all these people that have promise today and are creative, had that moment of peace . . . to continue with their work. So, I feel that that was a great benefit, a great contribution to our creative people and very important in the history of art. And not only in the visual arts but in the theater, and the folk arts, there wasn't a thing that they didn't touch on. . . . At that period, people in our country didn't have jobs and the head of government was able so intelligently to use mankind and manpower. I think it's a high-light of our American history.

The Federal Writers' Project provided support for scores of talented novelists and poets, editors and literary critics, men like Ralph Ellison and Nelson Algren, John Cheever and Saul Bellow. These writers turned out an exceptional set of state guides, with such features as Conrad Aiken's carefully delineated portrayal of Deerfield, Massachusetts, and special volumes like *These Are Our Lives,* a graphic portfolio of life histories in North Carolina, and *Panorama,* in which Vincent McHugh depicts "the infinite pueblo of the Bronx." Project workers transcribed chain-gang blues songs, recovered folklore that would otherwise have been lost, and collected the narratives of elderly former slaves, an invaluable archive later published in *Lay My Burden Down.* When the magazine *Story* conducted a contest for the best contribution by a Project employee, the prize was won by an unpublished 29-year-old black who had been working on the essay on the Negro for the Illinois guide. With the prize money for his stories, subsequently published as *Uncle Tom's Children*, Richard Wright gained the time to complete his remarkable first novel, *Native Son*.

Some thought it an ill omen that the Federal Theatre Project's first production was Shakespeare's *Comedy of Errors*, but that agency not only gave employment to actors and stage technicians but offered many communities their first glimpse of live drama. The "boy wonder" Orson Welles directed and acted in the Federal Theatre, which also discovered such unknowns as Joseph Cotten. Its Dance Group revealed the virtuosity of Katherine Dunham, Doris Humphrey, and Charles Weidman. The Federal Theatre sponsored the first U.S. presentation of T. S. Eliot's *Murder in the Cathedral*, and its Detroit unit staged the original professional production of Arthur Miller's first play.

If the creation of America's first state theatre was an unusual departure, the New Deal's ventures in documentary films seemed no less surprising. With Resettlement Administration funds, Pare Lorentz produced *The Plow That Broke the Plains* in 1936 and the classic *The River* in 1937. He engaged cameramen like Paul Strand, who had won acclaim for his movie on a fisherman's strike in Mexico; invited the young composer Virgil Thomson, who had just scored Gertrude Stein's *Four Saints in Three Acts*, to compose the background music; and employed Thomas Chalmers, who had sung at the Metropolitan Opera in the era of Caruso, to read the narration. American government documentaries before the New Deal had been limited to short subjects on topics like the love life of the honeybee. *The River*, which won first prize in Venice at the International Exposition of Cinematographic Art in 1938, proved that there was an audience in the United States for wellwrought documentaries. By 1940 it had drawn more than 10 million people, while *The Plow That Broke the Plains*, said one critic, made "the rape of millions of acres . . . more moving than the downfall of a Hollywood blonde."

Lorentz's films suggest the concern of the New Deal for the American land. Roosevelt, it has been said, had a "proprietary interest in the nation's estate," and this helps account for the fact that the 1930s accomplished for soil conservation and river valley development what the era of Theodore Roosevelt had done for the forests. The Tennessee Valley Authority, which drew admirers from all over the world, put the national government in the business of generating electric power, controlled floods, terraced hillsides, and gave new hope to the people of the valley. In the Pacific Northwest the PWA constructed mammoth dams, Grand Coulee and Bonneville. Roosevelt's "tree army," the Civilian Conservation Corps, planted millions of trees, cleared forest trails, laid out picnic sites and campgrounds, and aided the Forest Service in the vast undertaking of establishing a shelterbelt—a windbreak of trees and shrubs: green ash and Chinese elm, apricot and blackberry, buffalo berry and Osage orange from the Canadian border to the

Texas panhandle. Government agencies came to the aid of drought-stricken farmers in the Dust Bowl, and the Soil Conservation Service, another New Deal creation, instructed growers in methods of cultivation to save the land. As Alistair Cooke later said, the favorite of the New Dealers was the farmer with the will to "take up contour plowing late in life."

These services to farmers represented only a small part of the government's program, for in the New Deal years, the business of agriculture was revolutionized. Roosevelt came to power at a time of mounting desperation for American farmers. Each month in 1932 another 20,000 farmers had lost their land because of inability to meet their debts in a period of collapsing prices. On a single day in May 1932, one-fourth of the state of Mississippi went under the sheriff's hammer. The Farm Credit Administration of 1933 came to the aid of the beleaguered farmer, and within eighteen months, it had refinanced one-fifth of all farm mortgages in the United States. In the Roosevelt years, too, the Rural Electrification Administration literally brought rural America out of darkness. At the beginning of the Roosevelt era, only one farm in nine had electricity; at the end, only one in nine did not have it. But more important than any of these developments was the progression of enactments starting with the first AAA (the Agricultural Adjustment Act) of 1933, which began the process of granting large-scale subsidies to growers. As William Faulkner later said, "Our economy is not agricultural any longer. Our economy is the federal government. We no longer farm in Mississippi cotton fields. We farm now in Washington corridors and Congressional committee rooms."

GOVERNMENT OF AND FOR MORE OF THE PEOPLE

At the same time that its realm was being expanded under the New Deal, the national government changed the composition of its personnel and of its beneficiaries. Before 1933, the government had paid heed primarily to a single group—white Anglo-Saxon Protestant males. The Roosevelt Administration, however, recruited from a more ethnically diverse group, and the prominence of Catholics and Jews among the President's advisers is suggested by the scintillating team of the Second Hundred Days, Corcoran and Cohen. The Federal Writers' Project turned out books on Italians and Albanians, and the Federal Theatre staged productions in Yiddish and wrote a history of the Chinese stage in Los Angeles. In the 1930s women played a more prominent role in government than they ever had before, as the result of such appointments as that of Frances Perkins as the first female cabinet member, while the influence of Eleanor Roosevelt was pervasive.

Before Eleanor Roosevelt, First Ladies had been content to preside over the social functions of the White House. But by 1940 Mrs. Roosevelt had travelled more than 250,000 miles, written 1 million words, and become the leading advocate within the administration for the underprivileged, especially blacks and unemployed youth. No one knew where she would turn up next. In the most famous cartoon of the decade, a begrimed coal miner in the bowels of the earth cries out in astonishment to a fellow miner, "For gosh sakes, here comes Mrs. Roosevelt." Admiral Byrd, it was said, always set up two places for dinner at the South Pole "in case Eleanor should drop in." She was renowned for her informality. When the King and Queen of England visited America, she served them hot dogs and beer, and when during World War II, she travelled to Australia and New Zealand, she greeted her Maori guide by rubbing noses. No one captured the goals of the New Deal better than Eleanor Roosevelt. "As I have said all along," she remarked, "you have got to have the kind of country in which people's daily chance convinces them that democracy is a good thing."

Although in some respects the New Deal's performance with regard to blacks added to the sorry record of racial discrimination in America, important gains were also registered in the 1930s. Blacks, who had often been excluded from relief in the past, now received a share of WPA jobs considerably greater than their proportion of the population. Blacks moved into federal housing projects; federal funds went to schools and hospitals in black neighborhoods; and New Deal agencies like the Farm Security Administration (FSA) enabled 50,000 Negro tenant farmers and sharecroppers to become proprietors. "Indeed," one historian has written, "there is a high correlation between the location of extensive FSA operations in the 1930s and the rapidity of political modernization in black communities in the South in the 1960s." Roosevelt appointed a number of blacks, including William Hastie, Mary McLeod Bethune, and Robert Weaver, to high posts in the government. Negroes in the South who were disenfranchised in white primaries voted in AAA crop referenda and in National Labor Relations Board plant elections, and a step was taken toward restoring their constitutional rights when Attorney General Frank Murphy set up a Civil Liberties Unit in the Department of Justice. The reign of Jim Crow in Washington offices, which had begun under Roosevelt's Democratic predecessor, Woodrow Wilson, was terminated by Secretary of the Interior Harold Ickes who desegregated cafeterias in his department. Ickes also had a role in the most dramatic episode of the times, for when the Daughters of the American Revolution (DAR) denied the use of their concert hall to the black contralto Marian Anderson, he made it possible for her to sing before thousands from the steps of Lincoln Memorial; and Mrs. Roosevelt joined in the rebuke to the DAR. Anderson's concert on Easter Sunday 1939 was heard by thousands at the Memorial, and three networks carried her voice to millions more. Blacks delivered their own verdict on the New Deal at the polling places. Committed to the party of Lincoln as late as 1932, when they voted overwhelmingly for Hoover, they shifted in large numbers to the party of FDR during Roosevelt's first term. This was a change of allegiance that many whites were also making in those years.

TIIE DURABLE LEGACY OF THE NEW DEAL

The Great Depression and the New Deal brought about a significant political realignment of the sort that occurs only rarely in America. The Depression wrenched many lifelong Republican voters from their moorings. In 1928, one couple christened their newborn son "Herbert Hoover Jones." Four years later they petitioned the court, "desiring to relieve the young man from the chagrin and mortification which he is suffering and will suffer," and asked that his name be changed to Franklin D. Roosevelt Jones. In 1932 FDR became the first Democrat to enter the White House with as much as 50 percent of the popular vote in eighty years—since Franklin K. Pierce in 1852. Roosevelt took advantage of this opportunity to mold "the FDR coalition," an alliance centered in the low-income districts of the great cities and, as recently as the 1980 election, the contours of the New Deal coalition could still be discerned. Indeed, over the past half-century, the once overpowering Republicans have won control of Congress only twice, for a total of four years. No less important was the shift in the character of the Democratic party from the conservative organization of John W. Davis and John J. Raskob to the country's main political instrumentality for reform. "One political result of the Roosevelt years," Robert Burke has observed, "was a basic change in the nature of the typical Congressional liberal." He was no longer a maverick, who made a fetish of orneriness, no longer one of the men Senator Moses called "the sons of the wild jackass," but "a party Democrat, labor-oriented, urban, and internationalist-minded."

Furthermore, the New Deal drastically altered the agenda of American politics. When Arthur Krock of the *New York Times* listed the main programmatic questions before the 1932 Democratic convention, he wrote: "What would be said about the repeal of prohibition that had split the Republicans? What would be said about tariffs?" By 1936, these concerns seemed altogether old fashioned, as campaigners discussed the Tennessee Valley Authority and industrial relations, slum clearance and aid to the jobless. That year, a Little Rock newspaper commented: "Such matters as tax and tariff laws have given way to universally human things, the living problems and opportunities of the average man and the average family."

The Roosevelt years changed the conception of the role of government not just in Washington but in the states, where a series of "Little New Deals"—under governors like Herbert Lehman in New York—added a thick sheaf of social legislation, and in the cities. In Boston, Charles Trout has observed, city council members in 1929 "devoted endless hours to street paving." After the coming of the New Deal, they were absorbed with NRA campaigns, public housing, and WPA allotments. "A year after the crash the council thought 5,000 dollars an excessive appropriation for the municipal employment bureau," but during the 1930s "the unemployed drained Boston's treasury of not less than 100,000,000 dollars in direct benefits, and the federal government spent even more."

In a cluster of pathbreaking decisions in 1937, the Supreme Court legitimized this vast exercise of authority by government at all levels. As late as 1936, the Supreme Court still denied the power of the United States government to regulate agriculture, even though crops were sold in a world market, or coal mining, a vital component of a national economy, and struck down a minimum wage law as beyond the authority of the state of New York. Roosevelt responded with a plan to "pack" the Court with as many as six additional Justices, and in short order the Court, in what has been called "the Constitutional Revolution of 1937," sounded retreat. Before 1937 the Supreme Court stood as a formidable barrier to social reform. Since 1937 not one piece of significant social legislation has been invalidated, and the Court has shifted its docket instead to civil rights and civil liberties.

What then did the New Deal do? It gave far greater amplitude to the national state, expanded the authority of the presidency, recruited university-trained administrators, won control of the money supply, established central banking, imposed regulation on Wall Street, rescued the debt-ridden farmer and homeowner, built model communities, financed the Federal Housing Administration, made federal housing a permanent feature, fostered unionization of the factories, reduced child labor, ended the tyranny of company towns, wiped out many sweatshops, mandated minimal working standards, enabled tenants to buy their own farms, built camps for migrants, introduced the welfare state with old-age pensions, unemployment insurance, and aid for dependent children, provided jobs for millions of unemployed, created a special program for the jobless young and for students, covered the American landscape with new edifices, subsidized painters and novelists, composers and ballet dancers, founded America's first state theater, created documentary films, gave birth to the impressive Tennessee Valley Authority, generated electrical power, sent the Civilian Conservation Corps boys into the forest, initiated the Soil Conservation Service, transformed the economy of agriculture, lighted up rural America, gave women greater recognition, made a start toward breaking the pattern of racial discrimination and segregation, put together a liberal party coalition, changed the agenda of American politics, and brought about a Constitutional Revolution.

But even this summary does not account for the full range of its activities. The New Deal offered the American Indian new opportunities for self-government and established the Indian Arts and Crafts Board, sponsored vaudeville troupes and circuses, taught counterpoint and solfeggio, was responsible for the founding of the Buffalo Philharmonic, the Oklahoma Symphony, and the Utah State Symphony, served hot lunches to school children and set up hundreds of nursery schools, sent bookmobiles into isolated communities, and where there were no roads, had books carried in by pack-horses. And only a truly merciful and farsighted government would have taken such special pains to find jobs for unemployed historians.

The New Deal accomplished all of this at a critical time, when many were insisting that fascism was the wave of the future and denying that democracy could be effective. For those throughout the world who heard such jeremiads with foreboding, the American experience was enormously inspiriting. A decade after the end of the age of Roosevelt, Sir Isaiah Berlin wrote:

> When I say that some men occupy one's imagination for many years, this is literally true of Mr. Roosevelt and the young men of my own generation in England, and probably in many parts of Europe, and indeed the entire world. If one was young in the thirties, and lived in a democracy, then, whatever one's policies, if one had human feelings at all, the faintest spark of social idealism, or any love of life whatever, one must have felt very much as young men in Continental Europe probably felt after the defeat of Napoleon during the years of the Restoration; that all was dark and quiet, a great reaction was abroad, and little stirred, and nothing resisted.

In these "dark and leaden thirties," Professor Berlin continued, "the only light in the darkness that was left was the administration of Mr. Roosevelt and the New Deal in the United States. At a time of weakness and mounting despair in the democratic world Mr. Roosevelt radiated confidence and strength. . . . Even to-day, upon him alone, of all the statesmen of the thirties, no cloud rested neither on him nor on the New Deal, which to European eyes still looks a bright chapter in the history of mankind."

For the past generation, America has lived off the legacy of the New Deal. Successive administrations extended the provisions of statutes like the Social Security Act, adopted New Deal attitudes toward intervention in the economy to cope with recessions, and put New Deal ideas to modern purposes, as when the Civilian Conservation Corps served as the basis for both the Peace Corps and the VISTA program of the War on Poverty. Harry Truman performed under the shadow of FDR, Lyndon Johnson consciously patterned his administration on Roosevelt's, Jimmy Carter launched his first presidential campaign at Warm Springs, and Ronald Reagan has manifested an almost obsessive need to summon FDR to his side. Carl Degler has observed:

> Conventionally the end of the New Deal is dated with the enactment of the Wages and Hours Act of 1938. But in a fundamental sense the New Deal did not end then at all. Americans still live in the era of the New Deal, for its achievements are now the base mark below which no conservative government may go and from which all new reform now starts. . . . The reform efforts of the Democratic Truman, Kennedy, and Johnson administrations have been little more than fulfillments of the New Deal.

The British historian David K. Adams has pointed out that the philosophy of the New Frontier has "conscious overtones of the New Deal" and indeed that John Kennedy's "New Frontier" address of 1960 was "almost a para-phrase" of an FDR speech of 1935. Theodore White has commented that both John and Robert Kennedy shared sentences from a Roosevelt address that reporters called the "Dante sequence." When at a loss for words, each was wont to quote a favorite passage from Franklin Roosevelt: "Govern-ments can err, Presidents do make mistakes, but the immortal Dante tells us that Divine Justice weighs the sins of the cold-blooded and the sins of the warm-hearted on a different scale. Better the occasional faults of a govern-ment living in the spirit of charity, than the consistent omissions of a govern-ment frozen in the ice of its own indifference."

By restoring to the debate over the significance of the New Deal acknowledgement of its achievements, we may hope to produce a more judicious estimate of where it succeeded and where it failed. For it unques-tionably did fail in a number of respects. There were experiments of the 1930s which miscarried, opportunities that were fumbled, groups who were neglected, and power that was arrogantly used. Over the whole perfor-mance lies the dark cloud of the persistence of hard times. The shortcomings of the New Deal are formidable, and they must be recognized. But I am not persuaded that the New Deal experience was negligible. Indeed, it is hard to think of another period in the whole history of the republic that was so fruit-ful or of a crisis that was met with as much imagination.

QUESTIONS TO CONSIDER

1. What criticisms of New Deal policies have historians long since accepted?
2. What moves did Roosevelt make to enhance the power of the presidency?
3. What New Deal programs especially benefited the common man?
4. What out-groups became more accepted under the New Deal?
5. What, then, did the New Deal do? Which of its accomplishments do you feel was most vital to the national well-being? Why?
6. How has this article affected your view of the New Deal?

11

The Centrality of the Bomb

GAR ALPEROVITZ AND KAI BIRD

Reprinted with permission from
Foreign Policy 94 (Spring 1994).
Copyright 1994 by the
Carnegie Endowment for
International Peace.

In 1945, the United States, United Kingdom, and USSR wound up a successful wartime alliance against the Axis powers, Germany, Japan, and Italy. By 1950, in a truly Orwellian switch (in fact, George Orwell wrote *1984* during this period), the United States and the United Kingdom counted Germany, Japan, and Italy as allies and condemned the USSR and their erstwhile ally China as enemies. Why had this dramatic change occurred? Why had the alliances of World War II been transformed into the new alignments of the Cold War? Who or what was at fault for the much-anticipated postwar peace giving way to a military arms race between East and West?

In this article, two analysts suggest that the atomic bomb—in particular, the American monopoly of the weapon from 1945 to 1949—determined the course of superpower relations in the years after World War II. Possession of the bomb freed President Harry Truman from the need to cooperate with the Soviet Union to ensure peace in Europe and thus led him into much more confrontational policies than would have been the case otherwise. With regard to the American character, the obvious question that arises is what sort of impact world power would have on it. Would the nation continue to show what Jefferson termed a "decent respect for the opinions of mankind," or would it become an international bully? Questions of this nature, first seriously raised in the context of the Spanish-American War in 1898 would haunt the world's most powerful nation after World War II.

Gar Alperovitz, president of the National Center for Economic Alternatives and a fellow of the Institute for Policy Studies, wrote the controversial *Atomic Diplomacy: Hiroshima and Potsdam* in 1965, advancing the argument that the bomb had been used not primarily to defeat Japan but to influence the Soviet Union's behavior after the war. That view has won at least partial, grudging acceptance by many historians. In 1995, he wrote the massive *The Decision to Use the Atomic Bomb and the Architecture of an American Myth*, further developing his theme. Kai Bird is the author of *John J. McCloy: The Making of the American Establishment*.

Russia and the United States [have] always gotten along for a hundred and fifty years history with Russia friendly and helpful. Our respective orbits do not clash geographically and I think on the whole we can probably keep out of clashes in the future.
— *Secretary of War Henry Stimson*
April 1945

Before the atom bomb was used, I would have said, yes, I was sure we could keep the peace with Russia. Now I don't know. . . . People are frightened and disturbed all over. Everyone feels insecure again.
— *General Dwight Eisenhower*
Visiting Moscow, August 1945

Even though the Cold War's abrupt, peaceful demise rendered useless most of the assumptions and theories advanced to explain that strange conflict, orthodox historians have kept on writing about it as if what actually happened had been inevitable. Moreover, they largely avoid the specific role the atomic bomb played in fueling the Cold War. In fact, the bomb was a primary catalyst of the Cold War, and, apart from the nuclear arms race, the most important specific role of nuclear weapons was to revolutionize American policy toward Germany. The bomb permitted U.S. leaders to do something no American president could otherwise have contemplated: rebuild and rearm the former Nazi state. That in turn had extraordinary, ongoing consequences.

The bomb also made the Korean and Vietnam wars possible: Had the weapon not been available to protect the U.S. global flank in Europe, such episodes would always have been "the wrong war in the wrong place at the wrong time," to use General Omar Bradley's words. Finally, those who believed early on that America and Russia could reach a great power accommodation were probably right—and such an accommodation may well have been delayed for four decades because the atomic bomb appeared precisely when America and the Soviet Union were beginning to feel their way to a new post–World War II relationship.

Not only does that explanation of the Cold War offer a good measure of common sense, but a vast body of new archival research lends powerful support to the hypothesis. This is not to say that frictions, rivalries, and areas of conflict would not have existed between the major powers had there been no atomic bomb. What needs to be explained is the extreme militarization of great power relations that came to be called "the Cold War."

Historians like to see patterns, trends, and continuity in long periods of development, but they rarely pause to reflect upon the extreme chanciness of the timing of historically important events. Consider the prehistory of nuclear weapons. Physicist Hans Bethe once observed that it was only very "slowly and painfully, through a comedy of errors, [that] the fission of uranium was discovered."

It was by mere chance, for instance, that Enrico Fermi made his critical 1934 discoveries about the capacity of the atom's nucleus to capture slow neutrons. Fermi's seemingly accidental findings built on a line of development that began with Albert Einstein's famous 1905 papers and continued with subsequent reports and inventions by scientists such as Leo Szilard (in connection with the cyclotron) and James Chadwick (in connection with the existence of the neutron).

Most accounts do not acknowledge that had twentieth-century physics not been moving at the particular rate it did, America would never have gotten to the 1939 Szilard–Einstein letter to President Franklin Roosevelt, the 1941 MAUD Committee report, and then the Manhattan Project—to a sufficiently advanced point, that is, where large sums of money and engineering expertise could have produced an atomic bomb by August 1945. As Bethe's remark suggests and others have noted, events might just as well have moved a decade or two slower or perhaps faster.

With that in mind, it is instructive to reflect on what might have happened (or, more precisely, what probably would not have happened) if the "independent track" of scientific historical development had not reached fruition in 1945. What might the postwar world have looked like in the absence of an early U.S. atomic monopoly?

GERMANY AND THE BOMB

At Yalta, Roosevelt had been quite clear about two fundamentals: First, given the domestic political concerns of a country taught to fear and hate Germany in the course of two world wars, he believed that the former Nazi state simply had to be eliminated as a serious security threat in the postwar period. It was both a strategic and an absolute political requirement. Second, as is well known, Roosevelt felt that the American people would not permit him to keep American troops in Europe for long after the war. Given strong "isolationist" sentiments that appeared in Congress and the popular press, he was almost certainly correct in his judgment.

Those constraints produced the main requirements of Roosevelt's postwar security policy: He needed a rough agreement with the other dominant military power—the Soviet Union—to control Germany directly, and he needed a concrete way (beyond rhetoric) to weaken Germany's underlying military potential. Exaggerated discussions of "pastoralization" apart, Roosevelt's strategy centered on the notion of "industrial disarmament" to weaken Germany's military-industrial complex—and simultaneously to cement American-Soviet cooperation. Reductions in German industry could also provide the short-term reparations Joseph Stalin desperately sought to help rebuild the war-torn Soviet Union.

Related to that strategy, of course, were implications for Roosevelt's de facto acceptance of a Soviet sphere of influence in Eastern Europe. To the extent Stalin was certain that Germany would not rise again, at least in theory Soviet policy could be more relaxed in Eastern Europe. The Yalta agreement embodied big-power control of Germany, large-scale reparations, and an extremely vague declaration on the status of Eastern Europe.

Often overlooked is that from the American point of view, the advent of nuclear weapons gave Washington an alternative to constructing a European peace in cooperation with the Soviet Union. At Yalta, Washington had essentially agreed to a neutralized Germany, but with the bomb U.S. policymakers realized they could afford the risks of acting unilaterally. The western portion of Germany could safely be reconstructed economically and, later, integrated into a West European military alliance. Only the atomic monopoly permitted that with little fear of German resurgence and without regard to Soviet security interests.

At Potsdam, American leaders explicitly understood that the atomic test the United States had conducted at Alamogordo, New Mexico, had upended the assumptions of policy. Compare, for instance, the views of President Harry Truman's closest adviser, James Byrnes, before and after Alamogordo. On June 6, 1945, six weeks before the blast, the diary of Ambassador Joseph Davies records that Byrnes, about to become secretary of state, "discussed the entire Russian situation at great length":

> It was clear that without Russian cooperation, without a primary objective for Peace, another disastrous war would be inevitable. . . . Nor did he think that our people on sober second thought would undertake fighting the Red Army and Russia for a hopeless cause of attempting to control the ideology or way of life which these various rival groups wished to establish in the various countries.

Although Russian cooperation was needed before the bomb, many scholars now recognize that the successful atomic test gave Truman "an entirely new feeling of confidence," as he put it. It provided Secretary of State Byrnes in particular with what he called "a gun behind the door" that he believed could make Russia "more manageable." One of many similar conversations from the period was recorded by Secretary of War Stimson in his diary shortly after Hiroshima: "Byrnes was very much against any attempt to cooperate with Russia. His mind is full of his problems with the coming meeting of foreign ministers and he looks to having the presence of the bomb in his pocket, so to speak, as a great weapon to get through the thing."

In connection with the U.S. approach to Germany, the atomic bomb altered policy in two quite specific ways that went to the heart of Rooseveltian strategy. Shortly after the atomic test Byrnes simply abandoned the Yalta understanding that had set German reparations at roughly $20 billion (half of which would go to the Soviet Union). Another Davies diary entry on July 28, 1945, shows that he did so explicitly relying on the atomic bomb: "[Byrnes] was having a hard time with reparations . . . , [but the] details as to the success of the atomic bomb, which he had just received, gave him confidence that the Soviets would agree as to these difficulties."

Moreover, according to Davies, the secretary of state was also quite clear about the shift in fundamental power relations in Europe: "Because of the New Mexico development [Byrnes] felt secure anyway." Byrnes suggested that "the New Mexico situation had given us great power, and that in the last analysis it would control." Several American policymakers (notably Benjamin Cohen, an assistant to Byrnes) had believed that international control of the Ruhr industrial heartland might be the key to a compromise approach. In principle, it could achieve security without necessarily weakening the German economic reconstruction effort. But—again, shortly after the report of the successful nuclear test—Byrnes rejected that proposal as well.

Many scholars now understand that the atomic bomb altered the Truman administration's general postwar approach to the USSR. What needs to be grasped is the specific implications the weapon had for the continuing U.S. approach to Germany. That there was a close link between the bomb and the German problem in the minds of U.S. policymakers was made quite explicit again, for instance, in two August 22, 1945, meetings with General Charles de Gaulle. Here Truman and Byrnes together urged that "the German danger should not be exaggerated." De Gaulle, however, continued to emphasize French fears—and, like Roosevelt's advisers and the Russians, urged direct security measures to manage the longer-term German threat (including international control of the Ruhr and severing the west bank of the Rhine from Germany). Finally, Truman and Byrnes—responding explicitly to de Gaulle's concern about Germany—became blunt: "The atomic bomb will give pause to countries which might [be] tempted to commit aggressions."

Although U.S. policymakers still worried about the potential power of a united German state, very early in the postwar period they clearly understood that Germany no longer presented a fundamental military threat. The new nuclear monopoly substantially relieved the Truman administration of the central foreign-policy and military concern of Roosevelt and his advisers. "In the last analysis it would control" as Byrnes said—even if the

American people forced the withdrawal of U.S. troops from the Continent, even if American-Soviet cooperation failed, and even if Germany were not disarmed industrially. Put another way, the bomb made it possible to pursue a policy described by scholars in recent years as "double containment"— that is, the division of Germany could be used to contain both the Germans and the Soviets.

SCARING STALIN

The problem was obviously not quite the same from the Soviet point of view. In the first place, the new weapon itself now posed a threat. Generalized fear provoked by the new weapon was only one aspect of the problem: In the fall of 1945 and spring of 1946, American policy moved slowly but steadily away from Roosevelt's approach to Germany. Partly as a result of French obstruction on the Allied Control Council, partly out of understandable fear of economic chaos and political disorder, and partly—but not at the outset—out of frustration with Soviet policy, U.S. policy shifted from industrial disarmament to rebuilding German economic power. A major turning point was probably the decision to stop reparation shipments in May 1946— dramatically followed by the tough speech Byrnes gave that September in Stuttgart.

That shift occurred at the same time that policymakers began to play up the bomb as a strategic factor. The U.S. stockpile of assembled weapons was actually quite small, but the potential of the nuclear monopoly was also obviously extraordinary—as was advertised by the atomic tests in June 1946 at Bikini Atoll in the Pacific. Code-named "Operation Crossroads," the blasts took place at the same time Byrnes and Soviet foreign minister Vyacheslav Molotov were again trying to reach agreement over Germany. *Pravda* took note of the mushroom cloud over Bikini and accused Washington of plotting an atomic war. And as the arsenal grew (50 weapons were available by 1948), the Truman administration steadily found the courage to act more forcefully and unilaterally in Germany.

Reams have been written about the extreme Russian security fears of the German threat. Stalin, in Nikita Khrushchev's judgment, "lived in terror of an enemy attack." The Soviet premier observed in April 1945 that Germany "will recover, and very quickly"—but apparently he initially believed that "quickly" meant as many as 10 or 15 years. Sometime at the end of 1947, as Michael McGwire observes in a recent study, "Stalin shifted focus . . . to the more immediate threat of war within 5–6 years against a capitalist coalition led by the Anglo-Saxon powers."

Recently released Soviet documents offer additional insight. Soviet ambassador to the United States Nikolai Novikov, for instance, painted a deeply disturbing picture of American intentions toward the Soviet Union in

1946. Citing the U.S. "establishment of a system of naval and air bases stretching far beyond the boundaries of the United States" and the "creation of ever newer types of weapons," Novikov believed that Washington was preparing for war. In the heart of Europe, he

> emphasized, America was "considering the possibility of terminating the Allied occupation of German territory before the main tasks of the occupation—the demilitarization and democratization of Germany—have been implemented. This would create the prerequisites for the revival of an imperialist Germany, which the United States plans to use in a future war on its side."

U.S. leaders fully understood Russian fears of Germany. Ambassador Averell Harriman, for instance, later recalled that "Stalin was afraid of Germany, Khrushchev was afraid of Germany, the present people [Brezhnev] are afraid of Germany—and I am afraid of Germany. . . . [The Soviets] have a feeling that the Germans can arouse a situation which will involve us and that will lead to a disaster."

Obviously, the critical turning point came with the decision to partition Germany and rearm West Germany. American leaders recognized that the Soviets would view even the restoration of significant German economic power as a threat—and that this would have painful repercussions in Eastern Europe. At a cabinet meeting in late 1947, Secretary of State George Marshall predicted that because of U.S. actions in Germany the Soviets would have to "clamp down completely" on Czechoslovakia, and that when they did, it would be a "purely defensive move."

Was Marshall's basic insight into a critical dynamic feature of the early Cold War correct? Was Soviet policy in Central and Eastern Europe primarily defensive and a reaction to American policy toward Germany? It is difficult to know, of course, but others also recognized the point early on. In his opinion columns at the time, Walter Lippmann, for instance, regularly pointed out the obvious connection between what happened in Germany and what happened in Eastern Europe. Unless the German problem were settled first, he urged, the Russians were unlikely ever to relax their hold on Eastern Europe. Lippmann believed that Byrnes's strategy of pressing forward on Eastern Europe without simultaneously promoting a reasonable settlement of the German issue was demanding too much. "We must not set up a German government in the two or three Western zones," Lippmann urged the Wall Street lawyer and future secretary of state John Foster Dulles in 1947. "We must not make a separate peace with it."

A steadily expanding body of research and documentary evidence suggests that Marshall's fundamental insight and Lippmann's early judgment offer the most plausible explanation for one of the most dramatic and painful features of the Cold War—Stalin's clampdown on Eastern Europe. The Soviet archives have yet to divulge anything definitive about Stalin's intentions at the end of World War II. However, even Harriman, who is usually portrayed as a hardliner in early postwar dealings with Moscow, thought the Soviet dictator had no firm plan at the outset: "I had a feeling," Harriman observed, "that they were considering and weighing the pros and cons of cooperating with us in the postwar world and getting the benefit of our cooperation in reconstruction."

Recent scholarship has uncovered far more indications of ambivalence—and, indeed, a great deal more caution and cooperation—in Soviet policy during 1945 and 1946 than is commonly recognized. A number of developments helped produce judgments about the Soviet Union like Harriman's:

- General elections in Hungary in the fall of 1945 held under Soviet supervision resulted in the defeat of communist-supported groups.
- In September 1945, Moscow unilaterally withdrew troops from Norway, despite its long-standing claims on Bear Island and Spitzbergen.
- In the wake of the December 1945 Moscow agreements, the government in Romania was enlarged to include noncommunists, after which both the United States and Great Britain recognized it.
- The Soviet military also withdrew from Czechoslovakia at that time, and free elections produced a coalition government of communists and noncommunists committed to keeping the country's doors open to both the East and the West.
- In the spring of 1946, Soviet troops left the Danish island of Bornholm.
- In accord with his "percentage agreement" with Winston Churchill, Stalin abandoned the Greek communists at a critical juncture in their civil war, leaving Greece within the Western sphere of influence.
- In Austria, the Soviet army supervised free elections in their occupation zone and, of course, withdrew after the signing of the Austrian Peace Treaty in 1955.
- The Soviets warned the French communist leader, Maurice Thorez, against attempting "to seize power by force since to do so would probably precipitate an international conflict from which the Soviet Union could hardly emerge victorious." (American intelligence obtained a report on that conversation in November 1946.)
- Despite a short delay, Soviet troops in 1946 did pull out of Iran—a country bordering the Soviet Union—after a brief and, in retrospect, rather modest international dispute.
- Perhaps most revealing, former Soviet officials who had defected to the West documented that important railway lines running from the Soviet Union through Eastern Europe were yanked up in the very early postwar period. The working assumption appeared to be that since there would be only a short occupation, Soviet forces should hurry to remove as much useful material as possible.
- Nor did Stalin pursue an aggressive policy in the Far East during the early years. Indeed, for a good period of time Stalin supported Nationalist Chinese leader Chiang Kai-shek—much to the lasting chagrin of Chinese communist leaders. And Red Army troops departed Manchuria in May 1946.

Many historians now accept that substantial evidence exists that Stalin neither planned nor desired the Cold War. Finland and Austria—neutral but free states—serve as alternative models for border-area countries that the Soviet Union might have accepted had a different dynamic been established after World War II.

Of course, Soviet policy in Eastern Europe was to shift dramatically, especially after 1947 and 1948. Along with the announcement of the Truman Doctrine, the Marshall Plan also appears to have been far more threatening to Stalin than was previously understood: It suggested the creation of a powerful "economic magnet" to draw Eastern Europe into the Western orbit. Once it was clear that Germany was to be rebuilt and later rearmed, the crackdown in Eastern Europe became irrevocable.

That interpretation returns us to a central point, namely that the U.S. decision to rearm West Germany was made possible only by the atomic bomb. Modern writers often forget the degree of concern in the U.S. foreign policy establishment and elsewhere about the former Nazi state in the early postwar years. Even after the outbreak of the Korean War—and even with the atomic bomb—Truman's high commissioner in Germany, John McCloy, initially opposed the creation of a German national army. So too did his successor, James Conant. And when they changed their minds, both men had to deal with the unrelenting opposition of the French. As late as August 1950, the State Department declared it "opposed, and still strongly opposes, the creation of German national forces."

Further, Truman himself was deeply worried about the Germans—again, even with the bomb. Among many indications of Truman's worry was a memo to Secretary of State Dean Acheson in June 1950:

> We certainly don't want to make the same mistake that was made after World War I when Germany was authorized to train one hundred thousand soldiers, principally for maintaining order locally in Germany. As you know, that hundred thousand was used for the basis of training the greatest war machine that ever came forth in European history.

Truman also recognized that he faced very powerful domestic political opposition to rearming a nation that had so recently caused the deaths of so many American boys. "From today's perspective, the rearmament of Germany seems natural and almost inevitable," writes historian Frank Ninkovich in a recent study.

> To achieve it, however, American policy makers had to clear a long series of hurdles, including self-doubts, widespread European reluctance, and Soviet obstructionism. . . . The amazing thing, then, is not that rearmament took place with such enormous difficulty, but that it happened at all.

Amazing, indeed! All but unimaginable in the absence of nuclear weapons or popular support for maintaining major conventional forces. As

Roosevelt had forecast, the American people overwhelmingly demanded rapid demobilization after the war. In June 1945, the United States had more than 12 million men and women under arms, but one year later the figure was only 3 million, and by June 1947 demobilization had left the armed services with no more than 1.5 million personnel. Congress defeated universal military training in 1947 and in 1948; defense spending in general declined rapidly during the first postwar years. Such domestic political realities left U.S. policymakers empty-handed: They did not have sufficient conventional forces to hold down the Germans.

Given such realities—and considering the extraordinary difficulty of achieving German rearmament even with U.S. possession of the atomic bomb—it is all but impossible to imagine the early rearmament of the former Nazi enemy had there been no atomic bomb. Put another way, had the scientific-technical track of development that yielded the knowledge required to make an atomic weapon not chanced to reach the point it had by 1939, the central weapon in America's postwar diplomatic arsenal would not have existed.

There is a further reason why we believe this hypothesis explains the early Cold War dynamic: German rearmament and the U.S. Cold War conventional buildup, many scholars recognize, probably could not have happened without the dramatic U.S. decision to enter the Korean War. That decision, in turn, was made possible only by the atomic bomb—and, hence, the train of subsequent events is difficult to imagine in the absence of the bomb.

Even with the atomic bomb virtually every important American military leader was extremely skeptical about a land war in Asia. The Korean peninsula, of course, had been arbitrarily divided in 1945 by Moscow and Washington, and both powers were well aware that their client regimes in Pyongyang and Seoul were committed to unifying the country under their own flags. Each regime had guerrilla units operating in the other's territory in what amounted to a simmering civil war. (Washington was actually restricting the supply of offensive weapons to the Syngman Rhee regime in South Korea for fear that they would be used in an invasion of the North.)

By late 1949, as is well known, Truman's National Security Council (NSC) advisers had concluded that Korea was of little strategic value to the United States and that a commitment to use military force in Korea would be ill-advised. Early in 1950, both Acheson and the chairman of the Senate Foreign Relations Committee, Tom Connally, had publicly stated that South Korea lay outside the perimeter of U.S. national security interests.

Most important, to pledge troops to a land war in Asia would expose the American "European flank," since moving troops to Asia would weaken the American presence on the Continent. As General Bradley recounted in his memoirs, "We still believed our greatest potential for danger lay in Soviet aggression in Europe." And, "to risk widening the Korean War into a war with China would probably delight the Kremlin more than anything else we could do." The famous Bradley comment quoted earlier summarized the general view within the Joint Chiefs of Staff: Fighting in Korea would involve the United States "in the wrong war, at the wrong place, at the wrong time, and with the wrong enemy." When an invasion of the South did occur in June 1950, the Truman administration's decision to intervene amounted to an astonishing policy reversal.

If, even with the atomic bomb, U.S. military leaders hesitated to pledge land forces to the defense of Korea, then without the atomic bomb—which to the generals would have meant a totally exposed European "flank"—a decision to protect South Korea would have been practically impossible.

And again, very few would disagree with the proposition that the Korean War, in turn, provided a crucial fulcrum upon which the Cold War pivoted. Most scholars accept that NSC-68, the document outlining a massive rebuilding of the U.S. military, was going nowhere in early 1950; the defense budget was being cut, not raised. The political drama surrounding the Korean War permitted an extraordinary escalation both in Cold War hysteria and in military spending. Before Korea such spending was around 4 percent of gross national product (GNP); during the war it peaked at nearly 14 percent. After Korea it stabilized to average roughly 10 percent of GNP during the 1950s—an unimaginable extravagance before that time. (The buildup, in turn, established a structure of forces and political attitudes without which the subsequent intervention in Vietnam is difficult to imagine.)

Most important, Germany almost certainly could only have been rearmed in the domestic political atmosphere that accompanied the chaotic Korean conflict, along with the qualitative political shift in Cold War tensions that the war brought. The entire scenario depended ultimately upon the odd historical timing that put nuclear weapons in American hands at a particular moment in the twentieth century.

What of "the Cold War" per se—the larger, overarching dynamic? Recall that the issue is not whether the usual tensions between great powers would or would not have existed. The issue is whether the relationship would have had to explode into the extremely militarized form it took.

Recently declassified archival materials from both sides should destroy the traditional assumption that the Soviet army at the end of World War II offensively threatened Western Europe. In 1945, roughly half the Soviet army's transport was horse-drawn, and it would remain so until 1950. Moreover, Soviet troops demobilized massively and dramatically in the early postwar period. Soviet documents suggest that Stalin's army shrank from 11,365,000 in May 1945 to 2,874,000 in June 1947.

While there is debate about how widely such information was known or heeded by top U.S. officials, a number of scholars have recently cited evidence suggesting that U.S. policymakers fully understood that the Soviet Union had neither the intention nor the capability to launch a ground invasion of Western Europe. In December 1945, for instance, the State Department circulated an intelligence estimate concluding that for at least five years "the United States need not be acutely concerned about the current intentions of the Soviet Union [and has] considerable latitude in determining policy toward the USSR." A Joint Chiefs of Staff report at the end of 1948 estimated the Soviets might be able to marshal only some 800,000 troops for an attack force. Two years later, the CIA used the same figure in its intelligence estimate. Similarly, documents recapped in Frank Kofsky's recent *Harry S. Truman and the War Scare of 1948* provide devastating proof that American military intelligence estimates consistently concluded that the Soviets could not and did not want to wage war. One illustration is a high-level briefing given directly to Truman in late 1948:

> The Russians have dismantled hundreds of miles of railroads in Germany and sent the rails and ties back to Russia. There remains, at the present time . . . only a single track railroad running Eastward out of the Berlin area and upon which the Russians must largely depend for their logistical support. This same railroad line changes from a standard gage going Eastward, to a Russian wide gage in Poland, which further complicates the problem of moving supplies and equipment forward.

George Kennan, for one, "never believed that they [the Soviets] have seen it as in their interests to overrun Western Europe militarily, or that they would have launched an attack on that region generally even if the so-called nuclear deterrent had not existed."

Credible documentation has also emerged from the Russian archives that Stalin repeatedly rejected North Korean leader Kim Il-Sung's requests for support of an invasion of South Korea. As one scholar, Kathryn Weathersby, has explained in a recent working paper, Stalin reluctantly "approved the plan only after having been assured that the United States would not intervene." Even then he apparently did so because Kim Il-Sung would otherwise have pursued the war anyway with support from the communist Chinese. As Weathersby concludes, "it was Soviet weakness that drove Stalin to support the attack on South Korea, not the unrestrained expansionism imagined by the authors of NSC-68."

Moreover, Bruce Cumings's sweeping, two-volume history, *The Origins of the Korean War*, demonstrates that the U.S. command in South Korea knew at the time that South Korean irregular army units had been provoking the North Koreans for months. A once clear-cut case of communist aggression is now seen by most knowledgeable historians as a complicated civil war that dated back at least to 1945.

The Russian archives also show that often neither Stalin nor his successors could control the regimes in Eastern Europe, Cuba, China, North Korea, or North Vietnam. "It's a big myth that Moscow directed a unified mono-lith of socialist states," argues Deborah Kaple of Columbia University's Harriman Institute. Newly uncovered documents, for instance, make it clear that the Sino-Soviet split existed almost from the day Mao Tse-tung seized power. And other recent archival discoveries suggest that East Germany's Walter Ulbricht largely initiated the Berlin crisis of 1958–1961, forcing a reluctant Khrushchev to engage in brinkmanship diplomacy.

All of these events suggest a broadly defensive post–World War II Soviet foreign policy that on occasion accommodated American security in-terests. The monolithic enemy of Cold War fame, many now agree, existed mainly in the imaginations of America's ardent anticommunist cold war-riors. At the very least, these events suggest Stalin appeared willing to cut a deal with Washington in the critical early postwar years.

This analysis does not suggest that the American-Soviet relationships could have been a tranquil sea of cooperation. But the unusual and danger-ous over-militarization of foreign policy during the Cold War demands an explanation on its own terms—and the atomic bomb is the first item in that lexicon.

This essay has not attempted to untangle the many factors that led to the end of the Cold War. One related issue, however, may be noted: The ad-vent of nuclear weapons (and the U.S. nuclear monopoly in particular) upset the balance of power in general and especially in Europe, where from the Soviet point of view the critical issue was Germany. However, once the Soviet Union had its own nuclear weapons and a credible way to deliver them—and Germany had no such weapons—then the implicit balance of power in general and in Europe, too, was essentially restored, albeit at a higher level.

Before that time the Soviets kept Germany relatively weak by occupa-tion, reparations, and tight control of the invasion routes. After the Soviet Union had secured nuclear weapons (and once the implications were di-gested and fought out by policy elites), Soviet policy could relax all three prongs of its earlier strategy. Old military and foreign policy *apparatchiks* did not easily abandon traditional assumptions, as the crackdown in Czechoslovakia in 1968 suggests. The preconditions for ending the Cold War, however, were established only after the basic power relationship between the Soviet Union and the United States was rebalanced.

Might history have taken a different course? Many high-level Western policymakers believed an accommodation with the Soviet Union was a rea-sonable possibility in the early postwar years. The United States was also in a position to encourage Soviet cooperation with the lure of desperately needed long-term economic aid. Indeed, had the United States lacked a nu-clear weapons monopoly—and given the rapid pace of U.S. demobilization and Congress's rejection of universal military training—such an approach might well have been the only acceptable option from the U.S. point of view.

All of this, of course, is "counter-factual" history. As the late philosopher Morris Cohen observed in 1942, however, "we cannot grasp the full significance of what happened unless we have some idea of what the situation would have been otherwise." But in a sense all history is implicitly counter-factual—including, above all, the counter-factual orthodox theory that had the United States not taken a tough stand after World War II, there would have been no "long peace" and disaster would inevitably have befallen the Continent, the world, and the United States.

In *A Preponderance of Power*, Melvyn Leffler concludes that because of its enormous strength the United States must also bear a preponderance of responsibility for the Cold War. That important judgment, like Stimson's rejected 1945 plea for an immediate, direct, and private effort to cut short what became the nuclear era, brings into focus the question of just how wise were the "wise men" who crafted America's Cold War policies at the moment when the two great tracks of twentieth-century scientific and global political development converged. At the very least, they failed to find a way to avoid one of history's most costly and dangerous—indeed, literally world-threatening—struggles.

QUESTIONS TO CONSIDER

1. What events do the authors suggest made the bomb possible?
2. How did possession of the bomb affect American policy toward Germany?
3. How did George Marshall and Walter Lippmann link the German issue to Eastern Europe in late 1947?
4. Besides the bomb, what American policies in 1947 and 1948 do the authors suggest made the Soviet crackdown on Eastern Europe irrevocable? Why?
5. How did the bomb affect American decision making in Korea and what were the implications of the Korean War for the development of the Cold War?
6. What evidence do the authors advance that communism was not a monolith, with the Soviet Union directing it?
7. How did Soviet nuclear weapons ease the basic East-West tensions in Europe?

12

Cracks in the Mold

SARA EVANS

Sara Evans (1943–   ), educated at Duke and the University of North
Carolina and now a professor of women's history at the University of
Minnesota, is the author of the highly regarded *Born for Liberty: A History
of Women in America* (1989). She first won acclaim in 1979 when her
autobiographical account, *Personal Politics*, was published. The book
provided a professional scholar's firsthand explanation of the intersection
of the church, the civil rights movement, the New Left, and the feminist
movement. A preacher's daughter who got into the civil rights movement
through the church, Evans found it to be as sexist as the establishment against which it was revolting. She discovered a striking parallel
with women in the abolitionist movement 130 years earlier. They had
found the oppression of slaves not dissimilar to their own second-class
status and launched the first women's movement in 1848 at Seneca Falls,
New York. Women in the modern civil rights movement also found many
similarities between black grievances and their own condition, and the
radical women's movement was born.

    In this selection, the prologue to her book, Evans explains how
many women in the 1950s recognized that they were limited to function-
ing as wives and mothers but were not finding fulfillment in those roles.
Her thorough analysis of the condition of women and their emancipation
when Betty Friedan wrote her best-selling *The Feminine Mystique* in 1963
merits close attention from students of the American character. But even
though women began to be heard after 1963, Evans explains the
essential conservatism of the career women who launched the National

Organization for Women (NOW). It was left to younger women, energized by the civil rights and New Left movements, to take the feminist movement in more radical directions, challenging not only the male monopoly of the mainstream but also the nature of the mainstream itself. The character of American women, neatly constricted by a "cult of true womanhood" in the nineteenth century and a similar "feminine mystique" after World War II, has emerged into an ongoing state of redefinition.

> Of the accomplishments of the American woman, one she brings off with the most spectacular success is having babies.
>
> —*Life* magazine, December 24, 1956

In the mid-1950s Betty Friedan wrote and edited articles entitled "Millionaire's Wife," "I Was Afraid to Have a Baby," and "Two Are an Island" for *Cosmopolitan, McCall's,* and *Mademoiselle*. Robin Morgan was a child-actress playing Dagmar on the popular TV series "I Remember Mama." Thousands of other future feminists lived in middle-class homes, growing up to be bright, popular, and good. Everything appeared to promise them a future of happy domesticity. Who would have guessed that within a decade they would rise up to challenge that promise, to name it fraud, and to demand fundamental changes in American society under the banner of women's liberation? Feminism had been dead for over thirty years. Even the word had become faintly embarrassing. Feminists were seen as unfulfilled, neurotic, grasping women.

When *Life* magazine produced a special issue on women in December 1956, Mrs. Peter Marshall charged in her introduction that "many of woman's current troubles began with the period of her preoccupation with her 'rights.'" She advised women to turn instead to the most satisfying and "completely fulfilling" moments of their lives: the first formal dance, the first embrace, the first baby. In the same issue Cornelia Otis Skinner denounced the "shrill ridiculous war over the dead issue of feminism." "Ladies," she appealed, "we have won our case, but for heaven's sake let's stop trying to prove it over and over again."

The odor of embarrassment surrounding women's changing roles lingered as a reminder of the acrid attack that had been launched more than a decade before when Philip Wylie had blamed "Mom" for all the evils of American society. Modern industrialization, the critics argued, had undermined the basic functions of the traditional home. Such changes induced severe neurosis in women, they said. According to Wylie, it transformed them into narcissistic "Moms" who devoured their sons and husbands, robbing them of independence and ego strength. Freudians like Marynia Farnham and Ferdinand Lundberg pointed to another "pathological" response in modern women: feminism. They recommended massive use of psychotherapy, government propaganda and awards for good motherhood, cash payments to mothers, and the restoration of such traditional home tasks as cooking, preserving, and decorating. Only through a return to the traditional home, "a social extension of the mother's womb," could "women's inner balance" be reclaimed and the level of hostility in the world reduced.

By the midfifties such worries seemed a bit misplaced. Women were marrying younger, having three and four children, and apparently loving it. The vast majority of American women identified themselves as housewives whether they worked outside the home or not. Although growing numbers of them attended college, educators assured the public that they were simply preparing to be better mothers and wives, nothing more. If pickling and preserving had become the province of automated canneries, the work of the suburban housewife expanded in other ways. *Life* described a "typical" housewife under the banner: "Busy Wife's Achievements: Marjorie Sutton is Home Manager, Mother, Hostess, and Useful Civic Worker." No longer a household drudge, Marjorie the housewife had became a glamorized "superwoman" whose husband made $25,000 a year. Married at sixteen, she managed her household with the help of a full-time maid, worked with the Campfire Girls, the PTA, did charity fund raising, and sang in the choir. She cooked, sewed clothes for her four children, entertained 1500 guests a year, and exercised on a trampoline "to keep her size 12 figure."

While alternative images of womanhood never disappeared altogether, for most people they scarcely existed. The mass media proclaimed the triumph of domesticity. Women's magazines displayed "feminine" fashions with cinched waists, billowing petticoats, and accented bustlines. The movie industry promoted blond, buxom, sexy-but-innocent stars like Marilyn Monroe and Jayne Mansfield. Advertisers peddled a host of new appliances and household products to improve the housewife's ability to serve her family with cleaner, whiter clothes, odor-free kitchens, and "Poppin' Fresh" breads. The family as firmament of a stable social order received a stream of paeans from noted figures who encouraged women to center their energies in the home. Adlai Stevenson, liberal hero and two-time Democratic Party nominee for president, exhorted Smith College graduates in 1955 to remember that marriage and motherhood gave them a unique political duty. A woman could "inspire in her home a vision of the meaning of life and freedom . . . help her husband find values that will give purpose to his specialized daily chores . . . [and] teach her children the uniqueness of each individual human being." Studies indicated that most young women intended to do just that.

How, then, shall we explain the fact that by the early 1960s Betty Friedan had issued her famous denunciation of the "feminine mystique"— her term for the identification of womanhood with the roles of wife and mother? Or that Robin Morgan would grow up to organize a demonstration against Miss America in 1968 and use her powerful skills as writer and poet to proclaim herself a radical lesbian feminist in the early 1970s? Or that newspapers would be filled with news of a revival of feminism while feminist organizations and projects sprouted in every city in the country?

The feminist resurgence in the 1960s and the 1970s makes sense only when one looks deeper under the surface of the apparent placidity of the 1950s, for there lay a dramatically changed reality for women, one that the old ideologies about women's place could not explain. The "feminine mystique" in operation offered a modernized version of the Victorian notion of women's sphere sharply separated from the public (male) realms of paid work, politics, and "historic" action. As an ideology it shaped women's and men's perceptions of reality, but its life was limited at the outset.

This undercurrent of change provoked Wylie's rage and Farnham and Lundberg's assault. And it prompted Adlai Stevenson to preface his remarks about the political power of homemakers with an acknowledgment that many women in that role "feel frustrated and far apart from the great issues and stirring debate for which their education has given them understanding and relish. Once they wrote poetry. Now it's the laundry list." The reassertion of domesticity and its apparent hegemony in the 1950s constituted an attempt to ignore and contain the altered conditions of the twentieth century that had begun to culminate in new life patterns for women. But women's lives could no longer be encompassed by the older definitions of a "woman's place."

Within the home women with more and more education found that they had less and less to do. Despite the baby boom, their families were smaller than their grandmothers' had been. Technology abbreviated the physical labor of housework while consumer items complicated and, in effect, expanded it again. Laundry could be done by an automatic machine, but it required the appropriate detergents, bleaches, and rinses to meet changing standards of cleanliness. Children spent their days in school and afternoons at the playground, but a model mother had to be constantly available, both physically—to drive car pools, lead Scout troops, entertain bored children—and emotionally to avoid inflicting irreparable psychic damage. The suburban supermom, as illustrated by Marjorie Sutton, fulfilled a complex round of community activities and enhanced her husband's career opportunities with her well-kept home and lavish entertaining. Other women attempting a similar burden with less money and no full-time maid felt anxious, guilty, and inadequate. For all their busyness, little of what they did felt like work. Women's function in the home had shifted from producing food and clothing for family use to maintaining the family as an emotional community, making sure that everyone was healthy and above all happy. Led to fantasize that marriage would provide them with total emotional and intellectual fulfillment, more and more women experienced acute disappointment and then guilt when it fell below the mark. In particular, educated suburban housewives, the women who attempted to live out the mystique in its fullest form, found that their goal had become a trap.

Large numbers of them now attended college, where they performed to intellectual standards that made no allowances for sex. Although educators defensively proclaimed that they were educating women to be better wives and mothers, they nonetheless offered women essentially the same training as that which prepared men for future careers in professions and business. Thus women entered marriage with heightened expectations of companionship and fulfillment and with a growing knowledge of their own diverse capabilities. Yet they arrived to find that suburbia had become a female ghetto. Their husbands worked miles away; parents and relatives lived in other cities. The social isolation of modern housewives and the automation of housework, combined with a rising awareness of what they were missing "out there," produced, inevitably, a high degree of loneliness and boredom. Life seemed to be passing them by: shopping trips became forays into the outside world, and husbands, who had less and less time to spend with their families, were now their major link to the public realm.

Even more important than these changes in the home was the fact that many housewives were also leaving home for up to eight hours a day to shoulder additional jobs as secretaries, social workers, teachers, sales clerks, stewardesses, and waitresses. These were not the dreaded "career women." They had jobs, not professions. But the fact that most of them were older, married women shattered the notion that work outside the home was a male preserve, to be shared only with young, single women filling in a gap between childhood and marriage. Furthermore, they were not all victims of grinding poverty. Throughout the fifties women from middle-income families entered the labor force faster than any other group in the population.

If Harvard seniors in 1955 were concerned to limit the boundaries of their future wives' aspirations, then they had reason to worry. "She can be independent on little things, but the big decisions will have to go my way," said one. "The marriage must be the most important thing that ever happened to her." Another would permit his wife to work until she had children, after which she must stay home. A third wanted an "Ivy League type," who "will also be centered in the home, a housewife." Writers like Ashley Montagu bemoaned women's failure to understand that homemaking was the world's most important occupation and exhorted them to look to the model of European women, who focused their lives on the happiness of their husbands and children. Such women, he noted wistfully, "seem to behave as if they love their husbands." The fear of female competition with men had become a thread running through contemporary fiction, while the funny pages featured strong-minded Blondies married to foolish, ineffectual Dagwoods.

Yet few of the women entering the labor force saw themselves engaged in a challenge to tradition. They were simply doing what they could to help their families. And the jobs open to them were generally accepted as appropriate "women's work," requiring attributes similar to those expected of women at home. A changing economy created new jobs in such fields as health care, education, child care, clerical work, social work, and advertising—many of them labeled "female" from the beginning. If there were not enough young single women available for them, employers would have to relinquish their prejudices against married women and women with children. And they did. Thus millions of families achieved their "middle-class" status in the surge of postwar prosperity because of the additional income brought in by women. By 1956, 70 percent of all families in the $7,000 to $15,000 annual income range had at least two workers in the family, and the second was most often a woman.

Such participation in the labor force widened women's horizons. It gave them new skills and a paycheck that enhanced their role in family decision-making. But the blessing was a mixed one. A woman's work was likely to be threatening to her husband. It implied that he was not being a "good provider." Her guilt required that she avoid planning, training, or high aspirations. As a result she could not challenge discrimination according to sex. The only jobs logically open to most women were repetitious and boring. This structural inability to take oneself seriously induced a deep insecurity and a negative self-image. The lack of seriousness with which women and their employers viewed their work reflected itself in their paychecks. In 1966 women received a smaller income relative to men than in 1939; and as the percentages of women in certain occupations rose, their incomes relative to men in the same occupations fell.

In this context it seems logical that between 1940 and 1960, while the overall percentage of women working outside the home was climbing rapidly, there should have been a "slight but persistent decline in the proportion of professional, technical, and kindred workers that were female." Professional women could not pretend that their work was secondary and inconsequential. They pursued their careers with drive and determination.

These professional women were the most unmistakably "deviant," and often harbored among themselves the few remnants of feminism left in the 1950s. Many found it difficult to accept their performance of formerly "male" roles and went out of their way to assure themselves and others that they were still truly "feminine." A study of female executives found that all of the women surveyed placed home and family ahead of business, but felt that they could do both jobs, "if they want to badly enough." Frances Corey, a senior vice-president at Macy's, argued that women were "equal-but-special." "My attitude is that I can contribute something as a woman," she said. "My reaction is much more emotional—and emotion is a necessary commodity. There are places where I can't fill the bill as well as a man and I don't try."

The next generation, daughters of the fifties, grew up with the knowledge that their identifying roles should be those of wife and mother, but they knew that they would probably have a job at some point as well. They frequently observed their mothers shouldering the double burden of work outside the home and continuing responsibility for housework. Many knew that their mothers worked hard and were good at what they did—running day-care centers and shops, working in factories or offices, as lawyers or musicians. But their pay stayed low and their jobs offered few independent rewards. The feminine mystique had not obliterated the reality of working women. Rather, it had absorbed them. In 1956, alongside its "typical housewife," *Life* magazine included six pages of pictures bearing the title: "Women Hold 1/3 of U.S. Jobs." The accompanying photographs showed masses of women in various occupations. None of the jobs was portrayed as inviting; none seemed in the pictures to imply creativity or excitement. For example, hundreds of nurses in identical uniforms sat in a large auditorium listening to a male doctor; 104 middle-aged teachers stared impassively into the face of a man lecturing them on mental tests given to girl students; a typing pool of 450 pounded away in one enormous room. The only lively picture of the lot showed scantily clad chorus girls. This dulling mosaic contrasted sharply with other articles describing the "rich experience" of having a baby, the "achievements" of the busy housewife, and the glistening kitchen of a "Housewife's House."

Both in the home and outside it, women experienced themselves in new ways, discovering their capacities; yet they remained enclosed in the straitjacket of domestic ideology. To challenge it openly would be too frightening. In a rapidly changing world, clouded with the threat of nuclear warfare and the early brushfires of racial discontent and urban decay, where corporate behemoths trained their bureaucrats into interchangeable parts, few were ready to face the unnerving necessity of reassessing the cultural definitions of femaleness and maleness. If the world was changing, at least men could know that they were men and women were women. But that could happen only if women continued to maintain the home as a nurturing center, a private enclave, symbol of security and stability.*

---

*The resurgence of domestic ideology in the 1950s had complex roots. In the broadest context it meshed with a national mood that denied change in all aspects of American life. In foreign policy the rhetoric of the cold war held out the threat of nuclear annihilation as the price for violation of the status quo. Domestically McCarthyism was only the most extreme form of "rooting out subversion from within," as even moderate arguments for change in areas like race relations, labor, and education were treated as serious threats. The permission granted by government leaders and mass media to ignore or deny threatening changes was received gratefully by the American middle class, which after a generation of depression and war wanted nothing more than security and stability. And nothing represented these more clearly than home and family.

In addition, the feminine mystique may have represented the projected needs of middle-class men unable to accept their own changing roles. Within the burgeoning corporate and governmental bureaucracies, the work of these "organization men" had become increasingly technical, specialized, rationalized, and separated from any tangible "product." Bureaucracy suppressed emotion and passion, training its members into "interchangeable parts." Bureaucratic values emphasized "female" traits of cooperation, passivity, and security. "Getting along" and being well-liked became new life goals. Yet the older definitions of masculinity remained, and few could recognize the contradictory fact that what one part of their consciousness valued, another part judged unmanly. Thus, if women would stay within their traditional role, men could receive reassurance both that the emptiness in their own lives would be cared for and that their "manhood" had not changed. In one last realm, the home, the man could maintain the illusion of control.

Yet even in that most intimate arena, newly recognized female potentials generated tremors. Alfred Kinsey let the cat out of the bag in 1953. A sexual revolution had been going on for most of the twentieth century. Women, it turned out, had orgasms; they masturbated, engaged frequently in heavy premarital petting and not uncommonly in premarital intercourse; they committed adultery; they loved other women, and as Kinsey pointed out "heterosexual relationships could . . . become more satisfactory if they more often utilized the sort of knowledge which most homosexual females have of female sexual anatomy and female psychology." One commentator noted that "the criticism here implied of heterosexual relationships on the average in our society is, to say the least, devastating to the male ego." Now the "togetherness" of the home required achievement of the simultaneous orgasm as proof of its felicity.

However, this too could be contained, at least temporarily. The romantic fantasy life fostered by popular culture reemphasized passivity rather than power in female sexuality. The seductive but innocent woman remained a child. Beauty pageants stressed the competitive display of women's bodies and jealously guarded the purity of the chosen queens. *Life* preceded its "typical housewife" and working women with a thirteen-page display on "The American Girl at Her Beautiful Best." Yet most of the ten "girls" were married and over twenty. Advertisements made sex itself a commodity and women's bodies the medium for an array of beauty-enhancing products. Titillation and suggestion were "in," but direct discussion of sexuality remained a (faltering) taboo.

The entire special issue of *Life* provides an interesting study in the contrasts and blandly unresolved ambivalences of the midfifties. In praising beauties and babies, the primacy of sex-stereotyped roles went largely unquestioned. Beyond the "housewife's house," however, lay an article entitled "My Wife Works and I Like It." Here a multitude of commentators examined, defended, and criticized women's status. Emily Kimbrough, prolific writer of witty travelogues and former editor for the *Ladies' Home Journal,* defiantly challenged those who urged women to return to the home. "All the Canutes in the world, lined up shoulder to shoulder, could not turn back this tide now." *Life* staff writer Robert Coughlan railed at length against that "fatal error" of feminism, "that common urban phenomenon known as the 'career woman.'" He found hope, however, in the reappearance of the three- to five-child family in upper- and upper-middle-class suburbs. This somewhat more optimistic replay of Farnham and Lundberg appeared in a magazine whose cover was graced by the profiles of a young mother and a five-year-old child, gazing fondly into each other's eyes. The caption read: "Working Mother."

Clearly the feminine mystique was already in the process of erosion, even as it reached its zenith. Emily Kimbrough was correct. The traditionalists could not win. But their temporary hegemony in the continuing domination of the feminine mystique laid the basis for the more explosive readjustment of a feminism reborn. The dilemma went underground and gathered force. It did not disappear.

Eventually the conflicts could no longer be contained. The feminine mystique's promise of "fulfillment" raised the expectations of middle-class women. Yet the social role of housewife as it shaped women's work both in the home and in the paid labor force generated disappointment as expectations continually fell short, and strain as large numbers of bored and restless women strove to meet the growing emotional demands placed upon them. Such pervasive unhappiness could not remain hidden. The illusion of the "happy housewife" began to crack along with the rest of the illusory equilibrium of the 1950s. Its solidity was undermined as on every level changing realities came crashing through old assumptions to expose the uncertainty and anxiety that lay beneath. Internationally, the upsurge of third world nationalism undermined the earlier cold war certainty of American superiority and "goodness." Domestically, a few Beatnik young people with disheveled lifestyles and writings on the problem of "meaninglessness" challenged the lives and dreams of middle Americans. Invisible to the general public, a much larger mass of affluent youth yearned for something they couldn't define, a purpose and goal beyond the material security their parents had achieved. More visibly, black Americans began to express their discontent with the barriers to full participation in the "mainstream." Signs of racial unrest began to multiply: in 1956 the Montgomery Bus Boycott; in 1957, Little Rock; and then early in 1960, the sit-in movement, which was to initiate directly that mass protest reverberating through the decade.

The election of John Fitzgerald Kennedy in 1960 marked a shift in the public mood. Change became a positive rather than a negative value. Together with the southern civil rights movement, programs like the Peace Corps and VISTA sparked a resurgence of idealism and active involvement in social change. The child-mother no longer fit the times. She was too static, too passive, maybe even too safe. A rising number of voices in the late 1950s urged the abandonment of outmoded myths, though usually with a qualifying clause about the importance of mothers to very young children and the primacy of the family. Many social scientists moved from using "role conflict" as an argument for women to refuse outside work, to a more realistic appraisal of the problems of the "working wife," who could not and would not evade such conflicts by returning to the home. Thus, such observers had finally achieved the level of adjustment to changing reality accomplished already by millions of American families. Jobs for women were becoming legitimate as extensions of the housewife role.

With the growing public acceptance of women's work outside the home, the mass media suddenly discovered the "trapped housewife." Betty Friedan pointed out that in 1960 the housewife's predicament was examined in *The New York Times*, *Newsweek*, *Good Housekeeping*, *Redbook*, *Time*, *Harper's Bazaar*, and on CBS Television. *Newsweek* entitled a Special Science Report and cover story: "Young Wives with Brains: Babies, Yes—But What Else?" The editors reported that the American middle-class woman "is dissatisfied with a lot that women of other lands can only dream of. Her discontent is deep, pervasive, and impervious to the superficial remedies which are offered at every hand." Both seriously and superficially, most articles in the issue treated women's problems of boredom, restlessness, isolation, overeducation, and low esteem.

Educators also responded to the changing mood. Beginning in about 1960, a series of educational experiments and innovations appeared to meet the newly recognized malaise of the middle-class housewife. The "continuing education movement" focused on shaping the educational system to meet the demands of women's "dual role." Educational and career interruptions due to marriage and children were presumed inevitable. The problem, therefore, was to allow middle-class educated women to reenter the work force either full or part time without being forced into low-skilled, low-paid work.

Even the federal government began to treat women's roles as a public issue and to explore public policy alternatives to meet changing conditions. On December 14, 1961, President Kennedy established the President's Commission on the Status of Women, chaired by Eleanor Roosevelt. The purpose, in fact, may have been to quell a growing pressure for an Equal Rights Amendment, but unwittingly the government organized its own opposition. The existence of the commission and in subsequent years of state commissions on the status of women provided a rallying point for professional women. Such commissions constituted a tacit admission that there was indeed a "problem" regarding women's position in American society, that the democratic vision of equal opportunity had somehow left them out. Furthermore, they furnished a platform from which inequities could be publicized and the need for women's rights put forth. The President's Commission's report, entitled *American Women* and published in 1963, was moderate in tone. Yet despite obeisance to the primacy of women's roles within the family, it catalogued in great detail the inequities in the lives of women, the discrimination women faced in employment, and the need for proper child-care centers.

The importance of the report and the commission itself lay less in the specific changes they generated directly than in the renewed interest in "women's place in society" which they reflected. The following year women's rights advocates gained a crucial legal victory in the passage of Title VII of the Civil Rights Act, which prohibited discrimination by private employers, employment agencies, and unions on the basis of sex as well as race, color, religion, and national origin. Though introduced by a southern senator [sic] in a facetious gesture of hostility to the entire act, Title VII provided women with a legal tool with which to combat pervasive discrimination in hiring and promotion in all aspects of the economy.

The renewed discussion and activism took place primarily among professional women, who did not see themselves as housewives. Precisely because these professional women thought their work important and because they resented being patronized as if they had fled housework to get a little excitement, they felt even more acutely the discrimination leveled against them. Having openly admitted a certain level of drive and ambition, they were far more likely to experience discriminatory hiring, training, promotion, and pay rates as unfair. Other women could justify their unwillingness to fight against such barriers by saying, "I wouldn't be here if I didn't have to be," or "I'm only doing this for my family, not for myself." But for professional women, long-term careers were involved. Discrimination could close off opportunities they had invested years of training and hard work to attain. And it could deny them the positive reinforcement of respect from their colleagues. Since they took their work seriously, they were more vulnerable to the contempt that underlies patronage.

In general such women embraced the American ideology of equal opportunity, believing in advancement according to individual merit and achievement. Between 1940 and 1960, while the numbers of professional women declined relative to men, they also grew in absolute numbers by 41 percent. With more and more women in professional jobs, there were more examples to prove that women could excel at any occupation they chose. The individual professional woman was not a fluke or a freak of nature. On the other hand, there were also multiplying examples of blatant discrimination as their salaries and promotions increasingly lagged behind those of men with the same training and experience.

The new public attention to women's roles finally generated an overtly feminist position in 1963 in Betty Friedan's book, *The Feminine Mystique*. In a brilliant polemic she declared that housework was intrinsically boring, that the home had become a "comfortable concentration camp" which infantilized women. She took dead aim at the educational establishment, Freudians, women's magazines, and mass advertising, which she believed had combined to limit women's horizons and to force them back into the home. More academic but equally critical reassessments of women's traditional roles soon followed.

By the mid-sixties these angry professional women were developing an oppositional ideology and a strong network within governmental commissions on the status of women. As participants and consultants, they articulated the discrepancy between the ideals of equal opportunity and the actual treatment of women by employers. They mobilized to press for the passage of Title VII and then for its enforcement. A growing circle of women, including Friedan, Rep. Martha Griffiths, and the lawyers Mary Eastwood and Pauli Murray, urged the creation of an action group to pressure a government that continued to issue provocative reports but showed little sign of taking effective action. When, at a national conference of state commissions on the status of women in 1965, activists were informed that they could pass no resolutions and take no action in their capacity as state commissioners, a group broke away to resolve to found the National Organization for Women (NOW). These women had become convinced that, for real change to occur, a new civil rights group must be formed that could pressure the government to enact and enforce laws against sexual discrimination. Thus NOW became the "women's rights" branch of a renewed feminism.

In general, the professional women who created NOW accepted the division between the public and private spheres and chose to seek equality primarily in the public realm. Betty Friedan's devastating critique of housewifery ended up with a prescription that women, like men, should be allowed to participate in both realms. In effect she urged women to do it all—to be superwomen—by assuming the dual roles of housewife and professional. She made no serious assault on the division of labor within the home. For Friedan it was easier to imagine a professional woman hiring a "professional housewife" to take her place in the home than to challenge the whole range of sex roles or the division of social life into home and work, private and public, female and male domains.

In contrast, however, the oppression of most American women centered on their primary definition of themselves as "housewife," whether they worked solely inside the home or also outside it. Although they could vote, go to college, run for office, and enter most professions, women's primary role identification created serious obstacles both internally and in the outside world. Within themselves, women were never sure that they could be womanly when not serving and nurturing. And such doubts were reinforced by a long series of experiences: the advice and urging of high school and college counselors; discrimination on the job; pressure from family and friends; a lack of social services such as child care; and social expectations on the job that continually forced women back into traditional roles. Somehow women in every position from secretary to executive all too often ended up making the coffee.

At the same time that women acknowledged the social judgment that their work counted for very little—by accepting lower pay and poor jobs outside the home, or describing themselves as "just a housewife"—they also felt uncomfortable in any role other than that of the housewife. To admit discontent was to face a psychic void. The choices were there in a formal sense, but the price they exacted was a doubled workload and loss of both self-approval and public approval. Thus, though the *Newsweek* article on "Young Women with Brains" generated a storm of response from women, many who responded in writing denied the existence of a problem altogether. Others advised volunteer work and hobbies to fill the time, or else criticized women for their unhappiness. Only a few women echoed the article and discussed their distress.

If women found housewifery unfulfilling, they also on some level believed it was their own fault, thus turning their guilt and anger back in upon themselves. In a culture that offered no support for serious alternatives, women clung to the older definitions. If such roles did not reflect changing options or their real desires, at least they were familiar.

The tenacity of traditional roles and their internalization by most women meant that any successful revolt that drew on women's discontent would finally neither accept a traditional view of "female nature" as particularly suited to home and motherhood nor restrict itself simply to a critique of inequities in the public realm. For this reason, the emergence of the National Organization for Women did not provoke a massive grass-roots feminist movement. As a civil rights lobbying group, it could and did raise the public policy issues of discrimination in education, employment, and media in accordance with its stated purpose:

> to take action to bring women into full participation in the mainstream of American society *now,* exercising all the privileges and responsibilities thereof in truly equal partnership with men.

But while the professional women in NOW's constituency militantly demanded equality in the public realm, they were not prepared to question the mainstream itself, nor to carry their critique into the operation of sex roles in every aspect of life.

Yet the initiation of a mass movement required that the problem be addressed at its core. The pressures on most women were building up not on the level of public discrimination but at the juncture of public and private, of job and home, where older structures and identities no longer sufficed but could not simply be discarded either. The growing emotional strains of providing nurture for others with nowhere to escape to oneself, of rising expectations and low self-esteem, of public activity and an increasingly private, even submerged, identity required a radical—in the literal sense—response. A new movement would have to transform the privacy and subjectivity of personal life itself into a political issue.

Once such issues were raised by the radical young feminists in the late sixties, the challenge to traditional roles penetrated the mainstream of American society within a few years. Outrageous assaults on such cultural icons as Miss America, motherhood, and marriage caught the attention of the mass media. Americans were both shocked and intrigued by the sudden questioning of fundamental assumptions. As ever-widening circles of women joined in the process, a range of institutions—from corporations to families—began to experience angry insurgency from within. The *Ladies' Home Journal,* its offices seized by female journalists, agreed to print in August 1970 a special section written and produced by feminists; soon afterwards, women at *Newsweek* and *Time* staged their own rebellions. No institution, it seemed, was sacred or safe. Nuns organized within the Catholic Church; female seminary students began to agitate for full equality within Protestant churches. In 1975 they wracked the Episcopal Church with controversy, when eleven women defiantly joined in an unauthorized ordination service. And in the privacy of thousands of bedrooms and kitchens across the country, revolutions over housework, child care, family decision-making, and sexuality raged on or reached quiet resolution.

The young are prominent in most revolutions. In this case in particular it seemed logical and necessary that the initiative should come from young women who did not have marriages and financial security to risk or years invested in traditional roles to justify. Within the context of cultural unrest and the attack on tradition made by women like Friedan, the catalyst for a profounder criticism and a mass mobilization of American women proved to be the young female participants in the social movements of the 1960s. These daughters of the middle class had received mixed, paradoxical messages about what it meant to grow up to be women in America. On the one hand, the cultural ideal—held up by media, parents, and school—informed them that their only true happiness lay in the twin roles of wife and mother. At the same time they could observe the reality that housewifery was distinctly unsatisfactory for millions of suburban women and that despite the best efforts of *Ladies' Home Journal,* most American women could expect to work outside the home a substantial part of their lives. Furthermore, having grown up in an era that commoditized sexual titillation while it reasserted repressive norms, they found themselves living on the ambiguous frontiers of sexual freedom and self-control opened up by the birth control pill. Such contradictions left young, educated women in the 1960s dry tinder for the spark of revolt.

The stage was set. Yet the need remains to unravel the mystery of how a few young women stepped outside the assumptions on which they had been raised to articulate a radical critique of women's position in American society. For them, a particular set of experiences in the southern civil rights movement and parts of the student new left catalyzed a new feminist consciousness. There they found the inner strength and self-respect to explore the meaning of equality and an ideology that beckoned them to do so. There they also met the same contradictory treatment most American women experienced, and it spun them out of those movements into one of their own.

QUESTIONS TO CONSIDER

1. Define the "feminine mystique." How and when did the term originate?
2. What was the role of education in creating anxiety in women?
3. Describe women's work in the 1950s.
4. How did *Life*'s special issue on women in 1956 reinforce the feminine mystique?
5. How did the feminine mystique relate to the Cold War and the organization man?
6. What events in the 1961–1964 period stimulated the emergence of women?
7. How did NOW differ from radical feminism in its critique of society?

13

Trumpet of Conscience

STEPHEN B. OATES

One of the enduring questions in history is whether the individual makes the times or the times make the individual. Probably a combination of the two provides the best answer: a significant leader can emerge if the times are right, but it doesn't always happen. Martin Luther King, Jr., provided critical leadership to the civil rights movement, personified civil rights in the minds of much of the nation, and pursued a strategy that astutely drew on northern white liberal support by his nonviolent approach to fighting injustice. Though recent scholarship has begun to focus on the many local leaders who made a difference in their communities, during the civil rights era King was unquestionably the preeminent national figure.

King called on the better side of the American character by dramatizing the ills of segregation as a simple case of justice against injustice and, in so doing, mobilized public opinion to support the most important popular movement of the century. In this article, Stephen B. Oates stresses the importance of King's ideas, both his Christianity and the more secular thinking derived from Gandhi and Thoreau, in shaping his response to the evils of segregation. His achievement was such that he is today the only American who was never a president with a national holiday in his honor.

Stephen B. Oates, since 1968 a history professor at the University of Massachusetts, wrote a full-length biography of King, *Let the Trumpet Sound: The Life of Martin Luther King, Jr.* (1982). He has won great acclaim for his two volumes on the coming and fighting of the Civil War told in the first person by major participants: *The Approaching Fury: Voices of the Storm, 1820–1861* (1997), and *The Whirlwind of War: Voices of the Storm, 1861–1865* (1998).

He was M.L. to his parents, Martin to his wife and friends, Doc to his aides, Reverend to his male parishioners, Little Lord Jesus to adoring churchwomen, De Lawd to his young critics in the Student Nonviolent Coordinating Committee, and Martin Luther King, Jr., to the world. At his pulpit or a public rostrum, he seemed too small for his incomparable oratory and international fame as a civil rights leader and spokesman for world peace. He stood only five feet seven, and had round cheeks, a trim mustache, and sad, glistening eyes—eyes that revealed both his inner strength and his vulnerability.

He was born in Atlanta on January 15, 1929, and grew up in the relative comfort of the black middle class. Thus he never suffered the want and privation that plagued the majority of American blacks of his time. His father, a gruff, self-made man, was pastor of Ebenezer Baptist Church and an outspoken member of Atlanta's black leadership. M.L. joined his father's church when he was five and came to regard it as his second home. The church defined his world, gave it order and balance, taught him how to "get along with people." Here M.L. knew who he was—"Reverend King's boy," somebody special.

At home, his parents and maternal grandmother reinforced his self-esteem, praising him for his precocious ways, telling him repeatedly that he was *somebody*. By age five, he spoke like an adult and had such a prodigious memory that he could recite whole Biblical passages and entire hymns without a mistake. He was acutely sensitive, too, so much so that he worried about all the blacks he saw in Atlanta's breadlines during the Depression, fearful that their children did not have enough to eat. When his maternal grandmother died, twelve-year-old M.L. thought it was his fault. Without telling anyone, he had slipped away from home to watch a parade, only to find out when he returned that she had died. He was terrified that God had taken her away as punishment for his "sin." Guilt-stricken, he tried to kill himself by leaping out of his second-story window.

He had a great deal of anger in him. Growing up a black in segregated Atlanta, he felt the full range of southern racial discrimination. He discovered that he had to attend separate, inferior schools, which he sailed through with a modicum of effort, skipping grades as he went. He found out that he—a preacher's boy—could not sit at lunch counters in Atlanta's downtown stores. He had to drink from a "colored" water fountain, relieve himself in a rancid "colored" restroom, and ride a rickety "colored" elevator. If he rode a city bus, he had to sit in the back as though he were contaminated. If he wanted to see a movie in a downtown theater, he had to enter through a side door and sit in the "colored" section in the balcony. He discovered that whites referred to blacks as "boys" and "girls" regardless of age. He saw "WHITES ONLY" signs staring back at him in the windows of barber shops and all the good restaurants and hotels, at the YMCA, the city parks, golf courses, swimming pools, and in the waiting rooms of the train and bus stations. He learned that there were even white and black sections of the city and that he resided in "nigger town."

Segregation caused a tension in the boy, a tension between his parents' injunction ("Remember, you are *somebody*") and a system that constantly demeaned and insulted him. He struggled with the pain and rage he felt when a white woman in a downtown store slapped him and called him "a little nigger" . . . when a bus driver called him "a black son-of-a-bitch" and made him surrender his seat to a white . . . when he stood on the very spot in Atlanta where whites had lynched a black man . . . when he witnessed nightriding Klansmen beating blacks in the streets. How, he asked defiantly, could he heed the Christian injunction and love a race of people who hated him? In retaliation, he determined "to hate every white person."

Yes, he was angry. In sandlot games, he competed so fiercely that friends could not tell whether he was playing or fighting. He had his share of playground combat, too, and could outwrestle any of his peers. He even rebelled against his father, vowing never to become a preacher like him. Yet he liked the way Daddy King stood up to whites: he told them never to call him a boy and vowed to fight this system until he died.

Still, there was another side to M.L., a calmer, sensuous side. He played the violin, enjoyed opera, and relished soul food—fried chicken, cornbread, and collard greens with ham hocks and bacon drippings. By his mid-teens, his voice was the most memorable thing about him. It had changed into a rich and resonant baritone that commanded attention whenever he held forth. A natty dresser, nicknamed "Tweed" because of his fondness for tweed suits, he became a connoisseur of lovely young women. His little brother A.D. remembered how Martin "kept flitting from chick to chick" and was "just about the best jitterbug in town."

At age fifteen, he entered Morehouse College in Atlanta, wanting somehow to help his people. He thought about becoming a lawyer and even practiced giving trial speeches before a mirror in his room. But thanks largely to Morehouse President Benjamin Mays, who showed him that the ministry could be a respectable forum for ideas, even for social protest, King decided to become a Baptist preacher after all. By the time he was ordained in 1947, his resentment toward whites had softened some, thanks to positive contact with white students on an intercollegiate council. But he hated his segregated world more than ever.

Once he had his bachelor's degree, he went north to study at Crozer Seminary near Philadelphia. In this mostly white school, with its polished corridors and quiet solemnity, King continued to ponder the plight of blacks in America. How, by what method and means, were blacks to improve their lot in a white-dominated country? His study of history, especially of Nat Turner's slave insurrection, convinced him that it was suicidal for a minority to strike back against a heavily armed majority. For him, voluntary segregation was equally unacceptable, as was accommodation to the status quo. King shuddered at such negative approaches to the race problem. How indeed were blacks to combat discrimination in a country ruled by the white majority?

As some other blacks had done, he found his answer in the teachings of Mohandas Gandhi—for young King, the discovery had the force of a conversion experience. Nonviolent resistance, Gandhi taught, meant non-cooperation with evil, an idea he got from Henry David Thoreau's essay "On Civil Disobedience." In India, Gandhi gave Thoreau's theory practical application in the form of strikes, boycotts, and protest marches, all conducted nonviolently and all predicated on love for the oppressor and a belief in divine justice. In gaining Indian independence, Gandhi sought not to defeat the British, but to redeem them through love, so as to avoid a legacy of bitterness. Gandhi's term for this—Satyagraha—reconciled love and force in a single, powerful concept.

As King discovered from his studies, Gandhi had embraced nonviolence in part to subdue his own violent nature. This was a profound revelation for King, who had felt much hatred in his life, especially toward whites. Now Gandhi showed him a means of harnessing his anger and channeling it into a positive and creative force for social change.

At this juncture, King found mostly theoretical satisfaction in Gandhian nonviolence; he had no plans to become a radical activist in the segregated South. Indeed, he seemed destined to a life of the mind, not of social protest. In 1951, he graduated from Crozer and went on to earn a Ph.D. in theology from Boston University, where his adviser pronounced him "a scholar's scholar" of great intellectual potential. By 1955, a year after the school desegregation decision, King had married comely Coretta Scott and assumed the pastorship of Dexter Avenue Baptist Church in Montgomery, Alabama. Immensely happy in the world of ideas, he hoped eventually to teach theology at a major university or seminary.

But, as King liked to say, the Zeitgist, or spirit of the age, had other plans for him. In December 1955, Montgomery blacks launched a boycott of the city's segregated buses and chose the articulate twenty-six-year-old minister as their spokesman. As it turned out, he was unusually well prepared to assume the kind of leadership thrust on him. Drawing on Gandhi's teachings and example, plus the tenets of his own Christian faith, King directed a nonviolent boycott designed both to end an injustice and redeem his white adversaries through love. When he exhorted blacks to love their enemies, King did not mean to love them as friends or intimates. No, he said, he meant a disinterested love in all humankind, a love that saw the neighbor in everyone it met, a love that sought to restore the beloved community. Such love not only avoided the internal violence of the spirit, but severed the external chain of hatred that only produced more hatred in an endless spiral. If American blacks could break the chain of hatred, King said, true brotherhood could begin. Then posterity would have to say that there had lived a race of people, of black people, who "injected a new meaning into the veins of history and civilization."

During the boycott King imparted his philosophy at twice-weekly mass meetings in the black churches, where overflow crowds clapped and cried as his mellifluous voice swept over them. In these mass meetings King discovered his extraordinary power as an orator. His rich religious imagery reached deep into the black psyche, for religion had been the black people's main source of strength and survival since slavery days. His delivery was "like a narrative poem," said a woman journalist who heard him. His voice had such depths of sincerity and empathy that it could "charm your heart right out of your body." Because he appealed to the best in his people, articulating their deepest hurts and aspirations, black folk began to idolize him; he was their Gandhi.

Under his leadership, they stood up to white Montgomery in a remarkable display of solidarity. Pitted against an obdurate city government that blamed the boycott on Communist agitation and resorted to psychological and legal warfare to break it, the blacks stayed off the buses month after month, and walked or rode in a black-operated carpool. When an elderly woman refused the offer of a ride, King asked her, "But don't your feet hurt?" "Yes," she replied, "my feet is tired but my soul is rested." For King, her irrepressible spirit was proof that "a new Negro" was emerging in the South, a Negro with "a new sense of dignity and destiny."

That "new Negro" menaced white supremacists, especially the Ku Klux Klan, and they persecuted King with a vengeance. They made obscene phone calls to his home, sent him abusive sickening letters, and once even dynamited the front of his house. Nobody was hurt, but King, fearing a race war, had to dissuade angry blacks from violent retaliation. Finally, on November 13, 1956, the U.S. Supreme Court nullified the Alabama laws that enforced segregated buses, and handed King and his boycotters a resounding moral victory. Their protest had captured the imagination of progressive people all over the world and marked the beginning of a southern black movement that would shake the segregated South to its foundations. At the forefront of that movement was a new organization, the Southern Christian Leadership Conference (SCLC), which King and other black ministers formed in 1957, with King serving as its president and guiding spirit. Operating through the southern black church, SCLC sought to enlist the black masses in the freedom struggle by expanding "the Montgomery way" across the South.

The "Miracle of Montgomery" changed King's life, catapulting him into international prominence as an inspiring new moral voice for civil rights. Across the country, blacks and whites alike wrote him letters of encouragement; *Time* magazine pictured him on its cover; the National

Association for the Advancement of Colored People (NAACP) and scores of church and civic organizations vied for his services as a speaker. "I am really disturbed how fast all this has happened to me," King told his wife. "People will expect me to perform miracles for the rest of my life."

But fame had its evil side, too. When King visited New York in 1958, a deranged black woman stabbed him in the chest with a letter opener. The weapon was lodged so close to King's aorta, the main artery from the heart, that he would have died had he sneezed. To extract the blade, an interracial surgical team had to remove a rib and part of his breastbone; in a burst of inspiration, the lead surgeon made the incision over King's heart in the shape of a cross.

That he had not died convinced King that God was preparing him for some larger work in the segregated South. To gain perspective on what was happening there, he made a pilgrimage to India to visit Gandhi's shrine and the sites of his "War for Independence." He returned home with an even deeper commitment to nonviolence and a vow to be more humble and ascetic like Gandhi. Yet he was a man of manifold contradictions, this American Gandhi. While renouncing material things and giving nearly all of his extensive honorariums to SCLC, he liked posh hotels and zesty meals with wine, and he was always immaculately dressed in a gray or black suit, white shirt, and tie. While caring passionately for the poor, the downtrodden, and the disinherited, he had a fascination with men of affluence and enjoyed the company of wealthy SCLC benefactors. While trumpeting the glories of nonviolence and redemptive love, he could feel the most terrible anger when whites murdered a black or bombed a black church; he could contemplate giving up, turning America over to the haters of both races, only to dedicate himself anew to his nonviolent faith and his determination to redeem his country.

In 1960, he moved his family to Atlanta so that he could devote himself fulltime to SCLC, which was trying to register black voters for the upcoming federal elections. That same year, southern black students launched the sit-in movement against segregated lunch counters, and King not only helped them form the Student Nonviolent Coordinating Committee (SNCC) but raised money on their behalf. In October he even joined a sit-in protest at an Atlanta department store and went to jail with several students on a trespassing charge. Like Thoreau, King considered jail "a badge of honor." To redeem the nation and arouse the conscience of the opponent, King explained, you go to jail and stay there. "You have broken a law which is out of line with the moral law and you are willing to suffer the consequences by serving the time."

He did not reckon, however, on the tyranny of racist officials, who clamped him in a malevolent state penitentiary, in a cell for hardened criminals. But state authorities released him when Democratic presidential nominee John F. Kennedy and his brother Robert interceded on King's behalf. According to many analysts, the episode won critical black votes for Kennedy and gave him the election in November. For King, the election demonstrated what he had long said: that one of the most significant steps a black could take was the short walk to the voting booth.

The trouble was that most blacks in Dixie, especially in the Deep South, could not vote even if they so desired. For decades, state and local authorities had kept the mass of black folk off the voting rolls by a welter of devious obstacles and outright intimidation. Through 1961 and 1962, King exhorted President Kennedy to sponsor tough new civil rights legislation that would enfranchise southern blacks and end segregated public accommodations as well. When Kennedy shied away from a strong civil rights commitment, King and his lieutenants took matters into their own hands, orchestrating a series of southern demonstrations to show the world the brutality of segregation. At the same time, King stumped the country, drawing on all his powers of oratory to enlist the black masses and win white opinion to his cause.

Everywhere he went his message was the same.

> The civil rights issue . . . is an eternal moral issue that will determine the destiny of our nation and our world. As we seek our full rights, we hope to redeem the soul of our country. For it is our country, too, and we will win our freedom because the sacred heritage of America and the eternal will of God are embodied in our echoing demands. We do not intend to humiliate the white man, but to win him over through the strength of our love. Ultimately, we are trying to free all of us in America—Negroes from the bonds of segregation and shame, whites from the bonds of bigotry and fear.
>
> We stand today between two worlds—the dying old order and the emerging new. With men of ill-will greeting this change with cries of violence, of interposition and nullification, some of us may get beaten. Some of us may even get killed. But if you are cut down in a movement designed to save the soul of a nation, no other death could be more redemptive. We must realize that change does not roll in "on the wheels of inevitability," but comes through struggle. So "let us be those creative dissenters who will call our beloved nation to a higher destiny, to a new plateau of compassion, to a more noble expression of humaneness."

That message worked like magic among America's long-suffering blacks. Across the South, across America, they rose in unprecedented numbers to march and demonstrate with Martin Luther King. His singular achievement was that he brought the black masses into the freedom struggle for the first time. He rallied the strength of broken men and women, helping them overcome a lifetime of fear and feelings of inferiority. After segregation had taught them all their lives that they were *nobody*, King taught them that they were *somebody*. Because he made them believe in themselves and in the beauty of chosen suffering, he taught them how to straighten their backs ("a man can't ride you unless your back is bent") and confront those who oppressed them. Through the technique of nonviolent resistance, he furnished them something no previous black leader had been able to provide. He showed them a way of controlling their pent-up anger, as he had controlled his own, and using it to bring about constructive change.

The mass demonstrations King and SCLC choreographed in the South produced the strongest civil rights legislation in American history. This was the goal of King's major southern campaigns from 1963 to 1965. He would single out some notoriously segregated city with white officials prone to violence, mobilize the local blacks with songs, scripture readings, and rousing oratory in black churches, and then lead them on protest marches conspicuous for their grace and moral purpose. Then he and his aides would escalate the marches, increase their demands, even fill up the jails, until they brought about a moment of "creative tension," when whites would either agree to negotiate or resort to violence. If they did the latter, King would thus expose the brutality inherent in segregation and so stab the national conscience so that the federal government would be forced to intervene with corrective measures.

The technique succeeded brilliantly in Birmingham, Alabama, in 1963. Here Police Commissioner Eugene "Bull" Connor, in full view of reporters and television cameras, turned firehoses and police dogs on the marching protestors. Revolted by such ghastly scenes, stricken by King's own searching eloquence and the bravery of his unarmed followers, Washington eventually produced the 1964 Civil Rights Act, which desegregated public facilities—the thing King had demanded all along from Birmingham. Across the South, the "WHITES ONLY" signs that had hurt and enraged him since boyhood now came down.

Although SNCC and others complained that King had a Messiah complex and was trying to monopolize the civil rights movement, his technique worked with equal success in Selma, Alabama, in 1965. Building on a local movement there, King and his staff launched a drive to gain southern blacks the unobstructed right to vote. The violence he exposed in Selma—the beating of black marchers by state troopers and deputized possemen, the killing of a young black deacon and a white Unitarian minister—horrified the country. When King called for support, thousands of ministers, rabbis, priests, nuns, students, lay leaders, and ordinary people—black and white alike—rushed to Selma from all over the country and stood with King in the name of human liberty. Never in the history of the movement had so many people of all faiths and classes come to the southern battleground. The Selma campaign culminated in a dramatic march over the Jefferson Davis Highway to the state capital of Montgomery. Along the way, impoverished local blacks stared incredulously at the marching, singing, flag-waving spectacle moving by. When the column reached one dusty crossroads, an elderly black woman ran out from a group of old folk, kissed King breathlessly, and ran back crying, "I done kissed him! The Martin Luther King! I done kissed the Martin Luther King!"

In Montgomery, first capital and much-heralded "cradle" of the Confederacy, King led an interracial throng of 25,000—the largest civil rights demonstration the South had ever witnessed—up Dexter Avenue with banners waving overhead. The pageant was as ironic as it was extraordinary, for it was up Dexter Avenue that Jefferson Davis's first inaugural parade had marched, and in the portico of the capitol Davis had taken his oath of office as president of the slave-based Confederacy. Now, in the spring of 1965, Alabama blacks—most of them descendants of slaves—stood massed at the same statehouse, singing a new rendition of "We Shall Overcome," the anthem of the civil rights movement. They sang, "Deep in my heart, I do believe, We have overcome—*today.*"

Then, within view of the statue of Jefferson Davis, and watched by cordons of state troopers and television cameras, King mounted a trailer. His vast audience listened, transfixed, as his words rolled and thundered over the loudspeaker: "My people, my people listen. The battle is in our hands. . . . We must come to see that the end we seek is a society at peace with itself, a society that can live with its conscience. That day will be a day not of the white man, not of the black man. That will be the day of man as man." And that day was not long in coming, King said, whereupon he launched into the immortal refrains of "The Battle Hymn of the Republic," crying out, "Our God is marching on! Glory, glory hallelujah!"

Aroused by the events in Alabama, Washington produced the 1965 Voting Rights Act, which outlawed impediments to black voting and empowered the attorney general to supervise federal elections in seven southern states where blacks were kept off the rolls. At the time, political analysts almost unanimously attributed the act to King's Selma campaign. Once federal examiners were supervising voter registration in all troublesome southern areas, blacks were able to get on the rolls and vote by the hundreds of thousands, permanently altering the pattern of southern and national politics.

In the end, the powerful civil rights legislation generated by King and his tramping legions wiped out statutory racism in America and realized at least the social and political promise of emancipation a century before. But King was under no illusion that legislation alone could bring on the brave new America he so ardently championed. Yes, he said, laws and their vigorous enforcement were necessary to regulate destructive habits and actions, and to protect blacks and their rights. But laws could not eliminate the "fears, prejudice, pride, and irrationality" that were barriers to a truly integrated society, to peaceful intergroup and interpersonal living. Such a society could be achieved only when people accepted that inner, invisible law that etched on their hearts the conviction "that all men are brothers and that love is mankind's most potent weapon for personal and social transformation. True integration will be achieved by true neighbors who are willingly obedient to unenforceable obligations."

Even so, the Selma campaign was the movement's finest hour, and the Voting Rights Act the high point of a broad civil rights coalition that included the federal government, various white groups, and all the other civil rights organizations in addition to SCLC. King himself had best expressed the spirit and aspirations of that coalition when, on August 28, 1963, standing before the Lincoln Memorial, he electrified an interracial crowd of 250,000 with perhaps his greatest speech, "I Have A Dream," in which he described in rhythmic, hypnotic cadences his vision of an integrated America. Because of his achievements and moral vision, he won the 1964 Nobel Peace Prize, at thirty-four the youngest recipient in Nobel history.

Still, King paid a high price for his fame and his cause. He suffered from stomachaches and insomnia, and even felt guilty about all the tributes he received, all the popularity he enjoyed. Born in relative material comfort and given a superior education, he did not think he had earned the right to lead the impoverished black masses. He complained, too, that he no longer had a personal self and that sometimes he did not recognize the Martin Luther King people talked about. Lonely, away from home for protracted periods, beset with temptation, he slept with other women, for some of whom he had real feeling. His sexual transgressions only added to his guilt, for he knew he was imperiling his cause and hurting himself and those he loved.

Alas for King, FBI Director J. Edgar Hoover found out about the black leader's infidelities. The director already abhorred King, certain that Communist spies influenced him and masterminded his demonstrations. Hoover did not think blacks capable of organizing such things, so Communists had to be behind them and King as well. As it turned out, a lawyer in King's inner circle and a man in SCLC's New York office did have Communist backgrounds, a fact that only reinforced Hoover's suspicions about King. Under Hoover's orders, FBI agents conducted a ruthless crusade to destroy King's reputation and drive him broken and humiliated from public life. Hoover's men tapped King's phones and bugged his hotel rooms; they compiled a prurient monograph about his private life and showed it to various editors, public officials, and religious and civic leaders; they spread the word, Hoover's word, that King was not only a reprobate but a dangerous subversive with Communist associations.

King was scandalized and frightened by the FBI's revelations of his extramarital affairs. Luckily for him, no editor, not even a racist one in the South, would touch the FBI's salacious materials. Public officials such as Robert Kennedy were shocked, but argued that King's personal life did not affect his probity as a civil rights leader. Many blacks, too, declared that what he did in private was his own business. Even so, King vowed to refrain from further affairs—only to succumb again to his own human frailties.

As for the Communist charge, King retorted that he did not need any Russians to tell him when someone was standing on his neck; he could figure that out by himself. To mollify his political friends, however, King did banish from SCLC the two men with Communist backgrounds (later he resumed his ties with the lawyer, a loyal friend, and let Hoover be damned). He also denounced Communism in no uncertain terms. It was, he believed, profoundly and fundamentally evil, an atheistic doctrine no true Christian could ever embrace. He hated the dictatorial Soviet state, too, whose "crippling totalitarianism" subordinated everything—religion, art, music, science, and the individual—to its terrible yoke. True, Communism started with men like Karl Marx who were "aflame with a passion for social justice." Yet King faulted Marx for rejecting God and the spiritual in human life. "The great weakness in Karl Marx is right here," King once told his staff, and he went on to describe his ideal Christian commonwealth in Hegelian terms: "Capitalism fails to realize that life is social. Marxism fails to realize that life is individual. Truth is found neither in the rugged individualism of capitalism nor in the impersonal collectivism of Communism. The kingdom of God is found in a synthesis that combines the truths of these two opposites. Now there is where I leave brother Marx and move on toward the kingdom."

But how to move on after Selma was a perplexing question King never successfully answered. After the devastating Watts riot in August 1965, he took his movement into the racially troubled urban North, seeking to help the suffering black poor in the ghettos. In 1966, over the fierce opposition of some of his own staff, he launched a campaign to end the black slums in Chicago and forestall rioting there. But the campaign foundered because King seemed unable to devise a coherent anti-slum strategy, because Mayor Richard Daley and his black acolytes opposed him bitterly, and because white America did not seem to care. King did lead open-housing marches into segregated neighborhoods in Chicago, only to encounter furious mobs who waved Nazi banners, threw bottles and bricks, and screamed, "We hate niggers!" "Kill the niggers!" "We want Martin Luther Coon!" King was shocked. "I've been in many demonstrations all across the South," he told reporters, "but I can say that I have never seen—even in Mississippi and Alabama—mobs as hostile and as hate-filled as I've seen in Chicago." Although King prevented a major riot there and wrung important concessions from City Hall, the slums remained, as wretched and seemingly unsolvable as ever.

That same year, angry young militants in SNCC and the Congress of Racial Equality (CORE) renounced King's teachings—they were sick and tired of "De Lawd" telling them to love white people and work for integration. Now they advocated "Black Power," black separatism, even violent resistance to liberate blacks in America. SNCC even banished whites from its ranks and went on to drop "nonviolent" from its name and to lobby against civil rights legislation.

Black Power repelled the older, more conservative black organizations such as the NAACP and the Urban League, and fragmented the civil rights movement beyond repair. King, too, argued that black separatism was chimerical, even suicidal, and that nonviolence remained the only workable way for black people. "Darkness cannot drive out darkness," he reasoned: "only light can do that. Hate cannot drive out hate: only love can do that." If every other black in America turned to violence, King warned, then he would still remain the lone voice preaching that it was wrong. Nor was SCLC going to reject whites as SNCC had done. "There have been too many hymns of hope," King said, "too many anthems of expectation, too many deaths, too many dark days of standing over graves of those who fought for integration for us to turn back now. We must still sing 'Black and White Together, We Shall Overcome.'"

In 1967, King himself broke with the older black organizations over the ever-widening war in Vietnam. He had first objected to American escalation in the summer of 1965, arguing that the Nobel Peace Prize and his role as a Christian minister compelled him to speak out for peace. Two years later, with almost a half-million Americans—a disproportionate number of them poor blacks—fighting in Vietnam, King devoted whole speeches to America's "immoral" war against a tiny country on the other side of the globe. His stance provoked a fusillade of criticism from all directions—from the NAACP, the Urban League, white and black political leaders, *Newsweek*, *Life*, *Time*, and the *New York Times*, all telling him to stick to civil rights. Such criticism hurt him deeply. When he read the *Times*'s editorial against him, he broke down and cried. But he did not back down. "I've fought too long and too hard now against segregated accommodations to end up segregating my moral concerns," he told his critics. "Injustice anywhere is a threat to justice everywhere."

That summer, with the ghettos ablaze with riots, King warned that American cities would explode if funds used for war purposes were not diverted to emergency antipoverty programs. By then, the Johnson administration, determined to gain a military victory in Vietnam, had written King off as an antiwar agitator, and was now cooperating with the FBI in its efforts to defame him.

The fall of 1967 was a terrible time for King, the lowest ebb in his civil rights career. Everybody seemed to be attacking him—young black militants for his stubborn adherence to nonviolence, moderate and conservative blacks, labor leaders, liberal white politicians, the White House, and the FBI for his stand on Vietnam. Two years had passed since King had produced a nonviolent victory, and contributions to SCLC had fallen off sharply. Black spokesman Adam Clayton Powell, who had once called King the greatest Negro in America, now derided him as Martin Loser King. The incessant attacks began to irritate him, creating such anxiety and depression that his friends worried about his emotional health.

Worse still, the country seemed dangerously polarized. On one side, back-lashing whites argued that the ghetto explosions had "cremated" non-violence and that white people had better arm themselves against black rioters. On the other side, angry blacks urged their people to "kill the Honkies" and burn the cities down. All around King, the country was coming apart in a cacophony of hate and reaction. Had America lost the will and moral power to save itself? he wondered. There was such rage in the ghetto and such bigotry among whites that he feared a race war was about to break out. He felt he had to do something to pull America back from the brink. He and his staff had to mount a new campaign that would halt the drift to violence in the black world and combat stiffening white resistance, a nonviolent action that would "transmute the deep rage of the ghetto into a constructive and creative force."

Out of his deliberations sprang a bold and daring project called the poor people's campaign. The master plan, worked out by February 1968, called for SCLC to bring an interracial army of poor people to Washington, D.C., to dramatize poverty before the federal government. For King, just turned thirty-nine, the time had come to employ civil disobedience against the national government itself. Ultimately, he was projecting a genuine class movement that he hoped would bring about meaningful changes in American society—changes that would redistribute economic and political power and end poverty, racism, "the madness of militarism," and war.

In the midst of his preparations, King went to Memphis, Tennessee, to help black sanitation workers there who were striking for the right to unionize. On the night of April 3, with a storm thundering outside, he told a black audience that he had been to the mountaintop and had seen what lay ahead. "I may not get there with you. But I want you to know tonight that we as a people *will* get to the promised land."

The next afternoon, when King stepped out on the balcony of the Lorraine Motel, an escaped white convict named James Earl Ray, stationed in a nearby building, took aim with a high-powered rifle and blasted King into eternity. Subsequent evidence linked Ray to white men in the St. Louis area who had offered "hit" money for King's life.

For weeks after the shooting, King's stricken country convulsed in grief, contrition, and rage. While there were those who cheered his death, the *New York Times* called it a disaster to the nation, the *London Times* an enormous loss to the world. In Tanzania, Reverend Trevor Huddleston, expelled from South Africa for standing against apartheid, declared King's death the greatest single tragedy since the assassination of Gandhi in 1948, and said it challenged the complacency of the Christian Church all over the globe.

On April 9, with 120 million Americans watching on television, thousands of mourners—black and white alike—gathered in Atlanta for the funeral of a man who had never given up his dream of creating a symphony of brotherhood on these shores. As a black man born and raised in segregation, he had had every reason to hate America and to grow up preaching cynicism and retaliation. Instead, he had loved the country passionately and had sung of her promise and glory more eloquently than anyone of his generation.

They buried him in Atlanta's South View Cemetery, then blooming with dogwood and fresh green boughs of spring. On his crypt, hewn into the marble, were the words of an old Negro spiritual he had often quoted: "Free at Last, Free at Last, Thank God Almighty I'm Free at Last."

QUESTIONS TO CONSIDER

1. How did King's background and upbringing prepare him for his leadership role?
2. Explain Satyagraha.
3. What does Oates call King's singular achievement? Why?
4. What was King's goal in his 1963–1965 campaigns? How well did he succeed? What specific legislation resulted?
5. In what way did challenges to King from the left (black militants) and right (the FBI) affect his campaigns?
6. What issue led to King's break with Lyndon Johnson's administration? Why? Was King becoming too radical for mainstream America by 1967?

14

"With One Hand Tied Behind Their Back"

ROBERT BUZZANCO

Reprinted from *Myth America,*
Brandywine Press, 1997,
by permission of the author.

While women and blacks were redefining the American character at home, the United States, mesmerized by anticommunism, blundered into the Vietnam War in the 1960s. The war undermined the Cold War consensus about the American role in the world: that the United States was the leader of the "free world" against the forces of darkness. The moral ambiguity of the Vietnam conflict, coupled with a frustrating inability to defeat an obscure third-world country, undermined support for the war in the United States and produced a growing and increasingly vocal antiwar movement. Supporters and opponents of the war cited atrocities by the other side to bolster their arguments, and for the first time it was unclear to a sizable segment of the population just who the "good guys" were in an American war.

Many Americans responded to the loss in Vietnam by arguing that the American military had been "stabbed in the back," much as Nazis claimed that politicians had sabotaged the German military in World War I. In this article, Robert Buzzanco argues that the military had harbored serious reservations about an American commitment as far back as 1950; were under no illusion that they would be able to win the war; and, whatever political limitations were placed on them, had access to and used a stunning array of military weaponry in an effort to win a military victory in a political war. A more critical consideration in the American defeat, had victory been feasible at all, was to be found in the interservice debate between the Marines, who wanted to focus on pacification to win the "hearts and minds" of the Vietnamese people, and the Army, who favored a war of attrition. The United States took the latter approach, and that war, in support of an "imagined" country like South Vietnam, was basically unwinnable. Both President Lyndon Johnson and the military paid a heavy price for the effort in America, although the Indochinese suffered far more.

Robert Buzzanco teaches at the University of Houston. A specialist on the topic of this article, he has written *Masters of War: Military Dissent and Politics in the Vietnam Era* (1996) and *Vietnam and the Transformation of American Life* (1999). In 1998 the Society for Historians of American Foreign Policy proclaimed him the foremost young diplomatic historian in the nation.

A s he unleashed American air power against the armed forces and people of Iraq in January 1991, President George Bush assured the nation that U.S. soldiers would not be inhibited by craven politicians or an ambivalent public. "Our troops," Bush explained, "will not be asked to fight with one hand tied behind their back." Just six weeks later, after the American destruction of Iraq, Bush explained that "by God, we've kicked the 'Vietnam Syndrome' once and for all."

The president's words were not coincidental. The use of Vietnam as a symbol of a lack of will and weakness has become common in American political discourse over the past two decades. The United States, many politicians, officers, and scholars have argued, did not suffer a military defeat in Indochina but was in fact undermined at home by weak political leaders and a large antiwar movement. "On the battlefield itself," retired Colonel Harry Summers asserted, "the [U.S.] Army was unbeatable," a view shared by many defenders of the war. Others criticized political leaders, particularly President Lyndon B. Johnson and Defense Secretary Robert Strange McNamara, for limiting the war geographically, needlessly restricting the U.S. air war against the Democratic Republic of Vietnam (DRVN) in the north, and failing to take the strategic initiative and employ more firepower more effectively. By the 1980s such views had become commonplace and powerful; thus candidate Ronald Reagan called the American intervention into Vietnam a "noble cause," and Defense Secretary Caspar Weinberger, amid a public discussion over military policy, explained that "we must never again send Americans into battle unless we plan to win."

Such views, though they may produce significant political currency, do not constitute good history. In fact, those individuals charged with conducting the war in Vietnam, senior American military officers, were in fact critical of and divided over U.S. intervention in Indochina throughout the 1950s and early 1960s. Once American combat troops were deployed to Vietnam, the brass remained pessimistic about U.S. prospects there and engaged in serious interservice arguments over the way the war should be fought.

In short, the U.S. armed services never agreed on either intervention or strategy. The American failure in Vietnam was thus not a case of "hands tied behind backs," but rather was due to a conscious political decision to go to war in an area of secondary importance where the possibilities for success, as the military itself recognized, were never great.

For over a decade after the end of World War II, American officers remained highly critical of plans to increase U.S. involvement in Vietnam. Although the revolutionary Viet Minh, a nationalist-Communist force led by Ho Chi Minh and supported by the Soviet Union and People's Republic of China, seemed likely victors in its war against French imperialists and Vietnamese collaborators that had begun in 1946, American military leaders urged a "hands off" policy. Indeed, in the early 1950s, service officials developed a critique of Vietnam that would remain valid for two decades. Above all, the brass opposed war in Indochina because the area was not a priority in national security policy and because the military understood the limits of American power. Accordingly, officers such as Air Force Chief of Staff Hoyt Vandenberg—concerned that French stability was the keystone to European security—warned in 1953 that the continued commitment in Vietnam amounted to "pouring money down a rathole."

American officers clearly understood that French imperialism had created an oppressive political environment for native Vietnamese. Ho Chi Minh enjoyed the support of eighty percent of the population, U.S. Army planners estimated, yet eighty percent of the Viet Minh's followers were not communists. Even France's biggest booster inside the military, Pacific Commander and later JCS Chair Admiral Arthur Radford, saw that "the French seem to have no popular backing from the local Indo-Chinese." By late 1954, Army analysts pointed out that the Viet Minh had grown to about 340,000 troops with about one-quarter *below* the seventeenth parallel, which divided North from South Vietnam.

Any American military commitment to Vietnam, ranking service officials added, would face enormous barriers to success. In March 1950, Army intelligence officers recognized that the "rugged terrain" in Vietnam was a great advantage to the Viet Minh, which was well-versed in jungle, guerrilla warfare. Air Force General Charles Cabell, a JCS official, also had a clear understanding of the hazards of combat in Vietnam. "Terrain difficulties, the guerrilla nature of Viet Minh operations, and the political apathy of the population," he explained in 1953, would make it impossible to clear the Viet Minh out of southern villages, unless "physically occupied" by numerous friendly forces. In his debriefing after leaving Vietnam, General Thomas Trapnell, leader of the U.S. military advisory effort there, cited Ho's followers for their "clever war of attrition" and explained that the Viet Minh, believing that time and public opinion was on its side, would simply continue its guerrilla operations. "A strictly military solution to this war," Trapnell warned, "is not possible."

More importantly, Army Chief of Staff Matthew B. Ridgway, who had been the United Nations commander in Korea after the dismissal of Douglas MacArthur, successfully challenged advocates of intervention in the Spring of 1954. President Dwight Eisenhower and Secretary of State John Foster Dulles were seeking support for American intervention to relieve besieged French troops at Dien Bien Phu, a village near the Laotian border. Such a military commitment in Vietnam, Ridgway emphatically charged, would be a "dangerous strategic diversion" because of limited U.S. resources and troops. It therefore made no sense to Ridgway to commit American soldiers to "a non-decisive theatre" where only "non-decisive local objectives" might be gained. More pointedly, General James Gavin, the Army's chief of planning observed that any U.S. commitment to protect Vietnam below the seventeenth parallel "involves the risk of embroiling [the] U.S. in the wrong war, in the wrong place, at the wrong time."

Despite the military's strong reservations about involvement in Vietnam throughout the early 1950s, the United States established a training mission to the nation below the seventeenth parallel it had ostensibly invented at the 1954 Geneva Conference, the Republic of Vietnam (RVN), and, as the American military leadership had warned, escalated the U.S. role there throughout the next two decades. Publicly, Vietnam declined quite a bit as a foreign policy issue after 1955, but in the later 1950s Generals Gavin and Ridgway continued to criticize American involvement in Indochina. Ridgway expressed his opposition to intervention in poignant yet ultimately empty words: "When the day comes for me to face my Maker and account for my actions, the thing I would be most humbly proud of was the fact that I fought against, and perhaps contributed to preventing, the carrying out of some hare-brained tactical schemes which would have cost the lives of thousands of men. To that list of tragic accidents that fortunately never happened, I would add the Indo-China intervention."

By the early 1960s, it was clear that Ridgway would have to change the script for his heavenly talk. Though America's military planners of the early 1950s had anticipated the serious if not insurmountable barriers to effective military action in Vietnam, Presidents John F. Kennedy and Lyndon B. Johnson progressively expanded the U.S. commitment to the RVN and Johnson eventually deployed ground troops and "Americanized" the war in 1965.

John F. Kennedy came to the White House promising to "pay any price" and "bear any burden" in the global fight against Communism. From his inaugural in January 1961 to his assassination in November 1963, the centerpiece of that Cold War policy would be Vietnam. Kennedy, especially after suffering an embarrassing political defeat at the Bay of Pigs in Cuba in April 1961, focused increasing amounts of resources and money on the effort to prevent Ho Chi Minh's victory in Vietnam. As a result, the Kennedy administration supported the corrupt and repressive regime of

Ngo Dinh Diem in the RVN; increased the number of military personnel in Vietnam from 800 to 16,000; allowed the military to use defoliation agents and napalm in southern villages; and authorized the use of helicopters and air support against the enemy, now referred to as the "Viet Cong" (VC). Although Oliver Stone, in his film *JFK,* and many others claim that the president was preparing to withdraw the United States from Vietnam after the 1964 elections, the historical record proves otherwise. Kennedy and McNamara were heading toward war in Vietnam.

U.S. military leaders, however, were not nearly so hawkish. The armed forces, afraid of being unfairly blamed for failure in Vietnam as they had been after the Bay of Pigs disaster, constantly tried to pin down the president regarding Vietnam policy, to make him establish, describe and take responsibility for any military involvement there. As General Charles Bonesteel of the JCS staff put it, the military needed Kennedy to offer an explanation of "real national intent" before developing its own proposals for Indochina. More specific criticism came from the military's Pacific Commander, Admiral Harry D. Felt, who "strongly opposed" the use of American troops in Vietnam out of fear that the United States would be seen as the aggressor in Vietnam and that world opinion would condemn the intervention of Caucasian soldiers in an Asian civil war. Several officers, after touring Vietnam in mid-1962, added that "the military and political situation in South Vietnam can be described in four words, 'it is a mess.'"

Such military pessimism remained in evidence throughout the Kennedy years. American officers, however, did not refuse to implement the president's policies in Indochina or even strongly challenge them. Rather, the military, for the most part, went along with civilian decisions on Vietnam, but always tried to make it clear that Kennedy and McNamara would be responsible if conditions there, as the brass expected, worsened. Perhaps the best example of this came from General Lionel McGarr, the head of the U.S. Advisory Group in Vietnam. McGarr warned that any military involvement would turn out badly and, as early as 1961, he saw a "slimmer and slimmer" chance to succeed in Vietnam. McGarr nonetheless was willing to accept Kennedy's commitment to the RVN, but even more he feared that the military would be blamed for the likely failure. "As I am jealous of the professional good name of our Army," he explained, "I do not wish it to be placed in the position of fighting a losing battle and being charged with the loss."

Despite such military reservations, U.S. policy in Vietnam did not change in the Kennedy years. The young president, convinced that he had to challenge Communism everywhere, kept increasing the American role in Indochina. Indeed, in interviews shortly before his death, Kennedy was still hawkish on Vietnam. Though he understood that the public might be anxious about war there, an American withdrawal "only makes it easier for the Communists." Problems may lie ahead, but "I think we should stay." Lyndon Johnson agreed.

Lyndon Johnson entered the White House committed to "seeing things through in Vietnam"; he would not, he pledged, "be the President who saw Southeast Asia go the way China went" and so he told his advisors to "tell those generals in Saigon that Lyndon Johnson intends to stand by our word." As a result, from late 1963 until the Tet Offensive in early 1968, Johnson daily confronted the growing crisis of the Vietnam War without essentially questioning the U.S. commitment there. During those years three developments characterized military policy with regard to Vietnam. First, U.S. military leaders in the 1960s continued to recognize the dangerous nature of the American role and the serious obstacles to future success in Vietnam. Second, military leaders understood from the war's beginning that—due to both domestic and international political factors—Lyndon Johnson would establish limits (in troop deployments and geographic areas of warfare) beyond which the U.S. combat commitment in Vietnam would not expand. And third, both the military and the president developed their strategies for Vietnam with politics in mind: understanding the limits imposed by the White House, and unsure of success in any case, the brass nonetheless continued requesting an escalated war, thus forcing the president to confront his shifting approach and be responsible for any U.S. failure in Vietnam.

These three factors would converge in the aftermath of the 1968 Tet Offensive. Not only did the military recognize at that point that Tet had exposed the unsound military strategy of attrition employed in Vietnam but, with its request for 206,000 more troops and a massive reserve callup, also made Johnson accountable for an ultimate decision regarding the war, and effectively transferred blame for the debacle in Vietnam to the White House. Accordingly, U.S. military leaders in the mid-1960s had laid the groundwork for the conservative revisionist critique of Vietnam—the "one hand tied behind their backs" argument—which has become so popular since then.

In the early days of the Johnson administration, the military was no more eager for war than it had been earlier. Thus, in 1963 the incoming Marine Commandant, Wallace M. Greene, Jr., feared that U.S. troops were already "mired down in South Vietnam." "Frankly," he told fellow officers at Quantico, "the Marines do not want to get any more involved in South Vietnam. . . . [W]e've got enough business right now." By early 1965, as U.S. leaders began to debate whether to commit combat forces to Vietnam, many military men—especially General Maxwell Taylor, the Ambassador to Saigon at the time—opposed such deployments. Both Taylor and the Commander of the U.S. Military Assistance Command, Vietnam [MACV], General William C. Westmoreland, recognized that large-scale intervention would lead to increased U.S. responsibility for the war, more casualties, and propaganda linking Americans to French imperialists. Combat intervention, a MACV study remarkably, and prophetically, concluded, "would at best buy time and would lead to ever-increasing commitments until, like the French, we would be occupying an essentially hostile foreign country."

Nonetheless, the White House deployed two Marine battalions to Danang in March 1965, the first American combat units to enter the RVN; their commander, General Fredrick Karch, arrived to find fellow officers "dismal" over U.S. prospects, the enemy VC holding the political and military initiative, and the southern Army of the Republic of Vietnam (ARVN) passive and corrupt. Vietnam, Karch would later charge, "was just one big cancer." And it was spreading. Throughout the first part of 1965 American political and military leaders recognized the imperiled U.S. position in Vietnam but nevertheless significantly expanded their commitment in July. The White House had made a "political calculation" that it could not withstand the domestic consequences of the "loss" of Vietnam to Communism, just as earlier the Truman administration had suffered the political fallout of the "loss" of China.

At the same time the Johnson administration did not want a wider war and did not want Vietnam to obstruct its political agenda at home. Such political concerns were evident in a frank 1964 memo from Johnson's advisor Jack Valenti, in which he recommended that the White House "sign on" the JCS before making any final decisions regarding Vietnam. By bringing the military into the process, Valenti pointed out, the Chiefs "will have been heard, they will have been part of the consensus, and our flank will have been covered in the event of some kind of flap or investigation later." Westmoreland understood that such political limits were affecting military policy. In December 1965 he admitted to Ambassador Henry Cabot Lodge that a reserve callup and extended terms of service would "require drastic action that could be politically difficult for the President." In addition, military leaders continued to recognize that circumstances inside Vietnam were retarding progress. Even Westmoreland's hawkish Chief of Plans, General William DePuy, expected the war to continue indefinitely because the RVN's government "is really bankrupt" while the VC "fight like tigers." Although the General hoped that political leaders would commit more forces to Vietnam, he recognized that additional troops would not be sent "unless there's been progress," which was not terribly likely.

As if DePuy's understanding of the military and political dilemmas of Vietnam was not ominous enough, the MACV was also suffering the effects of a serious interservice rivalry over strategy which began in 1965 and would continue throughout the war. In particular Marine leaders Wallace Greene and Pacific Commander Victor H. Krulak consistently attacked the Westmoreland, and Army, strategy of attrition, and called for an emphasis on pacification and political warfare. In a late 1965 appraisal of U.S. strategy, Krulak thus urged Westmoreland to "put the full weight of our top level effort into bringing all applicable resources . . . into the pacification process." Greene also championed counterinsurgency and compared Westmoreland's strategy of attrition to "a grindstone that's being turned by the Communist side, and we're backing into it and having our skin taken off of . . . our entire body without accomplishing a damn thing because they've got enough to keep the old stone going." The VC could thus tolerate losses twenty or thirty times greater than the U.S. because, the Commandant wisely understood, "in the end, although their casualty rate may be fifty times what ours is, they'll be able to win through their capability to wage a war of attrition. "Yet, Greene concluded, "this is a thing that apparently the Army doesn't understand." Krulak agreed, adding that "this is not the strategy for victory."

After barely two years in the White House, Lyndon Johnson had committed increasing resources and troops into Vietnam with a clear understanding of the troubles that lay ahead and the limits to future expansion of the war. At the same time, military leaders were equally aware of obstacles to future progress and of the political constraints on military policy, yet they would continue to seek more forces and bombs rather than develop alternative strategies. Thus, political considerations would increasingly determine the course of the war.

The president himself was growing more anxious about the political turmoil affecting policymaking as well. "General," Johnson told Westmoreland at Honolulu in early 1966, "I have a lot riding on you. I hope you don't pull a MacArthur on me." Westmoreland and his staff understood Johnson's concerns, but were aware of many of the problems in South Vietnam as well. In addition to continued instability and manpower shortages within the Vietnamese military, the U.S. Commander did not expect to receive the reinforcements he had been requesting. In fact, Westmoreland developed the American force structure while assuming "that there will be no major call up of reserves." Nevertheless he would continue to make that very request throughout the war. Wheeler was more anxious about the political factors driving the war. The civilian leadership, he understood, remained troubled by the lack of emphasis given to pacification, the continuing lack of military activity by the South Vietnamese, and growing Communist infiltration into southern Vietnam, which was offsetting the VC's huge losses.

Despite such candid and bleak evaluations, Westmoreland's staff continued to emphasize its accomplishments and to expect progress. In a January 1967 evaluation the military stressed that U.S. and ARVN forces were routing the enemy, many VC and Communist supporters were rallying to the RVN, and pacification was likely to improve markedly in the coming year. While the enemy's determination had not weakened, "the conflict has taken a decided turn for the best." At the same time, however, there was serious question as to whether the military expected its own programs to succeed. Westmoreland himself would later speculate that, "even had Washington adopted a strong bombing policy, I still doubt that the North Vietnamese would have relented." "The influx of men and materials" into the south, Admiral U.S.G. Sharp, the Pacific Commander, admitted, "has increased despite considerable air effort expended to hinder infiltration." Sharp also understood that the White House's reluctance to remove even more restrictions from the air war was "based primarily on political considerations."

Wheeler recognized it too. In early March, after revised MACV statistics showed that VC-initiated major unit attacks were actually about 400 percent higher than originally estimated, the obviously alarmed JCS Chair cabled Westmoreland that "if these figures should reach the public domain, they would, literally, blow the lid off of Washington." And surely the president was not ignorant of the reality of the war. Johnson "never intended" to escalate the war as the military was urging, and developments in Vietnam up to early 1967 had reinforced that position.

Nonetheless in April 1967 Westmoreland requested about 200,000 new troops for Vietnam. But McNamara, among others, had soured on the war and believed that attrition would fail "as a military strategy as well as a presidential policy for political survival." The president himself expressed serious misgivings in a meeting with Westmoreland and Wheeler in late April. Although the U.S. Commander claimed that his forces had eroded enemy strength to the "crossover point" at which its losses exceeded northern infiltration into the south, Johnson wondered "when we add divisions, can't the enemy add divisions? If so, when does it all end? . . . [A]t what point does the enemy ask for [presumably Chinese] volunteers?" The General's answers were not reassuring. Maintaining current levels would simply create a "meat grinder" in Vietnam, he told the president. Wheeler added that massive reinforcement might provoke the Soviet Union or China to retaliate in Europe, in Korea, or elsewhere in Southeast Asia. In addition, the JCS Chair admitted that the air war—the military's fundamental answer to the problems of Vietnam—"is reaching the point where we will have struck all worthwhile targets except the ports."

Such evaluations and continued candid reports out of Saigon thus prompted Johnson to reject Westmoreland's plan for full reinforcement. A full year before the crisis of Tet the White House, the JCS, and the MACV had clearly drawn the lines over which civil-military battles would be fought. The civilian leadership recognized that success was not close, but rejected fully unrestrained war. The military too was aware of the continued peril of war in Vietnam and also understood that it would not receive authorization to fight without constraints. Earle Wheeler was especially bleak, lamenting the White House's recognition that "the Main-Force war . . . is stalemated . . . and there is no evidence that pacification will ever succeed in view of the widespread rot and corruption of the government, the pervasive economic and social ills, and the tired, passive and accommodation prone attitude of the armed forces of South Vietnam."

Given such judgments it would take a rather great stretch of imagination to expect success in Vietnam. Yet the war continued, with the White House and the brass as concerned with avoiding blame for failure as with actually improving the situation on the battlefield. Army Chief Harold K. Johnson admitted as much, telling Wheeler that the war was being lost and that the military would "take the fall." Indeed, the service chiefs "now believed that they had been betrayed by their civilian leaders, that the war could not continue without an irrational loss of American lives, and that . . . there was little reason to hope for an eventual American victory." Neither the military nor White House, of course, publicly made such statements, and when Westmoreland made a public relations trip to Washington in late November 1967 he concluded that, despite problems, there was "light at the end of the tunnel."

Clearly Lyndon Johnson had to have such good news; his political career depended on it. But the light at the end of the tunnel, Westmoreland's critics later joked, was a train headed toward the general. And at the end of January 1968 it thundered through Vietnam. Taking advantage of a Tet New Year cease-fire, the VC and northern army struck virtually every military and political center of importance, even invading the U.S. embassy grounds. Within sixty days, Tet would bring down the president, finally force a reassessment of the war at the highest levels, and bring to a climax one of the gravest crises in civil-military relations in U.S. history. Tet, as it were, became the U.S. obituary in Vietnam.

Since 1968 the Tet Offensive has attained mythic status, with analysts of virtually every ideological stripe agreeing that Tet was—as Westmoreland and Johnson publicly claimed at the time—a great U.S. military victory, but political and psychological defeat. Such observations, however, neglect the military's own outlook on the war in February and March 1968. Indeed, throughout the Tet crisis, officials in the MACV and JCS as well as political leaders recognized America's perhaps-intractable dilemma in Vietnam. Just days after the attacks began, Westmoreland reported to Wheeler that, "from a realistic point of view, we must accept the fact that the enemy has dealt [South Vietnam] a severe blow," bringing the war to the people, inflicting heavy casualties and damage, and disrupting the economy. The Commander did end on an upbeat note, though, claiming that the enemy's own huge losses and failure to overthrow the southern government constituted the failure of the offensive. But he also recognized that the enemy's objectives "were primarily psychological and political." A week later Westmoreland would candidly explain, "we are now in a new ballgame where we face a determined, highly disciplined enemy, fully mobilized to achieve a quick victory." Such reports would continue throughout February 1968, leading an obviously alarmed Lyndon Johnson to despatch Wheeler to Saigon at the end of the month.

In his well-documented report, Wheeler found the enemy strong and capable of continuing its attacks. The ARVN meanwhile had lost about one-quarter of its pre-Tet strength. The pacification program had been badly undermined. And the government's effectiveness was obviously in question, especially as it confronted the massive problems of refugees and reconstruction. "In short," Wheeler concluded, "it was a very near thing." Harold K. Johnson did not resort to euphemism. "We suffered a loss," he cabled Westmoreland, "there can be no doubt about it." Clearly then, later

claims that Tet was a great U.S. victory are essentially moot. American leaders in early 1968 did not have time for the dust to settle in Vietnam for a
thorough analysis of the situation. With a barrage of candid and often pessimistic reports flowing from Saigon to Washington, policymakers could do
little more than seek an effective way to cut their losses in Vietnam.

Obviously such bleak views disturbed Washington, with the president
on 9 February wondering "what has happened to change the situation between then [initial optimism] and now?" At the end of February, however,
Johnson received an even greater shock when Wheeler and Westmoreland
again requested about 200,000 additional troops for Vietnam and the activa-
tion of almost 300,000 reservists. Even when the military's reports out of
Vietnam had been optimistic about future progress, such massive reinforcement was never realistically likely. Amid the crisis of Tet, it was impossible.
Westmoreland himself later admitted that he and the JCS Chair "both knew
the grave political and economic implications of a major call-up of reserves."
Nonetheless the military asked for a remarkable escalation of the war at the
very moment it had descended to its nadir.

Within the context of civil-military relations during the Vietnam War,
however, the reinforcement request had a certain logic. It was consistent
with long-term White House and military patterns of behavior toward the
war. By February and March 1968 military and civilian leaders understood
that reinforcement, especially in such vast numbers, was not politically feasible. But the military, rather than change course after Tet, sent notice that it
would continue its now-discredited war of attrition. In so doing, however,
the service leaders forced Lyndon Johnson to finally take decisive action
regarding Vietnam and bear responsibility for future failure.

The military realized that the request for more forces would cause a
political firestorm. The Army's Pacific Commander, General Dwight Beach,
when notified of Westmoreland's proposals, "had commented that it would
shock" government officials. Indeed, the military had reason to expect such
a reaction from Washington. Not only had the White House rejected
Westmoreland's previous proposals for such escalation, but the president
himself on 2 February had told reporters that he saw no reason to expand
troop levels beyond the 525,000 then deployed to Vietnam. Johnson was also
worried that the crisis of Tet might be politically devastating. At a meeting
with his advisors, he charged that "all of you have counseled, advised, con-
sulted and then—as usual—placed the monkey on my back again. . . . I do
not like what I am smelling from those cables from Vietnam."

Johnson's outburst may have been disingenuous but it was well-
founded. The monkey in fact belonged squarely on his back, but it was true
that his advisors had developed even more grave reservations about the
Vietnam War as a result of Tet. Thus, the president feared that the military
might be able to exploit White House division over Vietnam. "I don't want
them [U.S. military leaders] to ask for something," Johnson worried aloud,

"not get it, and have all the blame placed on me." Although not expecting such a huge reinforcement request, it was thus clear that the president understood the political implications of any future moves regarding Vietnam. Ambassador to Saigon Ellsworth Bunker understood as well, warning Westmoreland against asking for so many additional forces because reinforcement was now "politically impossible," even if Johnson had wanted it, which was also more unlikely than ever.

Indeed it was. Within the month, incoming Defense Secretary Clark Clifford would reassess the war, Johnson's informal advisors, the so-called Wise Men, would finally urge de-escalation, and U.S. military leaders would continue to provide candid evaluations of the enemy's capabilities and America's problems. By the end of March the President would lament that *"everybody is recommending surrender."* But it was Johnson himself who surrendered, withdrawing from the 1968 presidential campaign at the end of a 31 March national address. Finally forced to confront his failure to determine a consistent policy on Vietnam by the twin shocks of Tet and the huge reinforcement proposal, the president knew that time had run out on both his political career and the U.S. experience in Vietnam.

Although the United States would remain in Vietnam for five more years, until the Paris Peace Accords of January 1973, Tet in fact constituted the end of American illusions about "victory" in the Indochina War. The United States, after Tet, began its policy of "Vietnamization," which meant that the South Vietnamese themselves would be responsible for the war while American troops began to withdraw. At the same time, however, Johnson's successor Richard M. Nixon would significantly expand the conflict into neighboring Laos and Kampuchea and markedly escalate the air war. In the end, however, the ARVN was not able to withstand continuing pressure from the VC and northern Vietnamese forces and, despite massive American air strikes and aid to the RVN, crumbled before the Communist offensive which reunified the country in April 1975. In the end, Vietnamization, as Senator George McGovern charged, amounted to "changing the color of the corpses."

Nixon and his defenders, however, have steadfastly maintained that a more consistent application of air power and intervention into North Vietnam or Laos and Cambodia might have made a difference. Again, the military itself challenged such views. Indeed, the military did not seriously consider intervening in North Vietnam; the logistics needs alone would have been massive and troop morale could not have been taken for granted. With regard to the air war, Army Chief of Staff General Harold K. Johnson asserted that "if anything came out of Vietnam, it was that airpower couldn't do the job." Nor did the armed services possess the unity of purpose that would be essential to any successful strategy. The Army and Marines, it seemed, were fighting each other as much as they were jointly fighting against the enemy.

In the end, the United States suffered a military defeat in Vietnam. The "country" that American troops were defending, the RVN, never achieved political stability and its military seemed content to let U.S. soldiers fight and die for it. As for the United States, its political and military leaders often seemed more concerned with avoiding blame for failure as with developing strategy. U.S. troops thus did not fight with "one hand tied behind their back," as a popular myth would have it. The United States, in fact, dropped 4.6 million tons of bombs on Vietnam and another 2 million tons on Kampuchea and Laos (over twice the total dropped by the Allies in all theatres of World War II combined). In addition, U.S. forces sprayed 11.2 million gallons of Agent Orange, a dioxin-carrying herbicide, and dropped over 400,000 tons of napalm. The impact of such warfare was catastrophic. American firepower destroyed 9,000, out of 15,000 southern villages, 25 million acres of farmland, and 12 million acres of forests, while creating over 2.5 million bomb craters and leaving a significant amount of unexploded ordnance throughout Vietnam. The human toll was worse: perhaps 2 to 3 million Vietnamese, mostly civilians, were killed, while an additional 300,000 or so Kampucheans and Laotians died. Over 3 million Indochinese were wounded as well. And by 1975, there were about 15 million refugees in the area. If such activities amounted to fighting in a restrained and limited manner, with "hands tied behind backs," one can hardly imagine what total war in Vietnam would have been like.

QUESTIONS TO CONSIDER

1. Why was the American military reluctant to get involved in Vietnam in the early 1950s?
2. How did Kennedy's policy escalate the American effort? Does Buzzanco feel that Kennedy would have abandoned Vietnam had he lived?
3. How, according to Buzzanco, did military leaders in the mid-1960s lay the groundwork for their "stab-in-the-back" theory?
4. What was the nature of the marine-army debate over strategy? What are the main points on each side? How did that debate relate to the whole war effort?
5. What does Buzzanco call the American obituary in Vietnam? Why?
6. Why does Buzzanco argue that the American military did *not* fight with one hand tied behind their back?

15

The American Environment

JOHN STEELE GORDON

Reprinted by permission of
American Heritage, Magazine,
© Forbes, Inc., 1993.

Americans are prone to become caught up in crusades. In the late 1950s and well into the 1960s, civil rights dominated the nation's crusading spirit. Then, as the movement for black equality became less focused and more divisive, the drive to halt the war in Vietnam replaced it as the preeminent cause. But by 1973, the Americans were out of Vietnam and a new crusade was underway, one that would have much greater staying power—the environmental movement. The environment became a dominant issue of the 1970s, and well beyond.

The movement was based in the grass roots, with politicians reacting to the public's concerns rather than leading the way. As John Steele Gordon suggests, the nation had become in one century far more receptive to the environmental message. In 1864, George Perkins Marsh had published *The Earth as Modified by Human Action* to no effect whatsoever. Yet almost a hundred years later, Rachel Carson published *Silent Spring* in 1962, and her book launched Americans into a major readjustment of their behavior. In effect, she stimulated a transformation of the American character. Historically, Americans had disposed of waste by throwing it over "the nearest stone wall" and forgetting about it because there was an apparently infinite amount of land out there. Technological advances, however, had made it possible to transform even that much land, pollute endless quantities of water, and undermine the quality of life of the nation. Earth Day in 1970 launched the modern environmental movement, and Congress created the Environmental Protection Agency and passed the Clean Water Act and the Clean Air Act. The results of the movement have been heartening, as Gordon points out in this 1993 article, one that critics maintain is overly positive—although Americans talk a good environmental game, they are still not willing to make any significant sacrifices to protect the environment.

The Cuyahoga River died for our sins. In 1796 the Cuyahoga, which promised easy transportation into the wilderness of the Ohio country from Lake Erie, prompted the city of Cleveland into existence. Over the next 170 years a primitive frontier town grew into a mighty industrial city, one that stretched for miles along the banks of its seminal river.

By the midtwentieth century, however, the river no longer served as a major artery of transportation, having been superseded by railroads and highways. Now, instead of carrying the products of civilization into the vast interior, it carried the effluent of a far more technically advanced civilization out into the lake. The once crystalline waters of the river had become turbid and rank with its new cargo of chemicals and sewage. Its once abundant wildlife had long since fled, leaving only a few carps and suckers to eke out a living in the foul sullage on its bottom, testifying thereby to the very tenacity of life itself.

Finally, late in the morning of June 22, 1969, the Cuyahoga could no longer bear the burden humankind had placed upon it. In a sort of fluvial *cri de coeur,* the river burst into flames.

The fire was no will-o'-the-wisp flickering over a transient oil slick. Rather, it roared five stories into the sky, reduced wooden railroad trestles to ruins, and demonstrated to the people of Cleveland and the nation as no scientific study or news report ever could that the burden being placed on the environment was reaching limits that could be crossed only at the peril of the future.

Less than a year later, on April 22, 1970, Earth Day was held, one of the most remarkable happenings in the history of democracy. Fully 10 percent of the population of the country, twenty million people, demonstrated their support for redeeming the American environment. They attended events in every state and nearly every city and county. American politics and public policy would never be the same again.

Today, nearly a quarter-century after the fire, sunlight once more sparkles off the surface of the Cuyahoga. Boaters cruise its waters for pleasure, and diners eat at riverside restaurants. Mayflies—so characteristic of a Great Lakes spring—once more dance in the air above it in their millions while their larvae provide food for at least twenty-seven species of fish that have returned to its waters.

The Cuyahoga is not pristine, and barring an alteration in human priorities and circumstances beyond anything now imagined, it will not become so. But it has changed greatly for the better and continues to improve. It is once more a living river.

The Cuyahoga and its history is a microcosm of the American environment. For the history of that environment is the story of the interaction between a constantly changing, ever-more-powerful technology and an only slowly shifting paradigm of humankind's proper relationship with the natural world.

Human beings evolved in the Old World, a fact that more than once would have sudden and drastic consequences for the New.

The beginning of the Upper Paleolithic period was marked by a dramatic technological development as humans acquired tools and weapons that were far more sophisticated than any known before and became the most formidable hunters the world has ever known. In the Old World both our prey and our competitors, evolving alongside, quickly learned to treat the emerging biological superpower with the greatest respect, and most were able to adapt successfully. But the New World lay in innocence while human hunters perfected their newfound skills in the Old.

When the land bridge that was a temporary consequence of the last ice age allowed humans to migrate into it, the results were swift and devastating: much of the North American Pleistocene fauna went extinct. Horses, camels, mastodons, mammoths, true elephants, several species of deer, bison, and antelope, ground sloths, glyptodonts, and giant beavers vanished, as did their associated predators such as saber-toothed cats, giant lions, and cheetahs.

It cannot be known for sure to what extent the arrival of human hunters affected this great extinction, but there is little doubt that it was an important, perhaps fundamental, factor. But the evolutionary equilibrium that had been shattered by the arrival of the superhunters eventually returned, for the human population of the New World, limited by numerous other factors besides food supply, remained low. And the surviving among the species they had encountered quickly adapted to the new conditions.

Thus the next human culture that appeared in the New World, the Europeans, found it to possess a biological abundance and diversity of, to them, astounding proportions. But these newcomers failed almost entirely to appreciate this aspect of the New World, for hunting in their culture had been reduced to, at most, a secondary source of food.

They were heirs to the agricultural revolution that began in the Old World at the end of the last ice age. It, too, was marked by a profound leap in technology. In turn the more settled conditions of agricultural communities allowed the development of still more elaborate technologies as well as social and political organizations of unprecedented complexity. The result was what we call civilization.

But the early civilizations were acutely aware that they were small islands surrounded by vast seas of wilderness from which savage beasts, and savage men, might come at any time and wipe them out. Thus their inhabitants came to look on the wilderness as an alien place, separate and apart. Not surprisingly under these circumstances, the religions that developed in the Near East in the wake of the agricultural revolution reflected this world-view, sanctioned it, and codified it. Because it became, quite literally, Holy Writ, it persisted unquestioned for centuries.

The Book of Genesis, in fact, could hardly be more direct on the subject, "God said unto [man], Be fruitful, and multiply, and replenish [i.e., fill up] the earth, and subdue it: and have dominion over the fish of the sea, and over the fowl of the air, and over every living thing that moveth upon the earth."

Over the next more than two thousand years, humans operating with this worldview in mind transformed the continent of Europe, and by the time they began to expand overseas, wilderness had disappeared from all but the margins of that continent.

Thus the world they encountered in North America was unlike anything they had ever seen. The greatest temperate forest in the world, teeming with life, stretched almost unbroken from the Atlantic seaboard to well west of the Mississippi. The grasslands that filled the Great Plains in the rain shadow of the Rocky Mountains also abounded with animal life as millions of bison, pronghorn antelope, elk, white-tailed and mule deer roamed it, as did their associated predators, the wolf, the mountain lion, the bear, and the jaguar.

Farther west still, the forests of the Northwest and the deserts of the Southwest reached to the Pacific.

When the new settlers arrived, they did not see the beauty or abundance of the wilderness that greeted them. Far from it; they regarded it as barren and threatening because the ancient paradigm that dated to the dawn of civilization still molded their thinking. Thus they regarded their first task in the New World to be a re-creation of what they had known in the Old, an environment shaped by the hand of man, for man's benefit.

But while they sought, as nearly as possible, to re-create the Europe they had left behind, converting the "remote, rocky, barren, bushy, wild-woody wilderness" into a "second England for fertilness," there was one way in which the New World was utterly unlike the Old: it possessed an abundance of land so great that it seemed to the early settlers, and to their descendants for many generations, to verge upon the infinite. "The great happiness of my country," wrote the Swiss-born Albert Gallatin, Jefferson's Secretary of the Treasury, "arises from the great plenty of land."

Because the supply seemed without end, the value placed on each unit was small. It is only common sense to husband the scarce and let the plentiful take care of itself. Caring for the land, an inescapable necessity in Europe, was simply not cost-effective here. After all, the settlers could always move on to new, rich land farther west. For three hundred years they did exactly that, with ever-increasing speed.

Americans also developed other habits in the early days that stemmed directly from the wealth of land and scarcity of the population. Today, when American archaeologists investigate a site, they know that the place to look for the garbage dump is on the far side of the fence or stone wall that was nearest to the dwelling. In Europe that was likely to belong to a neighbor; in America it was often wilderness and thus beyond the human universe. This out-of-sight-out-of-mind attitude would have no small consequences when technology increased the waste stream by orders of magnitude.

The early settlers, while they greatly altered the landscape of the Eastern seaboard, clearing whole stretches of the primeval forest and converting the land to fields, pastures, and meadows, did not greatly diminish the biological diversity. They opened up the best land for farming but left untouched the steep or rocky areas as well as, to a great extent, the wetlands and mountains. Indeed in some ways the early settlers increased the diversity by expanding habitat for such grassland species as bluebirds, ground hogs, and meadowlarks. The ecosystem as a whole remained intact.

Only in the South, where plantation agriculture became the rule in areas to which it was suited, did monocultural husbandry greatly diminish the fertility and texture of the soil. Virginia, the largest and, thanks to its tobacco exports, most powerful of the colonies, found its yields declining sharply toward the end of the eighteenth century as the best land was exploited and exhausted. Erosion became an increasing problem. As early as the 1780s Patrick Henry thought that "the greatest patriot is he who fills the most gullies."

Meanwhile, as a new civilization was being built out of the wilderness of North America, new attitudes toward wilderness itself were emerging in Europe. The ancient paradigm that had gripped Western thinking since Genesis was beginning, partially, to shift at last.

In the seventeenth century, wilderness had been universally regarded as at best a waste, if not an evil. In the eighteenth, however, it began to be seen for the first time as a thing of beauty. Mountains came to be viewed as majestic, not just as an impediment to travel or a barrier against invasion.

In Britain the aristocracy began to lay out gardens, such as those by Capability Brown, that were highly stylized versions of nature itself, rather than the direct refutation of it that seventeenth-century gardens, like those at Versailles, had been.

Biology became a systematic science (although the word itself would enter the language only in the early nineteenth century). Linnaeus studied the relationships of plants and animals. Georges Cuvier, William Smith, and others began to examine fossils and to sense, for the first time, a history of the earth that was at variance with the account given in Genesis.

The new attitude toward wilderness soon came to this country and contributed to the growing American sense of uniqueness. James Fenimore Cooper's novels and Thoreau's essays displayed a love of wilderness that would have been inconceivable a century earlier.

Of course, in Europe wilderness was largely an abstraction. In America it was just down the road. At the end of the Revolution, it nowhere lay more than a few days on horseback from the Atlantic shore, and Thomas Jefferson, no mean observer, thought it would be "a thousand years" before settlement reached the Pacific.

Jefferson was wrong. He did not realize—no one could have—that a third technological revolution was just getting under way, one that would give humankind the power to transform the world far beyond anything provided by the first two. It had taken millennia to reshape the face of Europe to human ends. North America would be transformed in less than a century. But there would be a vast price to pay for this miracle.

The steam engine and its technological successors allowed energy in almost unlimited quantity to be brought to bear on any task. So forests could be cut, fields cleared, dams built, mines worked with unprecedented speed. As a result, in less than a single human lifetime an area of eastern North America larger than all Europe was deforested. Virtually uninhabited by Europeans as late as 1820, the state of Michigan by 1897 had shipped 160 billion board feet of white pine lumber, leaving less than 6 billion still standing.

But the new engines needed fuel. At first waste wood supplied much of it, and later coal and then oil. The by-products of this combustion were dumped into the atmosphere as they had always been, but now their quantity was increasing geometrically. In 1850 Americans were utilizing more than eight million horsepower, animal and mechanical. By 1900 nearly sixty-four million, almost all mechanical, was being used by what economists call prime movers.

The factory system and mechanization brought many commodities within the financial reach of millions, while new transportation systems created national markets and made economies of scale both possible and necessary. This, in turn, caused the demand for raw materials to soar. The great mineral wealth that was being discovered under the American landscape was exploited with ever-increasing speed. Again the waste products were dumped at the lowest possible cost, which meant, in effect, on the far side of the nearest stone wall.

Increasing wealth and the new technologies allowed cities to bring in fresh, clean water for their rapidly increasing populations. This water was used to flush away the dirt and sewage of human existence, but only into the nearest body of water. The quality of life in the human environment was immeasurably improved by this, as the squalor that had characterized the urban landscape since Roman times disappeared. But the quality of the nation's waterways sharply deteriorated.

The new technology allowed us to turn more and more of the landscape to human use. The old-fashioned moldboard plow, in use since medieval times, could not deal easily with the rich, heavy soils and deep sod of the American Midwest. The steel plow invented by John Deere in 1837 quickly opened up what would become the breadbasket of the world. Wetlands could now be drained economically and made productive. Millions of acres vanished, and their vast and wholly unappreciated biological productivity vanished too.

So rapid an alteration of the landscape could only have a severe impact on the ecosystem as a whole. The loss of so much forest caused runoff to increase sharply, eroding the land and burdening the waters with silt, destroying more wetlands. Many animals' habitats disappeared. And because the ancient biblical notion that humans had dominion over the earth still held, others vanished entirely.

The beautiful Carolina parakeet, North America's only native parrot, proved a major agricultural pest. Because it lived in large, cohesive flocks, it made an easy target for farmers with the shotguns that the Industrial Revolution made cheap. It was extinct in the wild by the turn of the century; the last known specimen died in the Cincinnati Zoo in 1914.

Another avian casualty was the passenger pigeon, one of the great natural wonders of America, as amazing as Niagara Falls or the Grand Canyon. The passenger pigeon almost certainly existed in larger numbers than any other bird in the world. Moreover, it was concentrated in flocks of unbelievable immensity. Audubon reported one flock that took a total of three days to pass overhead and estimated that, at times, the birds flew by at the rate of three hundred million an hour.

The passenger pigeon nested in heavily forested areas in colonies that were often several miles wide and up to forty miles long, containing billions of birds. Trees within the colony each had hundreds of nests, and limbs often broke under the weight. The squabs, too heavy to fly when abandoned by their parents at the end of the nesting season, were easy prey. With railroads able to ship the fresh-killed birds to the great Eastern cities quickly, hunters slaughtered them in the millions to meet the demand.

Unfortunately it turned out that passenger pigeons needed the company of huge numbers of their fellows to stimulate breeding behavior. Once the size of the flocks fell below a certain very large minimum, the birds stopped reproducing, and the population crashed. Just as with the Carolina parakeet, the last passenger pigeon died in the Cincinnati Zoo in 1914.

The herds of the Great Plains also fell to hunters. It is estimated that upward of thirty million bison roamed the grasslands of North America in the middle of the nineteenth century. By the dawn of the twentieth, less than a thousand remained alive.

As early as the 1850s it was clear to the more thoughtful that something precious and irreplaceable was rapidly disappearing. The wilderness that had helped define the country seemed ever more remote. It was now recognized the natural world could provide refreshment whose need was becoming more and more keenly felt.

Urban parks, such as New York City's incomparable Central and Prospect parks, were intended to provide the population with a taste of nature that many could now obtain no other way. But these parks were, like the aristocratic gardens created in eighteenth-century Britain, wholly man-made and no more truly natural than a sculpture is a rock outcropping.

Movements began to take hold to preserve portions of the fast-vanishing wilderness itself. As early as the 1830s the painter George Catlin put forward the idea of a wild prairie reservation, a suggestion that, alas, was not implemented before nearly all of the country's prairie ecosystem was destroyed. But the movement took root, and in 1864 the first act of preservation was undertaken when ownership of the Yosemite Valley and a stand of sequoias was transferred from the public lands of the United States to the state of California.

In 1872 the first national park in the world was created when reports of the splendors of Yellowstone were delivered to Congress. James Bryce, British ambassador to the United States, called the national parks the best idea America ever had. Certainly they have been widely copied around the world. Today American national parks protect 47,783,680 acres, an area considerably larger than the state of Missouri.

States, too, began to set aside land to protect what was left of the wilderness. New York turned five million acres—15 percent of the state's land area—into the Adirondack Park and Forest Preserve, to remain "forever wild."

In the 1870s Carl Schurz, Secretary of the Interior, began moving for the preservation of federally owned forests. Born in Europe, where forests had long since become scarce and thus precious, and where forest-management techniques were far more advanced than those in this country, Schurz and many others helped create a new concern for America's fast-dwindling woodlands. By the end of Theodore Roosevelt's Presidency, almost sixty million acres were in the forest reserve system.

Today hundreds of millions of acres in this country enjoy various levels of protection from development, and more are added every year. But while the parks and reserves created by this movement are national treasures that have greatly enriched the quality of life, their creation was predicated on the part of the ancient paradigm that still survived. That part held that the natural world and the human one were two separate and distinct places. And it was still thought that each had little effect on the other.

It was George Perkins Marsh, lawyer, businessman, newspaper editor, member of Congress, diplomat, Vermont fish commissioner, and lover and keen observer of nature, who first recognized the folly of this unexamined assumption. Growing up in Vermont, he had seen how the clear-cutting of the forests and poor farming practices had degraded the state's environment.

In 1864 he published *Man and Nature,* which he expanded ten years later and published as *The Earth as Modified by Human Action.* Individual instances of human effect on the natural world had been noted earlier, but Marsh, like Darwin with evolution, gathered innumerable examples together and argued the general case. He decisively demonstrated that the impress of humankind on the whole world was deep, abiding, and, because it was largely unnoticed, overwhelmingly adverse. "Man is everywhere a disturbing agent," he wrote. "Wherever he plants his foot, the harmonies of nature are turned to discords."

Recognizing that technology, energy use, population, food production, resource exploitation, and human waste all were increasing on curves that were hyperbolic when plotted against time, he feared for the future. "It is certain," he wrote, "that a desolation, like that which overwhelmed many once beautiful and fertile regions of Europe, awaits an important part of the territory of the United States . . . unless prompt measures are taken."

Darwin's book *On the Origin of Species* provoked a fire storm of controversy in the intellectual world of his time when it was published in 1859. It changed humankind's perception of the world profoundly and immediately. But *Man and Nature* changed nothing. Published only five years later, it met with profound indifference, and its author sank into the undeserved oblivion of those who are out of sync with their times. As late as 1966, when the science of ecology he was instrumental in founding was already well developed, so commodious a reference work as the *Encyclopaedia Britannica* made no mention of him whatever.

Perhaps the difference was that Darwin's ideas had only philosophical, religious, and scientific implications. Marsh's ideas, on the other hand, had profound economic consequences. An America rapidly becoming the world's foremost industrial power did not want to hear them, even though as early as 1881 the mayor of Cleveland could describe the Cuyahoga River as "an open sewer through the center of the city."

In fact, the seeds of the country's first great man-made ecological disaster were being planted even as Marsh wrote.

In the 1860s railroads pushed across the Great Plains and opened them up to settlement by connecting them to Eastern markets. On the high plains toward the Rockies, as hunters slaughtered bison and pronghorns by the millions, ranchers replaced them with cattle, which overgrazed the land. Then farmers began moving in.

World War I greatly increased the demand for wheat, while the tractor made plowing the tough, deep sod of the high plains a more practical proposition. The number of farms in the area east of the Rocky Mountains burgeoned in the 1920s, taking over more and more of the ranchland.

The mean annual rainfall in this area varied between ten and twenty inches, not enough for crop farming except in the best of years. But the early decades of the century happened to see many such years. Then, in the late twenties, the rains slacked off, and drought swept the plains.

This had happened hundreds of times in the past, and the plants and animals that had evolved there were adapted to it. Wheat and cattle were not. Worse, over the last few years, the sod, the deep net of grass roots that had bound the soil together, had been broken over millions of acres by the farmers with their plows. The topsoil, without which no plant can grow nor animal live, now lay exposed to the ceaseless, drying winds.

In 1933 no rain fell for months in western Kansas, and little elsewhere. The crops withered, the livestock died of thirst or starvation, and the dust, bound by neither sod nor moisture, began to blow. On November 11 a howling, rainless storm sprang up. "By midmorning," a reporter wrote of a farm in South Dakota, "a gale was blowing cold and black. By noon it was blacker than night, because one can see through the night and this was an opaque black. It was a wall of dirt one's eyes could not penetrate, but it could penetrate the eyes and ears and nose. It could penetrate to the lungs until one coughed up black. . . .

"When the wind died and the sun shone forth again, it was on a different world. There were no fields, only sand drifting into mounds and eddies that swirled in what was now but an autumn breeze. There was no longer a section-line road fifty feet from the front door. It was obliterated. In the farmyard, fences, machinery, and trees were gone, buried. The roofs of sheds stuck out through drifts deeper than a man is tall."

The dust of this storm, uncountable millions of tons of topsoil, darkened the skies of Chicago the following day and those of Albany, New York, the day after that. Terrible as it was, the storm proved but the first of many that ravaged the high plains in the next several years, as the drought tightened its grip and the unforgiving winds blew and blew. In the middle years of the 1930s, they laid waste thousands of square miles of what had been, just a few years earlier, a vibrant ecosystem. It was now the Dust Bowl. Upward of two hundred thousand people were forced to abandon their farms and trek westward in desperate search of the necessities of life itself.

The rains finally came again, and in the 1940s the discovery of the Oglala aquifer, a vast reservoir of water that underlies much of the Midwest, rescued the farmers who remained. Tapped by ever-deeper wells, the aquifer is now seriously depleted. And economics is slowly rescuing the land as the price of water increases every year.

It was always marginal for farming, and so it remains. Even with many, though mostly ill-conceived, federal programs, the farmers on the high plains are finding it ever harder to compete in world markets. Every year more and more farms are abandoned, and the land reverts to what in a perfect world it would never have ceased to be—shortgrass prairie.

The technological leap that had begun in Jefferson's day only accelerated in the twentieth century. The burdens that had been placed on the environment in the nineteenth century by such things as fuel use and sewage disposal increased sharply as the population expanded and new technologies spread across the land.

The limits of the ability of the environment to cope with the load were being reached more and more often. In October 1947 a thermal inversion settled over Donora, Pennsylvania. The town is set in a natural basin and was home to much heavy industry. The layer of cold air trapped the effluent of that industry and of the cars and furnaces of the population. By the time the inversion ended, four days later, twenty people were dead and six thousand ill enough to require treatment.

To an astonishing extent—at least as viewed from today's perspective— the people of the time accepted such happenings as the price of the Industrial Revolution that had brought them so much wealth and material comfort. A *New Yorker* cartoon of the day showed a woman sitting at a table set for lunch in the garden of a New York brownstone. "Hurry, darling," she calls to her unseen husband, "your soup is getting dirty."

New burdens were also added. The chemical industry grew quickly in this century, fueled by an explosion in knowledge. The disposition of chemicals was, as always, over the nearest stone wall: into a landfill or convenient body of water.

Agriculture became more businesslike as farms grew in size, became much more mechanized, and increasingly specialized in one or two crops. Of course, even Patrick Henry had known, two centuries earlier, that monocultural farming depletes the soil and is vulnerable to insects and other pests. But now the chemical industry could overcome this, thanks to synthetic fertilizers and pesticides.

Such chemicals as DDT were greeted as miracles of modern science when they first became available, and their use spread rapidly. In 1947 the United States produced 124,259,000 pounds of chemical pesticides. Only thirteen years later, in 1960, production was up to 637,666,000 pounds of often far more potent pesticides.

Diseases such as malaria and agricultural pests such as the boll weevil were declared on the verge of eradication. And the "control of nature," the final realization of the dominion enjoined by Genesis, was said to be at hand. DDT and other pesticides sprayed from airplanes blanketed vast areas, to kill gypsy moths, budworms, and mosquitoes.

But there were troubling signs for the few who looked. The pesticides were nondiscriminatory; they killed all the insects they touched. Honeybees, essential for the pollination of many crops and innumerable natural plants, were often wiped out by spraying programs aimed at other insects. Bee-keepers began to fight back with lawsuits. "It is a very distressful thing," one beekeeper wrote, "to walk into a yard in May and not hear a bee buzz."

More than two hundred new pesticides were introduced in the years following World War II. The reason was that the older ones became increasingly ineffective. Many species of insects go through numerous generations a year and can evolve very rapidly, especially when a severe pressure such as a new pesticide is applied. In a monument to the vigor with which life clings to existence, they did exactly that.

And birdwatchers noticed a troubling decline in the numbers of some species, especially the large raptors that lived at the top of the food chains. Charles Broley, a retired banker, banded bald eagles in Florida beginning in 1939 as a hobby. He usually banded about a hundred and fifty young birds a year on the stretch of coast he patrolled. Beginning in 1947, more and more nests were empty or held eggs that had failed to hatch. In 1957 he found only eight eaglets, the following year only one.

But these troubling events were scattered, knowledge of them dispersed over a huge country and many scientific disciplines. They were no match for the chemical companies. But these, it turned out, were no match for a frail middle-aged woman named Rachel Carson.

Rachel Carson was trained as a marine biologist, but she was a born writer. In 1952 her book *The Sea Around Us* was published with a very modest first printing. To everyone's astonishment—most of all hers—it became a titanic bestseller that made its author famous across America. Ten years later she published *Silent Spring*. It changed the world.

Again a huge bestseller, *Silent Spring* detailed in lucid, often poetic, and always accessible prose how pesticides were playing havoc with the air, land, and water of the country and how their uncontrolled use was doing far more harm than good. Further, it introduced millions of Americans to the concept that the natural world was an intimately interconnected web. This web, Carson made clear, included humans quite as much as every other living thing that shared planet Earth. What killed insects would, if not handled carefully, one day kill us too. George Perkins Marsh had said much the same thing a hundred years earlier. This time the people read and believed.

The ancient paradigm from the dawn of civilization, when man was frail and nature omnipotent, was dead at last. Dead with it was what had been in theory a dream and in fact a nightmare—the control of nature. It had been, Rachel Carson wrote on the last page of *Silent Spring*, "a phrase conceived in arrogance."

Within a few years the public demand for action in behalf of the environment became irresistible, and it caught a complacent government by surprise. John C. Whitaker, Nixon's cabinet secretary, later recalled that "we were totally unprepared for the tidal wave of public opinion in favor of cleaning up the environment."

Earth Day cleared up any lingering doubts about the public's opinion on the matter. Federal government agencies such as the Environmental Protection Agency were created, and goals and timetables for air and water quality were established. We Americans set out on a crusade to rescue the land from ourselves. In many ways we shared the fervor with which the medieval world had set out to rescue the Holy Land from the infidel.

Today, nearly a quarter-century after the crusade to the new Jerusalem of a clean environment began, there is vast progress to report. In 1959, 24.9 million tons of particulate matter—soot—were emitted into the air in the United States. By 1985, 7.2 million were, and less every year. In 1970, 28.4 million tons of sulfur oxides, a prime contributor to smog, were released by power plants and automobiles. In 1990, 21.2 million tons were, a drop of nearly 25 percent. Carbon monoxide emission has fallen by 40 percent since 1970, and lead has been eliminated as an additive to gasoline.

Cars being manufactured in the 1990s emit only a fifth as much pollution as those made before 1975. Thus 80 percent of all automobile pollution today is generated by just 10 percent of the cars on the road. In the next few years, as these clunkers end up on the scrap heap, automobile pollution will decrease sharply.

Already the number of days per year when the air quality is below standards in most of the country's cities has fallen significantly, by 38 percent in the 1980s alone. Even Los Angeles, the smog capital of the country thanks to its geography and automobile-oriented infrastructure, has enjoyed a 25 percent decline in smog-alert days.

In 1960 only about 50 million Americans were served by municipal sewage plants that provided secondary or tertiary treatment. Today more than half the population is. As a result, many urban waterways are now cleaner than they have been since the early 1800s. New York used to dump the sewage of eight million people into the Hudson, Harlem, and East rivers. Today, in a development that would have stunned turn-of-the-century New Yorkers, there is an annual swimming race around Manhattan Island.

Rural rivers too have greatly benefited. Most of the Connecticut River's four-hundred-mile length was declared "suitable only for transportation of sewage and industrial wastes" in the 1960s. Today 125 new or upgraded water treatment plants, costing $900 million, have transformed it. Fishing and swimming are now allowed almost everywhere, and wildlife such as ospreys, bald eagles, blue crabs, and salmon has returned in numbers.

The sludge that is the end product of sewage treatment was until very recently dumped in the ocean or into landfills. Now it is increasingly being sought by farmers as a cheap fertilizer and soil conditioner. New York City produces 385 tons a day, all of it once dumped beyond the continental shelf. One hundred tons of that is being used by farmers in Colorado and Arizona. Initially skeptical, fifty of those farmers recently sent New York's mayor a letter asking for more. He's likely to oblige. Boston sludge now fertilizes Florida citrus groves. And because sewage sludge not only fertilizes but improves soil quality, it is displacing chemical fertilizers.

As old factories reach the end of their productive lives and are replaced by new ones built under stringent controls, the non-sewage pollution of the waterways is also steadily declining. The violation rate (the percentage of tests where the amount of pollutants was found to be above standards) for lead and cadmium fell to less than one percent. Dissolved oxygen is an important measure of a water body's biological viability. The percentage of times it was found to be below standard fell 60 percent in the 1980s.

Many bodies of water, such as Lake Erie, declared dead in the 1970s, have bounded back with the improved situation and with the help of life's ferocious determination to go on living. The amounts of pesticides being used every year fell by more than a quarter in the 1980s, and those in use today are far less persistent and far less toxic than most of those in widespread use in the 1960s. The level of DDT present in human fatty tissue, a fair measure of its presence in the environment, was 7.95 parts per million in 1970. By 1983 it had fallen to 1.67 parts per million. Today, ten years later, no one even bothers to gather the statistic.

The land, too, has improved. In the eastern part of the United States, the area of forest land has been increasing for more than a century, as clear-cut areas have been allowed to regenerate. It will be another hundred years, at least, before they reach the climax stage, but they are on their way. And today 28 percent of all farmland is no longer plowed at all, and the percentage is growing quickly. Conservation tillage is used instead; the method sharply reduces erosion and improves soil quality while slashing costs, producing crops for as much as 30 percent less.

Programs to reduce the use of chemical fertilizers are being tried in more and more areas as farmers learn new techniques. In Iowa in 1989 and 1990 a joint EPA-state program helped farmers cut their use of nitrogen fertilizer by four hundred million pounds without sacrificing crop yields. Because agricultural fertilizers and pesticides now account for more than 65 percent of all water pollution (factories account for only 7 percent), this trend has no small implication for the future.

Wildlife is on the mend in many ways. To be sure, the number of species on the endangered list has grown sharply in the last two decades, but that is much more an artifact of increased knowledge than of a still-deteriorating situation.

Many species have rebounded sharply, thanks in some cases to protection and in others to the explosion of biological and ecological knowledge that has so marked the last twenty-five years. To give just two examples, alligators, once hunted mercilessly for their skins, are no longer on the list at all. And peregrine falcons, almost extirpated in the Eastern United States by DDT, have been with infinite care and effort put on the road to recovery. Today there is a pair nesting on the Verrazano Bridge at the entrance to New York's Upper Bay, and there is even a pair nesting on the top of the Met Life (formerly Pan Am) building in midtown, exploiting the distinctly unendangered local pigeon population.

Nor has public interest in rescuing the environment slackened. *The New York Times Index* for 1960 needed less than 19 inches to list all the references to air pollution that year, and only 15 for water pollution. In 1991 the two subjects required 87 and 107 inches, respectively. Local organizations monitoring local situations have multiplied across the country. Many hire professionals, such as the Hudson River Fisherman's Association, whose "riverkeeper" patrols the Eastern seaboard's most beautiful waterway.

And public opinion has become a powerful force. In the fall of 1992 the governor of Alaska proposed culling the number of wolves in the state in order to increase the number of moose and caribou for human hunters. It was not long before he wished he hadn't. The state, heavily dependent on tourist dollars, was soon backpedaling furiously before the onslaught of intensely negative public reaction.

So is the American environment once more pristine? Of course not. Many pollutants have proved unexpectedly stubborn and persistent. Many businesses have resisted changing their ways. In most cities the storm and waste sewers are still one and the same, and sewage overflows in bad weather. It will take many years and billions of dollars to correct that. An unknowable number of species are still threatened by human activity.

But the nation's water, air, land, and wildlife all are better, in many respects, than they have been in a century, and they continue to improve. To put it another way, if the task of cleaning up the American environment were a journey from Boston to Los Angeles, we would be well past the Appalachians and might even have the Mississippi in sight.

Then why is the impression so widespread that we are, at best, entering Worcester, if not actually marching backward somewhere in Maine? There are many reasons, and as so often happens, human nature lies at the root of all of them.

A first reason is that environmental bureaucrats, like all bureaucrats, want to maximize the personnel and budgets of their departments. So from their point of view, it simply makes good sense to highlight new problems and to minimize news about the old ones that have been successfully addressed. Similarly, environmental organizations live and die by fundraising. The-sky-is-falling stories are simply far more effective in getting someone to reach for a checkbook than are things-are-looking-up stories. And environmental bureaucrats and lobbyists alike know that they must struggle hard to maintain their constituencies and budgets to fight the serious problems that do persist. They fear, not without reason, that if they don't play up the troubles that endure, they may lose the ability to address them at all—and we might lose much of what we've won.

A second reason is that the media have often failed to evaluate environmental stories with scientific competence and sometimes even honesty. As in fundraising, bad news sells better than good news.

As a result, tentative data have often been presented as irrefutable fact, and short-term or local trends have been extrapolated into global catastrophes. In the 1970s there were many stories about the coming ice age. Ten years later global warming was destined to extinguish civilization.

A third reason that things often seem to be getting worse here at home is extremists. Extremists are always present in great reform movements, and the goal of environmental extremists is not a clean environment but a perfect one. They are few in number, compared with the legions now dedicated to cleaning the American environment, but like many extremists, they are often gifted propagandists and they are willing to use ignoble means to further noble ends.

Consider the support given by some environmental organizations to the Delaney Clause. The law, passed in 1958, requires that even the slightest residue of pesticides that have been shown to cause cancer in laboratory animals may not be present in processed foods. The Delaney Clause made some sense in the 1950s, when our ability to detect chemicals was limited to about one part in a million and our knowledge of carcinogenesis rudimentary at best. Today it is nothing short of ludicrous, for we can now detect chemicals in amounts of one part in a quintillion. To get some idea of what that means, here is the recipe for making a martini in the ratio of 1:1,000,000,000,000,000,000: Fill up the Great Lakes—all five of them—with gin. Add one tablespoon of vermouth, stir well, and serve.

As a result, to give just one example, propargite, a nonpersistent pesticide that controls mites on raisins, can't be used because it has been shown to cause cancer when fed to rats in massive doses. But a human being would have to eat eleven tons of raisins a day to ingest the amount of propargite needed to induce cancer in laboratory rats. Had it been available in the 1950s, propargite's use would have been perfectly legal because the infinitesimal residue would have been completely undetectable.

Every first-year medical student knows it is the dosage that makes the poison. Yet many environmental organizations are adamantly against any revision of the Delaney Clause for reasons that amount to nothing less than scientific know-nothingism. They are wasting time, money, and, most important, credibility on the chimera of perfection.

But time, money, and most of all credibility are precious commodities. For even if we are at the Mississippi on the journey to clean up the American environment, we still have two thirds of the journey to go. And it will be the most difficult part.

For as we proceed, the problems will become more and more intractable, and thus more and more expensive to deal with. For instance, it was easy to get a lot of lead out of the atmosphere. We simply stopped adding it to gasoline as an antiknock agent, virtually the sole source of atmospheric lead. But getting the fertilizers and pesticides out of agricultural runoff—now far and away the greatest source of water pollution in the country—will be another matter altogether, especially if we are to keep the price of food from rising sharply.

Part of the problem is the iron law of diminishing returns. Getting, say, 90 percent of a pollutant out of the environment may be easy and relatively cheap. But the next 9 percent might cost as much as the first 90, and so might the next .9 percent, and so on. At some point we have to say, "That's clean enough." Where that point will be, in case after case, is going to have to be decided politically, and democratic politics requires give and take on all sides to work.

Another part of the problem is that, increasingly, environmental regulations have been impinging on private-property rights. In the early days, the environmental movement was largely about cleaning up the commons—the air and water that belong to us all. The rule of thumb was easy: He who pollutes—whether the factory owner or the commuter in his automobile—should bear the cost of cleaning up now and of preventing that pollution in the future. Today, however, new regulations are more likely to affect the ways in which someone can use his or her own property and thus gravely affect its economic value.

There is a genuine clash of basic rights here. One is the individual right to hold, enjoy, and profit from private property. The other is the general right to pass on to our children a healthy and self-sustaining environment.

To give just one specific example of how these rights can clash, a man in South Carolina bought beachfront property in the 1980s for $600,000. The property was worth that much because it consisted of two buildable lots. He intended to build two houses, one for himself and one to sell. But the state then changed the regulations, to protect the delicate shoreline ecosystem, and his property became unbuildable. Its value plummeted from $600,000 to perhaps $30,000.

Not surprisingly, the owner sued for the economic loss he had suffered. But the state ruled that it was merely regulating in the public interest and that no compensation was due as it was not a "taking": the property still belonged to the owner. The property owner argued that the regulations, however valuable a public purpose they served, had indeed effected a taking, because the state had sucked the economic value out of his property, leaving him the dried husk of legal title.

This case is still in the courts, and cases like it are multiplying. A general acknowledgment of the validity of both sides' rights and motives is necessary if difficult matters such as these are to be resolved successfully.

Still a third problem is that, increasingly, environmental issues are global issues, beyond the reach of individual sovereign states. Worse, scientists have been studying the earth as a single, interlocking ecosystem for only the last few decades. Global weather and ocean temperature data nowhere stretch back more than a hundred and fifty years and usually much less. The amount of data we possess, therefore, is often insufficient to allow for the drawing of significant conclusions. Has the recent increase in atmospheric carbon dioxide caused an increase in average temperatures, or has a normal cyclical increase in temperature caused an increase in carbon dioxide? We just don't know the answer to that question. But billions, perhaps trillions of dollars in spending may depend on the answer.

Another issue is growth versus the environment. Many feel that economic growth and increased pollution are two sides of the same coin, that it is impossible to have the one without the other. Others feel that economic growth is the very key to cleaning up the environment because it alone can provide the wealth to do so.

Obviously, in some absolute sense, the more production of goods and services, the more waste products that must be dealt with. But if the wealth produced greatly exceeds the pollution produced, the pollution can be dealt with while standards of living continue to rise. Certainly among the world's densely populated countries, the correlation between wealth and environmental quality is striking. People cannot worry about the problem of tomorrow's environment if the problem of tonight's supper looms large. It is landless peasants, more than timber barons, who are cutting down the Amazon rain forest.

So far there has been no flagging of the pace or weakening of the spirit on the crusade to a clean American environment. The commitment of the American people is firm. Doubtless it will remain firm, too, if, in the midst of the ferocious political debates sure to come, we all keep in mind the fact that honorable people can disagree about means without disagreeing about ends; that there is more than one road to the New Jerusalem; and, especially, that cleaning up the American environment is far too important to be left to bureaucrats, activists, journalists, and fanatics. This is our crusade.

QUESTIONS TO CONSIDER

1. When and for what purpose was the first Earth Day?
2. How had European civilization and religion traditionally regarded wilderness? How did that affect the treatment of America?
3. What development made possible the rapid transformation of North America in the nineteenth century? What was its impact?

4. How did the United States, beginning in the 1860s, begin to try to preserve the natural habitat?

5. What was the country's first great man-made environmental disaster? How did it happen?

6. What does Gordon mean by "the nearest stone wall"? Give several examples.

7. What improvements have been seen in the environment since 1970?

8. Why is there a limited perception of environmental progress, in Gordon's view?

16

E Pluribus Unum?

ARTHUR SCHLESINGER, JR.

Reprinted by permission
of the author.

Arthur Schlesinger, Jr. (1917–), served as an aide in the Kennedy White House and subsequently wrote the award-winning 1965 treatment of JFK's presidency, *A Thousand Days*. A Harvard professor prior to his Washington service, Schlesinger has held the Albert Schweitzer Chair in the Humanities at City University of New York since 1966. One of the most gifted writers among eminent historians, he has written many other noteworthy books, including *The Age of Jackson* (1945), *The Age of Roosevelt* (3 vols., 1957–1960), *The Imperial Presidency* (1973), and *Robert F. Kennedy and His Times* (1978). He has been an outspoken and articulate defender of modern liberalism.

The clash of cultures has been a theme in the forging of the American character, beginning with the encounter of Columbus with the American natives, going through bouts of nativism in the 1850s and the 1920s, and reemerging in the rise of ethnicity in the past few decades. Sociologist Milton Gordon suggested in *Assimilation in America* that three models of assimilation have dominated the nation's past: the melting pot, Anglo-conformity, and cultural pluralism. In this selection, taken from the introduction and conclusion of his 1991 book, *The Disuniting of America: Reflections on a Multicultural Society,* Schlesinger makes an impassioned argument for the melting pot as the ideal that has held a disparate nation together. Full of commonsense responses to the flaws in multiculturalism, the book provides some solid food for thought about the nature of the United States and the national character as the country begins the third millennium.

At the beginning America was seen as a severing of roots, a liberation from the stifling past, an entry into a new life, an interweaving of separate ethnic strands into a new national design. "We have it in our power," said Thomas Paine for the revolutionary generation, "to begin the world all over again." The unstated national motto was "Never look back." "The Past is dead, and has no resurrection," wrote Herman Melville. ". . . The Past is the text-book of tyrants; the Future the Bible of the Free."

And the future was America—not so much a nation, Melville said, as a world. "You can not spill a drop of American blood without spilling the blood of the whole world. On this Western Hemisphere all tribes and people are forming into one federated whole. . . ." For Ralph Waldo Emerson too, like Crèvecoeur, like Melville, America was the distillation of the multifarious planet. As the burning of the temple at Corinth had melted and intermixed silver and gold to produce Corinthian brass, "a new compound more precious than any," so, Emerson wrote in his journal, in America, in this "asylum of all nations, the energy of Irish, Germans, Swedes, Poles, & Cossacks, & all the European tribes—of the Africans, & of the Polynesians, will construct a new race . . . as vigorous as the new Europe which came out of the smelting pot of the Dark Ages. . . ."

Melville was a novelist, Emerson an essayist; both were poets. But George Washington was a sternly practical man. Yet he believed no less ardently in the doctrine of the "new race." "The bosom of America," Washington said, "is open . . . to the oppressed and persecuted of all Nations and Religions." But immigrants who nestled as clannish groups in the national bosom retained the "Language, habits and principles (good or bad) which they bring with them." Let them therefore settle as individuals, prepared for "intermixture with our people." Then they would be "assimilated to our customs, measures and laws: in a word, soon become *one people.*"

John Quincy Adams, another sternly practical man, similarly insisted on the exclusiveness of the new American identity. When a German baron contemplating emigration interviewed Adams as secretary of state, Adams admonished his visitor that emigrants had to make up their minds to one thing: "*They must cast off the European skin, never to resume it.* They must look forward to their posterity rather than backward to their ancestors. . . ."

But how could Crèvecoeur's "promiscuous breed" be transformed into a "new race"? How was Emerson's "smelting pot" to fuse such disparate elements into Washington's "one people"? This question preoccupied another young Frenchman who arrived in America three quarters of a century after Crèvecoeur. "Imagine, my dear friend, if you can," Alexis de Tocqueville wrote back to France, "a society formed of all the nations of the world . . . people having different languages, beliefs, opinions: in a word, a society without roots, without memories, without prejudices, without routines, without common ideas, without a national character, yet a hundred times happier than our own." What alchemy could make this miscellany into a single society?

The answer, Tocqueville concluded, lay in the commitment of Americans to democracy and self-government. Civic participation, Tocqueville argued in *Democracy in America*, was the great educator and the great unifier.

> How does it happen that in the United States, where the inhabitants have only recently immigrated to the land which they now occupy, and brought neither customs nor traditions with them there; where they met one another for the first time with no previous acquaintance; where, in short, the instinctive love of country can scarcely exist; how does it happen that every one takes as zealous an interest in the affairs of his township, his country, and the whole state as if they were his own? It is because everyone, in his sphere, takes an active part in the government of society.

Immigrants, Tocqueville said, become Americans through the exercise of the political rights and civic responsibilities bestowed on them by the Declaration of Independence and the Constitution.

Half of a century later, when the next great foreign commentator on American democracy, James Bryce, wrote *The American Commonwealth*, immigration had vastly increased and diversified. Bryce's European friends expected that it would take a very long time for America to assimilate these "heterogeneous elements." What struck Bryce, on the contrary, was what had struck Tocqueville: "the amazing solvent power which American institutions, habits, and ideas exercise upon newcomers of all races . . . quickly dissolving and assimilating the foreign bodies that are poured into her mass."

A century after Tocqueville, another foreign visitor, Gunnar Myrdal of Sweden, called the cluster of ideas, institutions, and habits "the American Creed." Americans "of all national origins, regions, creeds, and colors," Myrdal wrote in 1944, hold in common "the *most explicitly expressed* system of general ideals" of any country in the West: the ideals of the essential dignity and equality of all human beings, of inalienable rights to freedom, justice, and opportunity.

The schools teach the principles of the Creed, Myrdal said; the churches preach them; the courts hand down judgments in their terms. Myrdal saw the Creed as the bond that links all Americans, including nonwhite minorities, and as the spur forever goading Americans to live up to their principles. "America," Myrdal said, "is continuously struggling for its soul."

The American Creed had its antecedents, and these antecedents lay primarily in a British inheritance as recast by a century and a half of colonial experience. How really new then was the "new race"? Crèvecoeur's vision implied an equal blending of European stocks, and Emerson's smelting pot generously added Cossacks, Africans, and Polynesians. In fact, the majority of the population of the 13 colonies and the weight of its culture came from Great Britain.

Having cleared most of North America of their French, Spanish, and Dutch rivals, the British were free to set the mold. The language of the new nation, its laws, its institutions, its political ideas, its literature, its customs, its precepts, its prayers, primarily derived from Britain. Crèvecoeur himself wrote his book not in his native French but in his acquired English. The "curse of Babel," Melville said, had been revoked in America, "and the language they shall speak shall be the language of Britain."

The smelting pot thus had, unmistakably and inescapably, an Anglo-centric flavor. For better or worse, the white Anglo-Saxon Protestant tradition was for two centuries—and in crucial respects still is—the dominant influence on American culture and society. This tradition provided the standard to which other immigrant nationalities were expected to conform, the matrix into which they would be assimilated.

But as the nineteenth century proceeded, non-Anglo immigration gathered speed. European peasants who may never have dared go twenty miles from their birthplaces now undertook the unimaginable adventure of a journey across perilous seas to a strange land in search of a new life. The land was indeed strange; and they could not but feel a need for reassurance and security. So at first they tended to cling to their compatriots and to the language, schools, churches they brought with them. These ethnic enclaves served as staging areas for regrouping and basic training before entry was made into the larger and riskier American life.

These immigrants came principally from western and northern Europe. The Anglos often disliked the newcomers, disdained their uncouth presence, feared their alien religions and folkways. Germans and Scandinavians were regarded as clannish in their fidelity to the language and customs of the old country. The German fondness for beer gardens and jolly Sundays excited puritanical disapproval. The Irish were regarded as shiftless and drunken; moreover, they were papists, and their fealty to Rome, it was said, meant they could never become loyal Americans. They were subjected to severe discrimination in employment and were despised by genteel society. W. E. B. Du Bois, the black scholar, testified that when he grew up in Great Barrington, Massachusetts, in the 1870s, "the racial angle was more clearly defined against the Irish than against me."

As the flow of immigrants increased, so did resentment among the old-timers. By the 1850s immigrants made up half the population of New York and outnumbered native-born Americans in Chicago. Nativist organizations sprang up, like the Supreme Order of the Star-Spangled Banner and its political front, the American Party, calling for a lengthened naturalization process and curtailment of the political rights of the foreign-born. They were referred to as Know-Nothings because members of the Supreme Order, when asked about their secret oaths and rituals, would reply, "I know nothing."

In 1856 the Know-Nothings even ran a former president, Millard Fillmore, as their presidential candidate. "Our progress in degeneracy appears to me to be pretty rapid," observed Abraham Lincoln. "As a nation, we began by declaring that *'all men are created equal.'* We now practicably read it 'all men are created equal, *except negroes.'* When the Know-Nothings get control, it will read 'all men are created equal, except negroes, *and foreigners, and catholics.'"*

But the Know-Nothing party fell as quickly as it rose. In the century and a half since, despite recurrent xenophobic outbursts, no nativist political party has appeared to take its place. However prejudiced white Anglo-Saxons were in practice, they were ashamed to endorse nativism in principle. Equally important, an expanding economy in an underpopulated country required a steady influx of new hands. Immigration alleviated the labor shortage, and economic need overpowered moral and aesthetic repugnance.

The pre–Civil War immigrants steadily turned into Americans. "The frontier," in the words of its great historian, Frederick Jackson Turner, "promoted the formation of a composite nationality. . . . In the crucible of the frontier the immigrants were Americanized, liberated, and fused into a mixed race, English in neither nationality nor characteristics." In the crucible of the cities too assimilation proceeded apace. Even "the Irish immigrant's son," Bryce reported in 1888, "is an American citizen for all other purposes, even if he retain, which he seldom does, the hereditary Anglophobia."

After the Civil War came the so-called "new" immigration from southern and eastern Europe. Over 27 million arrived in the half-century from Lee's surrender at Appomattox to America's entry into the First World War—more than the total population of the country in 1850. The new immigrants—Italians, Poles, Hungarians, Czechs, Slovaks, Russians, Jews—settled mainly in the cities, where their bizarre customs, dress, languages, and religions excited new misgivings.

Yet the old faith in the power of Bryce's "amazing solvent" to fulfill Washington's conception of Americans as "one people" held fast. However much they suffered from social prejudice, the newcomers were not barred from civic participation, and civic participation indoctrinated them in the fundamentals of the American Creed. They altered the ethnic composition of the country, but they preserved the old ambition to become Americans.

The fastidious Henry James, revisiting his native land in 1904 after many years abroad, was at first dismayed by the alien bustle of Ellis Island. But he soon understood and appreciated "the ceaseless process of the recruiting of our race, of the plenishing of our huge national *pot-au-feu,* of the introduction of fresh . . . foreign matter into our heterogeneous system." Though he wondered at times what immigration would do to Americans "ethnically, and thereby physiognomically, linguistically, *personally,*" though he saw at times "the 'ethnic' apparition" sitting like a skeleton at the feast, he was more impressed by the "colossal" machinery that so efficiently converted the children of immigrants into Americans—the political and social habit, the common school, the newspaper, all so reliably producing what James called "the 'ethnic' synthesis." He spoke with something like awe about "the cauldron of the 'American' character."

New race, one people, smelting pot, *pot-au-feu*, cauldron—the original faith received its most celebrated metaphor a few years after James's visitation. In 1908 a play by Israel Zangwill, an English writer of Russian Jewish origin, opened in Washington. *The Melting-Pot* tells the story of a young Russian Jewish composer in New York. David Quixano's artistic ambition is to write a symphony expressing the vast, harmonious interweaving of races in America, and his personal hope is to overcome racial barriers and marry Vera, a beautiful Christian girl. "America," David cries, "is God's crucible, the great Melting-Pot where all the races of Europe are melting and reforming! . . . Here you stand in your fifty groups, with your fifty languages . . . and your fifty blood hatreds. . . . A fig for your feuds and vendettas! Germans and Frenchmen, Irishmen and Englishmen, Jews and Russians— into the Crucible with you all! God is making the American."

The climatic scene takes place on the roof garden of a lower-Manhattan settlement house. In the background the Statue of Liberty gleams in the sunset. The composer, alone with Vera, gestures toward the city:

> There she lies, the great Melting-Pot—listen! Can't you hear the roaring and the bubbling? Ah, what a stirring and a seething! Celt and Latin, Slav and Teuton, Greek and Syrian,—black and yellow—
>
> VERA *(softly nestling to him):*   Jew and Gentile—
>
> DAVID: Yes, East and West, and North and South, the palm and the pine, the pole and the equator, the crescent and the cross. . . . Here shall they all unite to build the Republic of Man and the Kingdom of God. Ah, Vera, what is the glory of Rome and Jerusalem where all nations and races come to worship and look back, compared with the glory of America, where all races and nations come to labour and look forward! . . . *(Far back, like a lonely, guiding star, twinkles over the darkening water the torch of the Statue of Liberty. From below comes up the softened sound of voices and instruments joining in 'My Country, 'tis of Thee.' The curtain falls slowly.)*

When the curtain fell in Washington and the author walked onstage, President Theodore Roosevelt called from his box: "That's a great play, Mr. Zangwill, that's a great play." "I'm not a Bernard Shaw man or Ibsen man, Mrs. Zangwill," T. R. later told the playwright's wife. "No, *this* is the stuff." Zangwill subsequently dedicated the printed play to Roosevelt. *The Melting-Pot* played before rapt audiences across the country. Jane Addams of Hull-House in Chicago observed that Zangwill had performed "a great service to America by reminding us of the high hopes of the founders of the Republic."

Yet even as audiences cheered *The Melting-Pot*, Zangwill's metaphor raised doubts. One had only to stroll around the great cities, as Basil March did in William Dean Howell's *A Hazard of New Fortunes*, to see that the melting process was incomplete. Ethnic minorities were forming their own *quartiers* in which they lived in their own way—not quite that of the lands they had left but not that of Anglocentric America either: Little Italy, Chinatown, Yorkville, Harlem, and so on.

Nor was the WASP culture showing great inclination to ease their access into Anglo-America. And when it did, when barriers fell, when new immigrants gained acceptance through money or celebrity, there loomed the prospect of intermarriage. In having his drama turn on marriage between people of different races and religions, Zangwill, who had himself married a Christian, emphasized where the melting pot must inexorably lead: to the submergence of separate ethnic identities in the new American race.

Was such a result desirable? Many immigrants doubtless thought so. In the early twentieth century, most of their children certainly did. But soon ethnic spokesmen began to appear, moved by real concern for distinctive ethnic values and also by real if unconscious vested interest in the preservation of ethnic constituencies. Jewish reviewers castigated Zangwill: "All the worse for you and me, brother," wrote one, "who are to be cast into and dissolved in the crucible." Even some of Anglo-Saxon descent deplored the obliteration of picturesque foreign strains for the sake of insipid Anglocentric conformity.

The impression grew that the melting pot was a device to impose Anglocentric images and values upon hapless immigrants—an impression reinforced by the rise of the "Americanization" movement in response to the new polyglot immigration. Americanization programs, benign in intent, sought to expedite assimilation by offering immigrants special education in language, citizenship, and American history. The outbreak of war in 1914 gave Americanization a more coercive edge. Even presidents as friendly to immigrants as Theodore Roosevelt and Woodrow Wilson worried whether in crisis "hyphenated" Americans might not be more loyal to the old country than to their adopted land.

Three days after a German submarine sank the *Lusitania*, Wilson addressed an audience of recently naturalized citizens in Philadelphia. "You cannot become thorough Americans," he told them, "if you think of yourselves in groups. America does not consist of groups. A man who thinks of himself as belonging to a particular national group in America has not yet become an American."

"We can have no 'fifty-fifty' allegiance in this country," Theodore Roosevelt said two years later. "Either a man is an American and nothing else, or he is not an American at all." He condemned Americans who saw the world from the standpoint of another nation. "We Americans are children of the crucible," T. R. said. "The crucible does not do its work unless it turns out those cast into it in one national mould."

"One national mould"? Not everyone agreed. In 1915 Horace Kallen, a Jewish-American philosopher, wrote an essay for *The Nation* entitled "Democracy versus the Melting-Pot." The melting pot, Kallen argued, was valid neither as a fact nor as an ideal. What impressed him was, on the contrary, the persistence of ethnic groups and their distinctive traditions. Unlike freely chosen affiliations, Kallen said, the ethnic bond was both involuntary and immutable. "Men may change their clothes, their politics, their wives, their religions, their philosophies, to a greater or lesser extent: they cannot change their grandfathers. Jews or Poles or Anglo-Saxons, in order to cease being Jews or Poles or Anglo-Saxons, would have to cease to be. . . . "

Ethnic diversity, Kallen observed, enriches American civilization. He saw the nation not as one people, except in a political and administrative sense, but rather "as a federation or commonwealth of national cultures . . . a democracy of nationalities, cooperating voluntarily and autonomously through common institutions . . . a multiplicity in a unity, an orchestration of mankind." This conception he came to call "cultural pluralism."

Kallen was unclear on the question of how to encourage ethnic separatism without weakening the original ideal of a single society. One critic warned that cultural pluralism would "result in the Balkanization of these United States." But Kallen made his attack on Anglo-centered assimilation at a time when critics of the melting pot could reasonably assume the solidity of the overarching framework. Because he considered political unity a given, he put his emphasis on the protection of cultural diversity.

The gospel of cultural pluralism was at first largely confined to academics, intellectuals, and artists. The postwar years saw much popular disenchantment with Europe, a Red Scare directed largely against aliens, the rise of the anti-Catholic Ku Klux Klan, and a campaign, realized in the Immigration Act of 1924, to freeze the ethnic composition of the American people. The new law established quotas on the basis of the national origins of the population in 1890, thereby drastically reducing the flow from southern and eastern Europe.

The xenophobic nationalism of the 1920s was followed in the 1930s by crises that, on some levels divisive, nevertheless strengthened the feeling that all Americans were in the same boat and might as well pull together. The Great Depression and the Second World War showed the desperate necessity of national cohesion within the frame of shared national ideals. "The principle on which this country was founded and by which it has always been governed," Franklin D. Roosevelt said in 1943, "is that Americanism is a matter of the mind and heart; Americanism is not, and never was, a matter of race and ancestry. A good American is one who is loyal to this country and to our creed of liberty and democracy."

Gunnar Myrdal in 1944 showed no hesitation in declaring the American Creed the common possession of all Americans, even as his great book

An American Dilemma provided a magistral analysis of America's most conspicuous failure to live up to the Creed: the treatment by white Americans of black America.

Noble ideals had been pronounced as if for all Americans, yet in practice they applied only to white people. Most interpretations of the national identity from Crèvecoeur on were for whites only. Even Horace Kallen, the champion of cultural pluralism, made no provision in his "democracy of nationalities" for black or red or brown or yellow Americans.

Tocqueville was an exception in factoring persons of color into the American equation. With his usual prescience, he identified racism as the irremediable flaw in American democracy. This "most grasping nation on the globe" had doomed the red man to extinction; and the presence of a black population was "the most formidable of all the ills that threaten the future of the Union." The more optimistic Emerson and Zangwill had thrown nonwhite nationalities into their smelting or melting pots, but Tocqueville saw racist exclusion as deeply ingrained in the national character.

History supported this judgment. White settlers had systematically pushed the American Indians back, killed their braves, seized their lands, and sequestered their tribes. They had brought Africans to America to work their plantations and Chinese to build their railroads. They had enunciated glittering generalities of freedom and withheld them from people of color. Their Constitution protected slavery, and their laws made distinctions on the basis of race. Though they eventually emancipated the slaves, they conspired in the reduction of the freedmen to third-class citizenship. Their Chinese Exclusion acts culminated in the total prohibition of Asian immigration in the Immigration Act of 1924. It occurred to damned few white Americans in these years that Americans of color were also entitled to the rights and liberties promised by the Constitution.

Yet what Bryce had called "the amazing solvent power" of American institutions and ideas retained its force, even among those most cruelly oppressed and excluded. Myrdal's polls of Afro-America showed the "determination" of blacks "to hold to the American Creed." Ralph Bunche, one of Myrdal's collaborators, observed that every man in the street—black, red, and yellow as well as white—regarded America as the "land of the free" and the "cradle of liberty." The American Creed, Myrdal surmised, meant even more to blacks than to whites, since it was the great means of pleading their unfulfilled rights. Blacks, new immigrants, Jews, and other disadvantaged groups, Myrdal said, "could not possibly have invented a system of political ideals which better corresponded to their interests."

The Second World War gave the Creed new bite. Hitler's racism forced Americans to look hard at their own racial assumptions. How, in fighting against Hitler's doctrine of the Master Race abroad, could Americans maintain a doctrine of white supremacy at home? How, with China a faithful American ally, could Americans continue to forbid Chinese to become

American citizens? If the war did not end American racism, at least it drove much racial bigotry underground. The rethinking of racial issues challenged the conscience of the majority and raised the consciousness of minorities.

Emboldened by the Creed, blacks organized for equal opportunities in employment, opposed segregation in the armed forces, and fought in their own units on many fronts. After the war, the civil rights revolution, so long deferred, accelerated black self-reliance. So did the collapse of white colonialism around the world and the appearance of independent black states.

Across America minorities proclaimed their pride and demanded their rights. Women, the one "minority" that in America constituted a numerical majority, sought political and economic equality. Jews gained new solidarity from the holocaust and then from the establishment of a Jewish state in Israel. Changes in the immigration law dramatically increased the number arriving from Hispanic and Asian lands, and, following the general example, they asserted their own prerogatives. American Indians mobilized to reclaim rights and lands long since appropriated by the white man; their spokesmen even rejected the historic designation in which Indians had taken deserved pride and named themselves Native Americans.

The civil rights revolution provoked new expressions of ethnic identity by the now long-resident "new migration" from southern and eastern Europe—Italians, Greeks, Poles, Czechs, Slovaks, Hungarians. The ethnic enthusiasm was reinforced by the "third-generation" effect formulated in Hansen's Law, named after Marcus Lee Hansen, the great pioneer in immigration history: "What the son wishes to forget the grandson wishes to remember."

Another factor powerfully nourished the passion for roots: the waning American optimism about the nation's prospects. For two centuries Americans had been confident that life would be better for their children than it was for them. In their exuberant youth, Americans had disdained the past and, as John Quincy Adams urged, looked forward to their posterity rather than backward to their ancestors. Amid forebodings of national decline, Americans now began to look forward less and backward more. The rising cult of ethnicity was a symptom of decreasing confidence in the American future.

Ethnic as a word has had a long history. It originally meant "heathen" or "pagan" but soon came to mean anything pertaining to a race or nation. In this sense everyone, even the Lowells and the Cabots, were ethnics. By the time Henry James used the word in *The American Scene,* however, "ethnic" had acquired an association with foreignness. As applied since the 1960s, it definitely means non-Anglo minorities—a reversion to the original sense of being beyond the pale.

The noun *ethnicity* meanwhile made its modern debut in 1940 in W. Lloyd Warner's Yankee City series. From its modest beginning in that sociological study, "ethnicity" moved vigorously to center stage in popular discourse. The bicentennial of American independence, the centennial of the Statue of Liberty, the restoration of Ellis Island—all turned from tributes to the melting pot into extravaganzas of ethnic distinctiveness.

The pressure for the new cult of ethnicity came less from the minorities en masse than from their often self-appointed spokesmen. Most ethnics, white and nonwhite, saw themselves primarily as Americans. "The cravings for 'historical identity,'" Gunnar Myrdal said at the height of the ethnic rage, "is not in any sense a people's movement. Those cravings have been raised by a few well-established intellectuals, professors, writers—mostly, I gather, of a third generation." Few of them, Myrdal thought, made much effort to talk to their own ethnic groups. He feared, Myrdal added with a certain contempt, that this movement was only "upper-class intellectual romanticism."

Still, ideologues, with sufficient publicity and time, could create audiences. Spokesmen with a vested interest in ethnic identification repudiated the ideal of assimilation. The melting pot, it was said, injured people by undermining their self-esteem. It denied them heroes—"role models," in the jargon—from their own ethnic ancestries. Praise now went to "the unmeltable ethnics."

In 1974, after testimony from ethnic spokesmen denouncing the melting pot as a conspiracy to homogenize America, Congress passed the Ethnic Heritage Studies Program Act—a statue that, by applying the ethnic ideology to all Americans, compromised the historic right of Americans to decide their ethnic identities for themselves. The act ignored those millions of Americans—surely a majority—who refused identification with any particular ethnic group.

The ethnic upsurge (it can hardly be called a revival because it was unprecedented) began as a gesture of protest against the Anglocentric culture. It became a cult, and today it threatens to become a counter-revolution against the original theory of America as "one people," a common culture, a single nation.

The attack on the common American identity is the culmination of the cult of ethnicity. That attack was mounted in the first instance by European Americans of non-British origin ("unmeltable ethnics") against the British foundations of American culture; then, latterly and massively, by Americans of non-European origin against the European foundations of that culture. As Theodore Roosevelt's foreboding suggests, the European immigration itself palpitated with internal hostilities, everyone at everybody else's throats—hardly the "monocultural" crowd portrayed by ethnocentric separatists. After all, the two great "world" wars of the twentieth century began as fights among European states. Making a single society out of this diversity of antagonistic European peoples is a hard enough job. The new salience of non-European, nonwhite stocks compounds the challenge. And the non-Europeans, or at least their self-appointed spokesmen, bring with them a resentment, in some cases a hatred, of Europe and the West provoked by generations of Western colonialism, racism, condescension, contempt, and cruel exploitation.

Will not this rising flow of non-European immigrants create a "minority majority" that will make Eurocentrism obsolete by the twenty-first century? This is the fear of some white Americans and the hope (and sometimes the threat) of some nonwhites.

Immigrants were responsible for a third of population growth during the 1980s. More arrived than in any decade since the second of the century. And the composition of the newcomers changed dramatically. In 1910 nearly 90 percent of immigrants came from Europe. In the 1980s more than 80 percent came from Asia and Latin America.

Still, foreign-born residents constitute only about 7 percent of the population today as against nearly 15 percent when the first Roosevelt and Wilson were worrying about hyphenated Americans. Stephan Thernstrom doubts that the minority will ever arrive. The black share in the population has grown rather slowly—9.9 percent in 1920, 10 percent in 1950, 11.1 percent in 1970, 12.1 percent in 1990. Neither Asian-Americans nor Hispanic-Americans go in for especially large families; and family size in any case tends to decline as income and intermarriage increase. "If today's immigrants assimilate to American ways as readily as their predecessors at the turn of the century—as seems to be happening," Thernstrom concludes, "there won't be a minority majority issue anyway."

America has so long seen itself as the asylum for the oppressed and persecuted—and has done itself and the world so much good thereby—that any curtailment of immigration offends something in the American soul. No one wants to be a Know-Nothing. Yet uncontrolled immigration is an impossibility; so the criteria of control are questions the American democracy must confront. We have shifted the basis of admission three times this century—from national origins in 1924 to family reunification in 1965 to needed skills in 1990. The future of immigration policy depends on the capacity of the assimilation process to continue to do what it has done so well in the past: to lead newcomers to an acceptance of the language, the institutions, and the political ideals that hold the nation together.

Is Europe really the root of all evil? The crimes of Europe against lesser breeds without the law (not to mention even worse crimes—Hitlerism and Stalinism—against Europeans) are famous. But these crimes do not alter other facts of history: that Europe was the birthplace of the United States of America, that European ideas and culture formed the republic, that the United States is an extension of European civilization, and that nearly 80 percent of Americans are of European descent.

When Irving Howe, hardly a notorious conservative, dared write, "The Bible, Homer, Plato, Sophocles, Shakespeare are central to our culture," an outraged reader ("having graduated this past year from Amherst") wrote, "Where on Howe's list is the *Quran,* the *Gita,* Confucius, and other central cultural artifacts of the peoples of our nation?" No one can doubt the importance of these works nor the influence they have had on other societies. But on American society? It may be too bad that dead white European males have played so large a role in shaping our culture. But that's the way it is. One cannot erase history.

These humdrum historical facts, and not some dastardly imperialist conspiracy, explain the Eurocentric slant in American schools. Would anyone seriously argue that teachers should conceal the European origins of American civilization? or that schools should cater to the 20 percent and ignore the 80 percent? Of course the 20 percent and their contributions should be integrated into the curriculum too, which is the point of cultural pluralism.

But self-styled "multiculturalists" are very often ethnocentric separatists who see little in the Western heritage beyond Western crimes. The Western tradition, in this view, is inherently racist, sexist, "classist," hegemonic; irredeemably repressive, irredeemably oppressive. The spread of Western culture is due not to any innate quality but simply to the spread of Western power. Thus the popularity of European classical music around the world—and, one supposes, of American jazz and rock too—is evidence not of wide appeal but of "the pattern of imperialism, in which the conquered culture adopts that of the conqueror."

Such animus toward Europe lay behind the well-known crusade against the Western-civilization course at Stanford ("Hey-hey, ho-ho, Western culture's got to go!"). According to the National Endowment for the Humanities, students can graduate from 78 percent of American colleges and universities without taking a course in the history of Western civilization. A number of institutions—among them Dartmouth, Wisconsin, Mt. Holyoke—require courses in third-world or ethnic studies but not in Western civilization. The mood is one of divesting Americans of the sinful European inheritance and seeking redemptive infusions from non-Western cultures.

One of the oddities of the situation is that the assault on the Western tradition is conducted very largely with analytical weapons forged in the West. What are the names invoked by the coalition of latter-day Marxists, deconstructionists, poststructuralists, radical feminists, Afrocentrists? Marx, Nietzsche, Gramsci, Derrida, Foucault, Lacan, Sartre, de Beauvoir, Habermas, the Frankfurt "critical theory" school—Europeans all. The "unmasking," "demythologizing," "decanonizing," "dehegemonizing" blitz against Western culture depends on methods of critical analysis unique to the West—which surely testifies to the internally redemptive potentialities of the Western tradition.

Even Afrocentrists seem to accept subliminally the very Eurocentric standards they think they are rejecting. "Black intellectuals condemn Western civilization," Professor Pearce Williams says, "yet ardently wish to prove it was founded by their ancestors." And, like Frantz Fanon and Leopold Senghor, whose books figure prominently on their reading lists, Afrocentric ideologues are intellectual children of the West they repudiate. Fanon, the eloquent spokesman of the African wretched of the earth, had French as his native tongue and based his analyses on Freud, Marx, and Sartre. Senghor, the prophet of Negritude, wrote in French, established the Senegalese educational system on the French model and, when he left the presidency of Senegal, retired to France.

Western hegemony, it would seem, can be the source of protest as well as of power. Indeed, the invasion of American schools by the Afrocentric curriculum, not to mention the conquest of university departments of English and comparative literature by deconstructionists, poststructuralists, etc., are developments that by themselves refute the extreme theory of "cultural hegemony." Of course, Gramsci had a point. Ruling values do dominate and permeate any society; but they do not have the rigid and monolithic grip on American democracy that academic leftists claim.

Radical academics denounce the "canon" as an instrument of European oppression enforcing the hegemony of the white race, the male sex, and the capitalist class, designed, in the words of one professor, "to rewrite the past and construct the present from the perspective of the privileged and the powerful." Or in the elegant words of another—and a professor of theological ethics at that: "The canon of great literature was created by high Anglican assholes to underwrite their social class."

The poor old canon is seen not only as conspiratorial but as static. Yet nothing changes more regularly and reliably than the canon: compare, for example, the canon in American poetry as defined by Edmund Clarence Stedman in his *Poets of America* (1885) with the canon of 1935 or of 1985 (whatever happened to Longfellow and Whittier?); or recall the changes that have overtaken the canonical literature of American history in the last half-century (who reads Beard and Parrington now?). And the critics clearly have no principled objection to the idea of the canon. They simply wish to replace an old gang by a new gang. After all, a canon means only that because you can't read everything, you give some books priority over others.

Oddly enough, serious Marxists—Marx and Engels, Lukacs, Trotsky, Gramsci—had the greatest respect for what Lukacs called "the classical heritage of mankind." Well they should have, for most great literature and much good history are deeply subversive in their impact on orthodoxies. Consider the present-day American literary canon: Emerson, Jefferson, Melville, Whitman, Hawthorne, Thoreau, Lincoln, Twain, Dickinson, William and

Henry James, Henry Adams, Holmes, Dreiser, Faulkner, O'Neill. Lackeys of the ruling class? Apologists for the privileged and the powerful? Agents of American imperialism? Come on!

It is time to adjourn the chat about hegemony. If hegemony were as real as the cultural radicals pretend, Afrocentrism would never have got anywhere, and the heirs of William Lyon Phelps would still be running the Modern Language Association.

Is the Western tradition a bar to progress and a curse on humanity? Would it really do America and the world good to get rid of the European legacy?

No doubt Europe has done terrible things, not least to itself. But what culture has not? History, said Edward Gibbon, is little more than the register of the crimes, follies, and misfortunes of mankind. The sins of the West are no worse than the sins of Asia or of the Middle East or of Africa.

There remains, however, a crucial difference between the Western tradition and the others. The crimes of the West have produced their own antidotes. They have provoked great movements to end slavery, to raise the status of women, to abolish torture, to combat racism, to defend freedom of inquiry and expression, to advance personal liberty and human rights.

Whatever the particular crimes of Europe, that continent is also the source—the *unique* source—of those liberating ideas of individual liberty, political democracy, the rule of law, human rights, and cultural freedom that constitute our most precious legacy and to which most of the world today aspires. These are *European* ideas, not Asian, nor African, nor Middle Eastern ideas, except by adoption.

The freedoms of inquiry and of artistic creation, for example, are Western values. Consider the differing reactions to the case of Salman Rushdie: what the West saw as an intolerable attack on individual freedom the Middle East saw as a proper punishment for an evildoer who had violated the mores of his group. Individualism itself is looked on with abhorrence and dread by collectivist cultures in which loyalty to the group overrides personal goals—cultures that, social scientists say, comprise about 70 percent of the world's population.

There is surely no reason for Western civilization to have guilt trips laid on it by champions of cultures based on despotism, superstition, tribalism, and fanaticism. In this regard the Afrocentrists are especially absurd. The West needs no lectures on the superior virtue of those "sun people" who sustained slavery until Western imperialism abolished it (and, it is reported, sustain it to this day in Mauritania and the Sudan), who still keep women in subjection and cut off their clitorises, who carry out racial persecutions not only against Indians and other Asians but against fellow Africans from the wrong tribes, who show themselves either incapable of operating a democracy or ideologically hostile to the democratic idea, and who in their tryannies and massacres, their Idi Amins and Boukassas, have stamped with utmost brutality on human rights.

Certainly the European overlords did little enough to prepare Africa for self-government. But democracy would find it hard in any case to put down roots in a tribalist and patrimonial culture that, long before the West invaded Africa, had sacralized the personal authority of chieftains and ordained the submission of the rest. What the West would call corruption is regarded through much of Africa as no more than the prerogative of power. Competitive political parties, an independent judiciary, a free press, the rule of law are alien to African traditions.

It was the French, not the Algerians, who freed Algerian women from the veil (much to the irritation of Frantz Fanon, who regarded deveiling as symbolic rape); as in India it was the British, not the Indians, who ended (or did their best to end) the horrible custom of *suttee*—widows burning themselves alive on their husbands' funeral pyres. And it was the West, not the non-Western cultures, that launched the crusade to abolish slavery—and in doing so encountered mighty resistance, especially in the Islamic world (where Moslems, with fine impartiality, enslaved whites as well as blacks). Those many brave and humane Africans who are struggling these days for decent societies are animated by Western, not by African, ideals. White guilt can be pushed too far.

The Western commitment to human rights has unquestionably been intermittent and imperfect. Yet the ideal remains—and movement toward it has been real, if sporadic. Today it is the *Western* democratic tradition that attracts and empowers people of all continents, creeds, and colors. When the Chinese students cried and died for democracy in Tiananmen Square, they brought with them not representations of Confucius or Buddha but a model of the Statue of Liberty.

The great American asylum, as Crèvecoeur called it, open, as Washington said, to the oppressed and persecuted of all nations, has been from the start an experiment in a multiethnic society. This is a bolder experiment than we sometimes remember. History is littered with the wreck of states that tried to combine diverse ethnic or linguistic or religious groups within a single sovereignty. Today's headlines tell of imminent crisis or impending dissolution in one or another multiethnic polity—the Soviet Union, India, Yugoslavia, Czechoslovakia, Ireland, Belgium, Canada, Lebanon, Cyprus, Israel, Ceylon, Spain, Nigeria, Kenya, Angola, Trinidad, Guyana. . . . The list is almost endless. The luck so far of the American experiment has been due in large part to the vision of the melting pot. "No other nation," Margaret Thatcher has said, "has so successfully combined people of different races and nations within a single culture."

But even in the United States, ethnic ideologues have not been without effect. They have set themselves against the old American ideal of assimilation. They call on the republic to think in terms not of individual but of group identity and to move the polity from individual rights to group rights. They have made a certain progress in transforming the United States into a more segregated society. They have done their best to turn a college generation against Europe and the Western tradition. They have imposed ethnocentric, Afrocentric, and bilingual curricula on public schools, well designed to hold minority children out of American society. They have told young people from minority groups that the Western democratic tradition is not for them. They have encouraged minorities to see themselves as victims and to live by alibis rather than to claim the opportunities opened for them by the potent combination of black protest and white guilt. They have filled the air with recrimination and rancor and have remarkably advanced the fragmentation of American life.

Yet I believe the campaign against the idea of common ideals and a single society will fail. Gunnar Myrdal was surely right: for all the damage it has done, the upsurge of ethnicity is a superficial enthusiasm stirred by romantic ideologues and unscrupulous hucksters whose claim to speak for their minorities is thoughtlessly accepted by the media. I doubt that the ethnic vogue expresses a reversal of direction from assimilation to apartheid among the minorities themselves. Indeed, the more the ideologues press the case for ethnic separatism, the less they appeal to the mass of their own groups. They have thus far done better in intimidating the white majority than in converting their own constituencies.

"No nation in history," writes Lawrence Fuchs, the political scientist and immigration expert in his fine book *The American Kaleidoscope*, "had proved as successful as the United States in managing ethnic diversity. No nation before had ever made diversity itself a source of national identity and unity." The second sentence explains the success described in the first, and the mechanism for translating diversity into unity has been the American Creed, the civic culture—the very assimilating, unifying culture that is today challenged, and not seldom rejected, by the ideologues of ethnicity.

A historian's guess is that the resources of the Creed have not been exhausted. Americanization has not lost its charms. Many sons and daughters of ethnic neighborhoods still want to shed their ethnicity and move to the suburbs as fast as they can—where they will be received with far more tolerance than they would have been 70 years ago. The desire for achievement and success in American society remains a potent force for assimilation. Ethnic subcultures, Stephen Steinberg, author of *The Ethnic Myth*, points out, fade away "because circumstances forced them to make choices that undermined the basis for cultural survival."

Others may enjoy their ethnic neighborhoods but see no conflict between foreign descent and American loyalty. Unlike the multiculturalists, they celebrate not only what is distinctive in their own backgrounds but what they hold in common with the rest of the population.

The ethnic identification often tends toward superficiality. The sociologist Richard Alba's study of children and grandchildren of immigrants in the Albany, New York, area shows the most popular "ethnic experience" to be sampling the ancestral cuisine. Still, less than half the respondents picked that, and only one percent ate ethnic food every day. Only one-fifth acknowledged a sense of special relationship to people of their own ethnic background; less than one-sixth taught their children about their ethnic origins; almost none was fluent in the language of the old country. "It is hard to avoid the conclusion," Alba writes, "that ethnic experience is shallow for the great majority of whites."

If ethnic experience is a good deal less shallow for blacks, it is because of their bitter experience in America, not because of their memories of Africa. Nonetheless most blacks prefer "black" to "African-Americans," fight bravely and patriotically for their country, and would move to the suburbs too if income and racism would permit.

As for Hispanic-Americans, first-generation Hispanics born in the United States speak English fluently, according to a Rand Corporation study; more than half of second-generation Hispanics give up Spanish altogether. When *Vista,* an English-language monthly for Hispanics, asked its readers what historical figures they most admired, Washington, Lincoln, and Theodore Roosevelt led the list, with Benito Juárez trailing behind as fourth, and Eleanor Roosevelt and Martin Luther King Jr. tied for fifth. So much for ethnic role models.

Nor, despite the effort of ethnic ideologues, are minority groups all that hermetically sealed off from each other, except in special situations, like colleges, where ideologues are authority figures. The wedding notices in any newspaper testify to the increased equanimity with which people these days marry across ethnic lines, across religious lines, even, though to a smaller degree, across racial lines. Around half of Asian-American marriages are with non-Orientals, and the Census Bureau estimates one million interracial—mostly black-white—marriages in 1990 as against 310,000 in 1970.

The ethnic revolt against the melting pot has reached the point, in rhetoric at least, though not I think in reality, of a denial of the idea of a common culture and a single society. If large numbers of people really accept this, the republic would be in serious trouble. The question poses itself: how to restore the balance between *unum* and *pluribus?*

The old American homogeneity disappeared well over a century ago, never to return. Ever since, we have been preoccupied in one way or another with the problem, as Herbert Croly phrased in 80 years back in *The Promise of American Life,* "of preventing such divisions from dissolving the society into which they enter—of keeping such a highly differentiated society fundamentally sound and whole." This required, Croly believed, an "ultimate bond of union." There was only one way by which solidarity could be restored, "and that is by means of a democratic social ideal. . . ."

The genius of America lies in its capacity to forge a single nation from peoples of remarkably diverse racial, religious, and ethnic origins. It has done so because democratic principles provide both the philosophical bond of union and practical experience of civic participation. The American Creed envisages a nation composed of individuals making their own choices and accountable to themselves, not a nation based on inviolable ethnic communities. The Constitution turns on individual rights, not on group rights. Law, in order to rectify past wrongs, has from time to time (and in my view often properly so) acknowledged the claims of groups; but this is the exception, not the rule.

Our democratic principles contemplate an open society founded on tolerance of differences and on mutual respect. In practice, America has been more open to some than to others. But it is more open to all today than it was yesterday and is likely to be even more open tomorrow than today. The steady movement of American life has been from exclusion to inclusion.

Historically and culturally this republic has an Anglo-Saxon base; but from the start the base has been modified, enriched, and reconstituted by transfusions from other continents and civilizations. The movement from exclusion to inclusion causes a constant revision in the texture of our culture. The ethnic transfusions affect all aspects of American life—our politics, our literature, our music, our painting, our movies, our cuisine, our customs, our dreams.

Black Americans in particular have influenced the ever-changing national culture in many ways. They have lived here for centuries, and, unless one believes in racist mysticism, they belong far more to American culture than to the culture of Africa. Their history is part of the Western democratic tradition, not an alternative to it. Henry Louis Gates Jr. reminds us of James Baldwin's remark about coming to Europe to find out that he was "as American as any Texas G.I." No one does black Americans more disservice than those Afrocentric ideologues who would define them out of the West.

The interplay of diverse traditions produces the America we know. "Paradoxical though it may seem," Diane Ravitch has well said, "the United States has a common culture that is multicultural." That is why unifying political ideals coexist so easily and cheerfully with diversity in social and cultural values. Within the overarching political commitment, people are free to live as they choose, ethnically and otherwise. Differences will remain; some are reinvented; some are used to drive us apart. But as we renew our allegiance to the unifying ideals, we provide the solvent that will prevent differences from escalating into antagonism and hatred.

One powerful reason for the movement from exclusion to inclusion is that the American Creed facilitates the appeal from the actual to the ideal. When we talk of the American democratic faith, we must understand it in its true dimensions. It is not an impervious, final, and complacent orthodoxy, intolerant of deviation and dissent, fulfilled in flag salutes, oaths of allegiance, and hands over the heart. It is an ever-evolving philosophy, fulfilling its ideals through debate, self-criticism, protest, disrespect, and irreverence; a tradition in which all have rights of heterodoxy and opportunities for self-assertion. The Creed has been the means by which Americans have haltingly but persistently narrowed the gap between performance and principle. It is what all Americans should learn, because it is what binds all Americans together.

Let us by all means in this increasingly mixed-up world learn about those other continents and civilizations. But let us master our own history first. Lamentable as some may think it, we inherit an American experience, as America inherits a European experience. To deny the essentially European origins of American culture is to falsify history.

Americans of whatever origin should take pride in the distinctive inheritance to which they have all contributed, as other nations take pride in their distinctive inheritances. Belief in one's own culture does not require disdain for other cultures. But one step at a time: no culture can hope to ingest other cultures all at once, certainly not before it ingests its own. As we begin to master our own culture, then we can explore the world.

Our schools and colleges have a responsibility to teach history for its own sake—as part of the intellectual equipment of civilized persons—and not to degrade history by allowing its contents to be dictated by pressure groups, whether political, economic, religious, or ethnic. The past may sometimes give offense to one or another minority; that is no reason for rewriting history. Giving pressure groups vetoes over textbooks and courses betrays both history and education. Properly taught, history will convey a sense of the variety, continuity, and adaptability of cultures, of the need for understanding other cultures, of the ability of individuals and peoples to overcome obstacles, of the importance of critical analysis and dispassionate judgment in every area of life.

Above all, history can give a sense of national identity. We don't have to believe that our values are absolutely better than the next fellow's or the next country's, but we have no doubt that they are better *for us*, reared as we are—and are worth living by and worth dying for. For our values are not matters of whim and happenstance. History has given them to us. They are anchored in our national experience, in our great national documents, in our national heroes, in our folkways, traditions, and standards. People with a different history will have differing values. But we believe that our own are better for us. They work for us; and, for that reason, we live and die by them.

It has taken time to make the values real for all our citizens, and we still have a good distance to go, but we have made progress. If we now repudiate the quite marvelous inheritance that history bestows on us, we invite the fragmentation of the national community into a quarrelsome spatter of enclaves, ghettos, tribes. The bonds of cohesion in our society are sufficiently fragile, or so it seems to me, that it makes no sense to strain them by encouraging and exalting cultural and linguistic apartheid.

The American identity will never be fixed and final; it will always be in the making. Changes in the population have always brought changes in the national ethos and will continue to do so; but not, one must hope, at the expense of national integration. The question America confronts as a pluralistic society is how to vindicate cherished cultures and traditions without breaking the bonds of cohesion—common ideals, common political institutions, common language, common culture, common fate—that hold the republic together.

Our task is to combine due appreciation of the splendid diversity of the nation with due emphasis on the great unifying Western ideas of individual freedom, political democracy, and human rights. These are the ideas that define the American nationality—and that today empower people of all continents, races, and creeds.

"What then is the American, this new man? . . . Here individuals of all nations are melted into a new race of men." Still a good answer—still the best hope.

QUESTIONS TO CONSIDER

1. What did Tocqueville and Myrdal see as the great exception to the American creed? Why? What event stimulated the rethinking of that exception? Why?
2. What was the source of the ethnic movement? What congressional act encouraged it? How?
3. How has European bashing distorted reality in academe?
4. In what ways do the sources and arguments of critics of Eurocentrism undermine themselves?
5. "Is the Western tradition a bar to progress and a curse on humanity?" Why or why not?
6. What evidence does Schlesinger advance for the shallowness of the ethnic craze? Are you convinced?
7. What is your response to Schlesinger's arguments?